—SECOND— EDITION

EVERYMAN IN EUROPE

ESSAYS IN SOCIAL HISTORY

Volume 1 — The Preindustrial Millennia

ALLAN MITCHELL
University of California at San Diego

ISTVAN DEAK
Columbia University

PRENTICE-HALL, INC., ENGLEWOOD CLIFFS, NEW JERSEY 07632

Library of Congress Cataloging in Publication Data

Mitchell, Allan, comp.
    Everyman in Europe.

    Includes bibliographies.
    CONTENTS: v. 1. The preindustrial millennia.
—v. 2.   Social history—Modern, 1500-   —Addresses,
essays, lectures—Collected works. I.   Deák, István.
HN13.M58 1981   940   80-26438
ISBN 0-13-293613-5 (v. 1)
ISBN 0-13-293621-6 (v. 2)

To Four Women: *Gloria, Catherine, Alexandra, and Eva*

Editorial production/supervision and interior design by Cyrus Veeser
Cover design by A Good Thing, Inc.
Manufacturing buyer: Edmund W. Leone

©1981 by Prentice-Hall, Inc., Englewood Cliffs, N.J. 07632

Printed in the United States of America

10   9   8   7   6   5   4   3   2   1

Prentice-Hall International, Inc., *London*
Prentice-Hall of Australia Pty. Limited, *Sydney*
Prentice-Hall of Canada, Ltd., *Toronto*
Prentice-Hall of India Private Limited, *New Delhi*
Prentice-Hall of Japan, Inc., *Tokyo*
Prentice-Hall of Southeast Asia Pte. Ltd., *Singapore*
Whitehall Books Limited, Wellington, *New Zealand*

CONTENTS

PREFACE

History books ordinarily record major events in a way that we learn not only what happened, and when, but also why. No one would deny that these are important things to know, and few would dispute that it is a necessary and proper function of historians to be concerned with the impact of such events. Yet there has been for some time a realization among professional historians, as well as among students, that history needs to be something more than an analysis of important changes in the conduct of our lives. These changes are brought about by outstanding individuals, by elite groups, or by the faceless masses descending in the streets or marching on the battlefields. If we are really to understand the past, then we ought to know much more about the majority of humankind, about the individuals who make up the faceless masses, about people who endured rather than instigated the events we read about in the books. It is the special concern, then, of this book to learn how most people lived rather than how a few acted.

Most men and women who populate this world have always been poor and uneducated. This is not to say that they have been altogether powerless and inarticulate. What it does mean is that they have tended to express themselves and their interests in social groups, of one sort or another, rather than as individuals. To comprehend their behavior it is therefore more useful to think in terms of social types than of personalities. In the pages that follow, proper names will consequently figure infrequently. As important as they are, it is not Pericles, Julius Caesar, Henry VIII, and Napoleon who stand here in the foreground; rather, it is the peasant, the worker, the woman, and the youth. In short, our chief protagonist is Everyman.

By the careful selection of articles and excerpts we have attempted to trace the changing circumstances and activities of ordinary people from Greek civilization to the present time. Our focus is Europe, and we have attempted to define Europe as broadly as possible, drawing our examples from Ireland to Russia. Too often Europe is conceived largely in terms of what is most familiar to us and to the majority of Western historians: Britain and France. By giving central and eastern Europe their due we hope to redress the balance and to suggest a truer picture of European society.

The attentive reader will quickly perceive that generalizations about Everyman in one area of Europe at a given time are not readily applicable to other areas and other times. Can we nonetheless say that the various social types under consideration have something in common? Is there any constant factor among so many people in such a multitude of times and places? If so, it is certainly *not* that they have been deaf and dumb throughout European history. To the contrary, in their own way they have often and unmistakenly expressed enthusiasm, or dissatisfaction, or just indifference. Even the ostensibly most random forms of violence and deviant modes of behavior have sometimes spoken eloquently as to the character of European society. Yet Everyman has hardly been the master of his own fate, and this has perhaps been the salient characteristic of most people all along: they usually take rather than give orders. They do not command; they obey—or at least they are expected to do so.

Is this, then, a history of the oppressed? That is a question that readers must finally answer for themselves. There is certainly much evidence to support an affirmative reply. Still readers cannot remain unaware of the relativity of such a notion as "oppression." What degree of consciousness of their deprived social status must oppressed people attain before they want to change it? What degree of liberty is required in order to escape oppression? These are not simple issues, and they are not much clarified by dogmatic assertions of whatever political persuasion. The historian is always on the side of complexity; the dogmatist will therefore find little support here for his terrible simplifications.

We have thus kept two objectives in view: to select essays that are adequate to the difficulty of the subject rather than to choose brief and random fragments, and to achieve a sense of variety by drawing on a broad sample of historical techniques. Readers should gain the altogether legitimate impression that social history is far from becoming a monolithic discipline that represents a fixed consensus of opinion or approach. Only a moribund intellectual enterprise might present such uniformity, and social history, we believe, is still in its adolescence.

The notion that European society was transformed in modern times by an "industrial revolution" need not be accepted without reservation. In the first place, the term "revolution" implies a rapid and thorough change, whereas the development of an industrial society in Europe has been slow, uneven, and incomplete. The transformation was, moreover, not exclusively a matter of industry: one must also take into account demographic, agricultural, and technological innovations of considerable magnitude and complexity. To separate cause from effect, or symptom from correlation, is no simple task.

Another preliminary word of caution: we are perhaps unduly conditioned to believe that history consists of winners and losers. Thus, we may be inclined, without a flicker of protest, to accept the assertion that modern times were marked by the "triumph" of the bourgeoisie. Yet we would do well to recall that the results of a protracted social evolution are seldom to be measured by box scores or body counts, as if history were an athletic contest or a formal military engagement. Even if we could derive a precise definition of "bourgeois"—which would hardly hold for the entire European continent—we cannot be quite certain what "to win" really means in social terms. We know only that industrialization has meant an important alteration in the quality of life for most Europeans. A careful study of the essays in this volume should enrich our understanding of that complex phenomenon.

The preparation of this volume, as well as the second one, was greatly facilitated by the superb editorial care of Pieter M. Judson and John S. Micgiel, doctoral candidates in history at Columbia University.

COMMON PEOPLE IN CLASSICAL TIMES

The shores of the Mediterranean formed the crucible of European civilization. Other great cultures had of course existed before that of the Greeks and Romans. We might search back to ancient China or India, to the various societies of Mesopotamia and Palestine, or to Egypt. But it is classical Greece to which we first turn in order to discover those social forms that were to be enduringly significant in the evolution of Europe. Chronologically, what we consider here as the classical age stretches from the Greek poet Homer's time, about 700 B.C., to the sacking of Rome by invading bands of Visigoths just after 400 A.D. Eleven centuries may seem an unimaginably long span of years, and yet the pace of social change, judged by our present standards, was then exceedingly slow.

The Mediterranean world of antiquity possessed several unifying elements: the sea, the moderate climate, the poverty, and consequently the necessity of scratching out a meager living, or tending small herds, or plying some primitive craft. Such was the lot of a society in which only a very few were in any sense wealthy and many remained not only wretchedly poor but enslaved as well. This was true of the tiny city-states of Greece. It continued to characterize the sprawling possessions of the Roman Empire, which eventually ringed the entire Mediterranean and stretched northward into the Continent and to the British Isles.

Rome drew heavily on the intellectual resources of Greece, and for many reasons regarded Athens as the most advanced exemplar of Greek civilization. Much more than rival Sparta, Athens contained a cosmopolitan, urbane, commercial population. Social stratification there was somewhat less rigid than elsewhere at the time, and the Athenian state was more susceptible to social reform. If democracy was a Greek word, however, so was aristocracy. We can think of Athenian society as relatively progressive, but we need not exaggerate the freedom or comfort of the common people. The same was largely true of Rome. The Roman Empire reached new heights of political and military power, but it did not represent any extraordinary advance in what we might call civil rights. As in ancient Greece, for example, slaves were employed by the Romans to perform menial tasks in harvesting olives and grapes or as household servants. They were a substratum of society upon which the entire civilization rested.

Women must also be reckoned among the underprivileged of classical culture. It was, as we shall find, not necessarily an advantage for females to live in a town rather than a village or a rural cottage. Nor was the Roman woman significantly better off than her earlier Greek counterpart. Both in Greece and Rome, men conducted business, fought wars, and controlled politics. Women were thought and kept inferior. Life was organized for the edification, predilection, and competition of males. They met in public, whereas women were usually confined to their quarters or at least to a closely circumscribed existence that left little possibility for self-realization or fulfillment.

We begin, then, with a society in many ways very different from our own. Does that mean that the study of Greece and Rome is without relevance for us? Not, the answer must be, if we realize that what we are is the distant result of the way they were.

SLAVES AND LABORERS

For those of us now living in the twentieth century it is difficult to imagine the circumstances and attitudes of a society in which slave labor was a commonplace. Yet Greek and Roman civilizations both utilized and accepted slavery as a matter of course. Not that slavery altogether escaped criticism from certain intellectuals and protest from some of the slaves themselves; rather, it was a part of everyday life, and those societies could scarcely have existed without it. The articles that follow illustrate how little the institution of slavery actually changed from the fourth century B.C. to the fourth century A.D. They also raise some nagging questions. To what extent can it be said that slavery was "fundamental" to classical civilization? What proportion of the population was regarded and treated as chattel? What social function did the slaves perform? What possibilities existed for their escape from the status of a slave?

Gustave Glotz describes the practice of slavery in Greece and attempts to answer some elementary queries. How were slaves recruited? What rights and protection did they have? What roles did they perform? His analysis provides an excellent introduction to the subject.

Moses I. Finley writes with a more polemical bite. He argues that Greek society and economy were founded on the institutionalized exploitation of slavery. He examines the fragmentary evidence of the mentality of slaves, both those who willingly submitted and those who attempted to escape. And he suggests why less attention ought to be paid to the alleged political effect of slavery and more to its social function.

Peter A. Brunt confirms that Roman attitudes towards slave labor hardly differed from Greek attitudes. He shows how the practice of slavery was altered only very slowly in a society that remained overwhelmingly agricultural. Unlike Finley, Brunt raises the question of morality and finds it worthwhile to ask whether slavery affected the decline and collapse of classical civilization.

Careful readers will easily note the variation of scholarly opinion on these issues. But more important, they should gain some impression of how deeply rooted in Western society is the notion that some persons are by birth inferior to others, an assumption that has survived in one form or another well into modern times and has not disappeared up to the present day.

—GUSTAVE GLOTZ————————————

THE GREEK SLAVES

In the eyes of the Greek no healthy, lasting society could dispense with slaves. To devote his forces and intelligence to the city, the citizen must be relieved of domestic occupations and manual labour. Slavery was a necessary institution. That it might be a legal institution there must be creatures made for servitude by a natural inferiority. These born slaves existed; they were the barbarians. So the life of the city necessitated and justified slavery. No one would see, neither philosopher nor common man, that the rights invoked were merely wants.

1. THE RECRUITING AND CONDITION OF THE SLAVES

Slavery came from three sources—birth, war, and judicial condemnation.

The slaves "born in the house" were not very numerous. In the deeds of manumission found at Delphi, out of 841 slaves freed there are 217 of this class; and it should be noted that a master was more willing to free servants whom he

From Gustave Glotz, *Ancient Greece at Work: An Economic History of Greece from the Homeric Period to the Roman Conquest,* trans. M. R. Dobie (London: Routledge & Kegan Paul, 1926), pp. 192-94, 195-96, 198-99, 200-208, by permission of the publisher.

had known since their childhood. The reason was that the breeding of human livestock was not a good speculation. Most of the newborn infants were killed or exposed; those who had the most chance of surviving were those who owed their birth to a caprice of the master.

The vast majority of slaves came from war. After a pitched battle those prisoners who could not buy their freedom were sold; after the assault of a city the men were put to the sword and the women and children divided among the victors by lot. To barbarians these laws were applied in all their brutality; after the Eurymedon campaign Cimon threw more than twenty thousand prisoners on the market. Towards Greeks certain scruples were felt, and neutral public opinion made mercy necessary. Furthermore, in barbarian countries slave-raiding was always allowed, and occasionally a little poaching was done on Greek soil. Wherever the power of the State did not make itself felt with energy, in Thessaly, in Ætolia, brigands and pirates acted as purveyors to the dealers in men.

Lastly, private law itself contributed to the recruiting of slaves. Athens caused individual liberty to be respected in almost all circumstances, but elsewhere subordination easily became servitude. Even in philanthropical Athens the father had a right to expose his children, and newborn infants were hardly ever picked up on roads and public places except to be made into slaves. In most cities a father could get rid even of the children whom he had brought up (a horrible temptation in time of need); Athens forbade this abominable traffic, but authorised the sale of a guilty daughter. The insolvent debtor fell into the power of his creditor, with his wife and children; Athens almost alone forbade loans on the person. Everywhere the State, arrogating to itself the right which it allowed to individuals, maintained penal slavery in the code of law; Athens confined this to the Metic who usurped the rank of citizen, but most cities made much use of it, and some made civic degradation or *atimia* an ingenious preliminary to slavery.

In general, most slaves came into their master's house by way of purchase. They were of very varied origins. Few were Greeks; these were often wastrels, criminals sold abroad. In 415 one set of sixteen slaves was composed of five Thracians, three Carians, two Syrians, two Illyrians, one Scythian, one Cholcidian, one Lydian, and one Maltese. To meet the increasing demand the recruiters gradually extended their field of operation, and procured Bastarnæ and Sarmatians, Persians and Arabs, Egyptians and Libyans. In origin the slaves were more or less equally distributed between the rude countries of the North and the more civilized East. In other words, the Greeks had almost as much need of strong arms for the mines and workshops as of pliant natures and quick wits for domestic service and business.

So the slave trade was very busy in Greece. Dealers rushed after the armies or entered into relations with the pirates. They operated chiefly in the neighbourhood of the barbarian lands. Chios, Ephesos, Byzantion, and Thessaly, these were the great markets of supply. The recruiters sometimes formed a syndicate covering a district. The importers sent almost all the goods to Attica. A monthly fair was held on the Agora of Athens. Part of the cargoes was sent to Sunion for the mines. The surplus of imports was re-embarked for Sicily. So Athens was the centre of this business. The slave-dealers there were very rich; they ordered their bust from the fashionable sculptor, and would one day be sufficiently powerful to give financial backing to a revolution. . . .

The ideas of the Greeks on the necessity and lawfulness of slavery determined the legal status of the slave. He was a living instrument. He belonged to another man, he was his chattel. But this chattel was alive and had a soul. According as the master's right was absolute and uncompromising, or took into account the exceptional nature of this kind of property, there were notable differences in law, and still more in practice; for we can hardly say that slavery had a legal position in the city; it was subject to household law, which the master interpreted according to his own ideas.

On principle the slave had no personality. He had no real name of his own. If two slaves cohabited this union, though tolerated, was not a marriage. Their issue was merely an increase in livestock which belonged to the owner of the woman. Not being a person, the slave had not the free disposal of his body. He might be made over to another or confiscated; he might become immovable property through the use to which he was put. Being property himself, he was incapable of exercising the right of property. He was allowed to save his earnings; sometimes he plied his trade outside and had the use of part of his salary; he might even make a fortune and show off his wealth. But his enjoyment of his property always depended on a permission which might be recalled. In law the master's authority came between the legally disqualified slave and third parties, whether they were private individuals or representatives of the State. The slave could not lodge an accusation without the master. But his responsibility also was very limited. He was covered by the orders which he had received. Since he owned nothing in law, he could not be subjected to pecuniary penalties; for him there was, instead, the whip. If a sentence for damages was given, it fell on the master; he paid the damages, or else gave up the slave altogether by noxal surrender.

The interest of the master was the slave's only safeguard. For Aristotle the slave is an instrument, and "one must take care of the instrument in the measure which the work requires." If a man has a good servant he will be wise to feed and dress him better, to allow him rest, to let him form a family, and to hold out a prospect of the supreme reward, freedom. Plato is hard enough on the "brute" who revolts against a natural inequality; but such a difficult piece of property must be treated well, "for our own advantage rather than for his."

One might suppose that in societies in which the law kept down the slaves with implacable logic, and philosophy sought no alleviation of their lot but in a better utilization of their labour, nothing could lighten the weight of their chains.

Yet the Athenian people had the merit of introducing humane considerations into its law and improving the condition of the slaves. It acted in obedience to economic and political necessities. In a country where there were many slaves, public safety required that they should not be kept in a permanent state of exasperation. But above all the democratic idea had its own special virtue, that thoughtful tenderness for the humble which is designated by the essentially Athenian word "philanthropy." From the citizens this idea went on to shed its blessing on those who had not the right of citizenship, nor any right at all. Aristotle observes contemptuously that "democracy is adapted to the anarchy of slaves"; but, an Athenian retorts, "it was not for the slaves that the lawgiver felt so much concern, . . . he considered that the man who in a democracy does outrage to anybody whomsoever is not fit to take part in civic life." So the slaves had a better time in Athens than in any other city, and it was said that they enjoyed there an amount of freedom which the poor citizens of many an oligarchic State might have envied them. . . .

. . . These features . . . give a picture which is no doubt too idyllic. Beneath the few slaves who were on familiar terms with their masters there were thousands of squalid creatures vegetating, especially in the mines, fed just enough to prevent their strength from diminishing, and resting from work only when they were beaten. We cannot forget that the slaves of the Athenians used to flee to Megara, that the appearance of the Spartans was for the workers of Laurcion the signal for desertion in a mass, and that in Attica itself many wretches bore on their forehead the brand of the runaway. But it is something that, in a realistic theatre, we hear slaves uttering praises of their masters.

2. SLAVE LABOUR

It would be very interesting to be certain of the number of slaves in the various cities of Greece. We hear of 470,000 slaves in Ægina, of 460,000 in Corinth, of 400,000 in Athens. The exaggeration is obvious. It may at least be taken as a rule that in the commercial and manufacturing cities the slave population was greater than the free. On the other hand, those districts which still lived by agriculture and stock-breeding had few slaves. When in the middle of the fourth century a landowner in Phocis had a thousand there was an outcry. Slavery, then, appears in Greece as a concomitant of trade and industry, varying according to their development. At the same points, once in Ionia, now on the Saronic Gulf, economic life and slave labour were concentrated. . . .

The whole of Greece needed slaves for domestic service. Almost all the work of providing food was done by the women. The maidservants made the bread and did the cooking. For big dinners special dishes were ordered from professional cooks, or else one of these artists was engaged for the day; and one or two great personages had a chef of their own. We hear of the chef of Alcibiades; and the story goes that the cook of Demetrios of Phaleron made enough in two years to buy three tenement houses. Round about the master cook there was a busy staff of slaves, scullions, bakers, and pastry cooks.

The clothing of the family was also made at home. Under the eye of their mistress the slave girls spun, wove, and embroidered. Their chief occupations were the manufacture of materials and sewing; that is why, once free, they generally lived by the textile industry.

Women in easy circumstances had several slaves in their service, and even the humblest always had one. The speeches of the orators give us some typical examples. Ciron, a landowner with a fortune of more than twenty-thousand drachmas, had three domestics. An honest farmer, whose wife had one single child, kept a cook (a woman), a chambermaid, and a nurse maid. The ordinary middle-class townsman had a serving man and women of two classes, those of the ground floor, who did the house work, and those of the first floor, who made the clothes. Diogenes Laertios takes us into the homes of the philosophers. Plato freed a woman in his will and left four slaves to his heirs. Aristotle, who found that with too many servants it was hard to organise work, nevertheless had nine slaves, not including children. Theophrastos, too, had nine. Straton's will mentioned seven, and Lycon's twelve. In sum, a man of average fortune employed in his house from three to twelve slaves of the two sexes. But three was on the small side. There were families in very difficult circumstances who could not do with less. Stephanos, who lived on his wits with his concubine and three children, placed at the disposal of this household a male slave and two servant women. In the *Plutos* of Aristophanes, when poor old Chremylos groans over his wretched lot he confides his woes in his serving man. People used to point out, as "characters," Diogenes, who did not need any one to keep his tub in order, Hippias, who made his own clothes and shoes, and Chrysippos, who took Odysseus for a model in the art of fending for himself.

The rich were obliged by the progess of luxury to live in great style, with chambermaids, wet-nurses, dry-nurses, housekeepers, lady's maids, valets, footmen, coachmen, grooms, and pedagogues. "Use slaves like the members of the body, one for each purpose." The precept comes from a philosopher. The division of labour which it proclaims produced in very wealthy families an extreme diversity of servile functions. That servants might be well trained they were sent to take lessons at the school of housekeeping or from a certificated master in the culinary art.

In houses with a large domestic staff it was found necessary to place a trustworthy person over them. Pericles had a steward who managed his estates and had charge of the personnel. Big landowners even had a female housekeeper in addition to the steward. Such a post was well suited to slaves; it was easy to get back from them anything which they should take improperly. For this very reason citizens looked down on it. Eutheros, to whom Socrates suggests this means of earning a living, thanks him for nothing. It was an important and delicate decision, to choose out of your slaves the man or woman who should be put over them. Xenophon gives minute advice on the subject. As housekeeper you must choose "the woman who seems least inclined to gluttony, drink, sleep, and running after men; she must also have an excellent memory, and she must be capable of either foreseeing the punishment which neglect will cost her or of thinking of ways of pleasing her masters and deserving their favour." But the masters too must treat her with sympathy, and interest her in her work and in their property, "by keeping her informed of their position and sharing their happiness with her." As steward, also, you must reject the idler, the drunkard, and the dissolute man, and look for intelligence, industry, loyalty, experience, and authority, without being too much afraid of love of gain, which is a stimulus.

Apart from this, the Greeks never attained the frightful squandering of labour of which the Roman town houses and villas were to boast. It is true that in the sixth century a Sybarite appeared at the court of Sicyon with a retinue of a thousand slaves; but these Greeks from the colonies wanted to dazzle the old world. It is also true that, two centuries later, a man in Phocis formed a troop of slaves who were likewise reckoned at a thousand head, but he meant them to work in the fields; the proof of it is that he was accused of taking the bread from the mouths of so many free men, and in the same country the wife of Philomelos attracted attention the first time she walked out accompanied by two servant-women. So it is not in thousands, nor even in hundreds, that we must count the slaves in the houses which were most largely supplied with them. It was even held, with Aristotle, that too many servants spoiled the service. Plato compares to "tyrants" (we should say, to princes) those private individuals who own fifty slaves or more. We find one rich Metic, in 415, with only sixteen slaves. In the next century the ostentatious Meidias perhaps owned more; he had three or four footmen following him and kept a number of servant-women; but if he had had a "tyrannical" household staff his opponent Demosthenes would have made the most of it, and he says nothing about it. The Athenians, who loved money in order to employ it usefully, took good care not to sink large capital in an over-grand style of housekeeping.

Agriculture did not make a very great use of slave labour. In the countries of big estates, Laconia, Messenia, and Thessaly, the lords of the land had it worked by serfs who must pay a fixed revenue. Countries of small farms are notoriously ill-adapted to slavery. Corn growing furnished only intermittent work. To feed slaves all the year round in order to employ them usefully for about seven weeks is bad business. If costs of this amount are not to absorb the return in advance, the estate must be extraordinarily fertile and very extensive. In Greece, where the soil was poor and the fallow in alternate years reduced the sown land by a half, the production of corn by slave labour could not be remunerative. The cultivation of the olive and vine requires great care and knowledge. It suited the small proprietor working his own land. One or two slaves, employed in the house when there was no work in the fields—no more were needed. And indeed, as Aristotle says, "with the poor, the ox takes the place of a slave." In other words, to have more than two slaves the farmer had to be in comfortable circumstances.

Therefore the slave population was insignificant in the agricultural districts. . . .

Even in the manufacturing and commercial countries the abundance of slave labor was of no benefit to agriculture. Attica had few rural slaves. Xenophon's model farm employs slave labour almost entirely, but it is economical with it. Not number but quality was sought; for the difference in productivity between the good and the bad worker was reckoned at nine tenths. Agricultural science already fixed the return to be expected per team of oxen and per worker; each knew exactly how many beasts and men he needed. Among the condemned men whose goods were sold in 415 only one possessed sixteen slaves, and he was a Metic from the Peiræus, who could not own land. All the others, those whose lands or crops, standing or ingathered, had been confiscated, either had no slaves at all or had one, two, three, or at the most four. In a list of 131 freedmen whose occupations are known there are 62 women, none of whom worked on the land, and 69 men, of whom 9 were farmers (almost all market-gardeners) and 2 vine-growers. A wise landowner did not keep permanently the whole staff needed at the time of the oil-pressing; he took on hired men by the job or the day. They were not always free men, it is true; they were often slaves, but they were hired out. Going from one farm to another, and doing different tasks as the seasons came round, these slaves brought their masters a return which was sufficiently regular to be remunerative. One Arethusios had two men whom he hired out for all agricultural tasks; his own part was confined to making the contracts and drawing his share of their wages. The organisation of labour by the hiring of slaves, which did great service in industry, was also applied, but in a limited form, in agriculture.

For industry was what required by far the most slaves. The industrial system was such that it could not work without the motive power of slave labour. The division of labour in the crafts required an ever greater variety of manual operations. But for want of machines, "instruments working by themselves" as Aristotle calls them, all the work was done by man power. The slave was an animated tool; a gang of slaves was a machine with men for parts. The more arduous or delicate a task was, the more need it had, failing powerful or ingenious machines, of numerous or skillful slaves. An Athenian could not imagine that any industry could keep going without them.

The smallest craftsman had a few slaves as workmen or at least one slave as mate. Whether the work was done in the workshop, on the site, or at the customer's place, whether the master worked with his men or no, it was to him that the fruit of their labour came. One Athenian who sends mattress-makers to private houses lives on their salaries. In a comedy a mother and daughter have no means of subsistence but the money earned by their slave. A craftsman must be very badly off to say, like Lysias' cripple, "I have a trade which brings me a small income, and I carry it on myself, for I cannot afford a slave to whom I could entrust it.''

The building industries employed slaves in the most varied fashion. In the accounts of the Erechtheion we find slaves of all kinds. One is a labourer at a drachma a day. Others are skilled workers, but are told off in case of need to set up or remove scaffolding. The majority work only at their own trade. Out of thirty-five marble workers about twenty are slaves; half of these work with their master, and one is the foreman of a gang. All are paid at the same rate as the free men and their master himself; but, if their pay is entered under their name, it does not follow that they keep it.

Slave labour, extensively used by small employers, held an almost exclusive place in those industries which were organised in workshops and factories. In Socrates' day the miller Nausicydes, the baker Cyrebos, the chiton-maker Demeas, and the cloak-maker Menon made their fortunes without employing one free man. Timarchos owned a shoemaking establishment with workers and foreman of slave condition. The orators tell us of slaves plying the trade of metal-workers, embroiderers, druggists, and perfumers. Sophocles' father had them in his forge and Isocrates' father in his lyre manufactory. On a vase painting the potter is surrounded by slaves whom he threatens or chastises. The patrimony of Demosthenes included a bed factory and an armour works, which were chiefly valuable for the personnel with which they were supplied. Manufactories of shields like those of Cephalos and Pasion owed their importance less to the premises and the stock than to the human machinery. There are abundant examples of the kind from Athens, and they are not lacking from other cities. In Megara dressmaking was done entirely by barbarian labour.

But, though the total number of industrial slaves was large, they were never grouped in masses. There was nothing comparable to the great factory of the present day. The absence of machinery, the necessity for keeping the permanent staff proportionate to the constant, certain demand, the difficulty of keeping effective control over workmen who had not the incentive of pay, everything prevented the concentration of industry and the collection of large bodies of labour. The shoemakers of Timarchos numbered nine or ten, Demosthenes' workshops contained twenty cabinetmakers and thirty-two armourers, and the great factory of Cephalos employed a hundred and twenty men.

The only industries which could employ multitudes of workers were those which required neither vast buildings nor skilled labour, the transport business and the mines. The transport of heavy material needed an enormous train of wagons and oxen; to load the wagons and to drive the beasts at least one man was needed for each team. At Laureion, both for extraction and for smelting, labour was entirely servile. A concession or a workshop was hired, complete with personnel. The normal concession included a gang of thirty miners, but a man could obtain a large number of concessions and employ a whole army of slaves. Nicias hired a thousand to Sosias, Hipponicos hired out six hundred, Philomenides three hundred. When the Spartans occupied Deceleia twenty thousand fugitive slaves came running up to them. Xenophon proposed that the State should buy and let out miners up to ten thousand; the project may be fantastic, but the figure is significant.

To sum up, industrial slavery is inevitably confined within fairly narrow limits. It assumes a certain development only when the division of labour ceases to be rudimentary, and it does not progress beyond a certain point. For the tasks which require only physical strength the number of slaves can always be increased until it is sufficient. But if complicated articles have to be manufactured in quantities, it is indispensable that each man should specialise in one operation, in one motion. This is only possible with machinery, for to turn the human tool into an automatic machine a course of training would be necessary which would cost too much for too little result. Now so long as a society enslaves man power, being ignorant of the use of machine power, it has such opportunity for obtaining plentiful, docile labour that it does not feel the necessity of supplementing it artificially. The absence of machinery is at once the cause and, to a certain extent, the effect of industrial slavery; the result is that slavery is an obstacle to industry and even prevents itself from extending indefinitely.

——MOSES I. FINLEY————————————————————

WAS GREEK CIVILISATION BASED ON SLAVE LABOUR?[1]

I.

Two generalisations may be made at the outset. First: at all times and in all places the Greek world relied on some form (or forms) of dependent labour to meet its needs, both public and private. By this I mean that dependent labour was essential, in a significant measure, if the requirements of agriculture, trade,

From M. I. Finley, "Was Greek Civilisation Based on Slave Labour?" *Historia*, 8 Wiesbaden, Germany: Franz Steiner Verlag GmbH (1959), 145–64, by permission of the publisher.

1   This is a slightly enlarged and revised version of a paper read at the triennial meeting of the Joint Committee of Greek and Roman Societies in Cambridge on 11 August 1958. No effort has been made to annotate fully or to provide more than a handful of modern references. I am grateful to Professors A. H. M. Jones and M. Postan in Cambridge, and Mr. G. E. M. de Ste. Croix of New College and Mr. P. A. Brunt of Oriel College, Oxford, for much helpful criticism.

manufacture, public works, and war production were to be fulfilled. And by dependent labour I mean work performed under compulsions other than those of kinship or communal obligations.[2] Second: with the rarest of exceptions, there were always substantial numbers of free men engaged in productive labour. By this I mean primarily not free hired labour but free men working on their own (or leased) land or in their shops or homes as craftsmen and shopkeepers. It is within the framework created by these two generalisations that the questions must be asked which seek to locate slavery in the society. And by slavery, finally, I mean roughly the status in which a man is, in the eyes of the law and of public opinion and with respect to all other parties, a possession, a chattel, of another man.[3]

How completely the Greeks always took slavery for granted as one of the facts of human existence is abundantly evident to anyone who has read their literature. In the Homeric poems it is assumed (correctly) that captive women will be taken home as slaves, and that occasional male slaves—the victims of Phoenician merchant-pirates—will also be on hand. In the seventh century B.C., when Hesiod, the Boeotian "peasant" poet, gets down to practical advice in his *Works and Days,* he tells his brother how to use slaves properly; that they will be available is simply assumed.[4] The same is true of Xenophon's manual for the gentleman farmer, the *Oeconomicus,* written about 375 B.C. A few years earlier, an Athenian cripple who was appealing a decision dropping him from the dole, said to the Council: "I have a trade which brings me in a little, but I can barely work at it myself and I cannot afford to buy someone to replace myself in it."[5] In the first book of the Pseudo-Aristotelian *Oeconomica,* a Peripatetic work probably of the late fourth or early third century B.C., we find the following proposition about the organisation of the household, stated as baldly and flatly as it could possibly be done: "Of property, the first and most necessary kind, the best and most manageable, is man. Therefore the first step is to procure good slaves. Of slaves there are two kinds, the overseer and the worker."[6] Polybius, discussing the strategic situation of Byzantium, speaks quite casually of "the necessities of life—cattle and slaves" which come from the Black Sea region.[7] And so on. . . .

---

2   I also exclude the "economic compulsion" of the wage-labour system.

3   It is obviously not a valid objection to this working definition to point out either that a slave is biologically a man none the less, or that there were usually some pressures to give him a little recognition of his humanity, such as the privilege of asylum or the de facto privilege of marriage.

4   I believe that the ἔριθος and perhaps the θῆς of 11. 602-3 were slaves, from the context, peculiar as that use of the two words may be. But even if one rejects my interpretation of these two lines, slaves are so repeatedly taken for granted in the poem that it is incorrect to imply a balanced alternative, as does W. L. Westermann, The Slave Systems of Greek and Roman Antiquity (Philadelphia 1955), 4, when he writes: "The peasant of modest means of the type of Hesiod might well have slaves but he also used hired labor."

5   Lysias 24.6.

6   Ps.-Aristotle, Oec. 1.5.1,1344a22.

7   Polyb. 4.38.4.

II.

With little exception, there was no activity, productive or unproductive, public or private, pleasant or unpleasant, which was not performed by slaves at some times and in some places in the Greek world. The major exception was, of course, political: no slave held public office or sat on the deliberative and judicial bodies (though slaves were commonly employed in the "civil service," as secretaries and clerks, and as policemen and prison attendants). Slaves did not fight as a rule, either, unless freed (although helots apparently did), and they were very rare in the liberal professions, including medicine. On the other side, there was no activity which was not performed by free men at some times and in some places. That is sometimes denied, but the denial rests on a gross error, namely, the failure to differentiate between a free man working for himself and one working for another, for hire. In the Greek scale of values, the crucial test was not so much the nature of the work (within limits, of course) as the condition or status under which it was carried on.[8] "The condition of the free man," said Aristotle, "is that he does not live under the restraint of another."[9] On this point, Aristotle was expressing a nearly universal Greek notion. Although we find free Greeks doing every kind of work, the free wage-earner, the free man who regularly works *for* another and therefore "lives under the restraint of another" is a rare figure in the sources, and he surely was a minor factor in the picture.[10]

The basic economic activity was, of course, agriculture. Throughout Greek history, the overwhelming majority of the population had its main wealth in the land. And the majority were smallholders, depending on their own labour, the labour of other members of the family, and the occasional assistance (as in time of harvest) of neighbours and casual hired hands. Some proportion of these smallholders owned a slave, or even two, but we cannot possibly determine what

8 See A. Aymard, "L'idée de travail dans la Grèce archaïque," J. de Psych. XLI (1948), 29-45.

9 Rhet. 1.9, 1367a32.

10 This statement is not invalidated by the occasional sally which a smallholder or petty craftsman might make into the labour market to do three days' harvesting or a week's work on temple construction; or by the presence in cities like Athens of a substantial number of men, almost all of them unskilled, who lived on odd jobs (when they were not rowing in the fleet or otherwise occupied by the state), those, for example, who congregated daily at Κολωνὸςμίσθιος (on which see A. Fuks, in Eranos XLIX (1951), 171-73). Nowhere in the sources do we hear of private establishments employing a staff of hired workers as their normal operation. Public works are frequently adduced as evidence to the contrary, but I believe without sufficient cogency. In the first place, the more common practice seems to have been a contract with an entrepreneur (even if he worked alone), not hire for wages; see P. H. Davis, "The Delian Building Accounts," Bull. Corr. Hell. LXI (1937), at pp. 110-20. Second, such evidence as we have—most fully from Delos—argues that such work was spasmodic and infrequent, and quite inconceivable as a source of livelihood for any but a handful of men. All this is consistent with the view that most of the craftsmen appearing in the accounts were independent masons and carpenters who occasionally accepted a job from the state just as they accepted orders from private clients. The key to the whole question is the absence of entrepreneurs whose regular labour force consisted of hired free men.

the proportion was, and in this sector the whole issue is clearly not of the greatest importance. But the large landholders, a minority though they were, constituted the political (and often the intellectual) elite of the Greek world; our evidence reveals remarkably few names of any consequence whose economic base was outside the land. This landholding elite tended to become more and more of an absentee group in the course of Greek history; but early or late, whether they sat on their estates or in the cities, dependent labour worked their land as a basic rule (even when allowance is made for tenancy). In some areas it took the form of helotage, and in the archaic period, of debt-bondage, but generally the form was outright slavery. . . .

I had better be perfectly clear here: I am not saying that slaves outnumbered free men in agriculture, or that the bulk of farming was done by slaves, but that slavery dominated agriculture insofar as it was on a scale that transcended the labour of the householder and his sons. Nor am I suggesting that there was no hired free labour; rather that there was little of any significance. Among the slaves, furthermore, were the overseers, invariably so if the property was large enough or if the owner was an absentee. "Of slaves," said the author of the *Oeconomica,* "there are two kinds, the overseer and the worker."

In mining and quarrying the situation was decisively one-sided. There were free men, in Athens for example, who leased such small mining concessions that they were able to work them alone. The moment, however, additional labour was introduced (and that was the more common case), it seems normally to have been slave. The largest individual holdings of slaves in Athens were workers in the mines, topped by the one thousand reported to have been leased out for this purpose by the fifth-century general Nicias.[11] It has been suggested, indeed, that at one point there may have been as many as thirty thousand slaves at work in the Athenian silver mines and processing mills.[12]

Manufacture was like agriculture in that the choice was (even more exclusively) between the independent craftsman working alone or with members of his family and the owner of slaves. The link with slavery was so close (and the absence of free hired labour so complete) that Demosthenes, for example, could say "they caused the *ergasterion* to disappear" and then he could follow, as an exact synonym and with no possible misunderstanding, by saying that "they caused the slaves to disappear."[13] On the other hand, the proportion of operations employing slaves, as against the independent self-employed craftsmen, was probably greater than in agriculture, and in this respect more like mining. In commerce and banking, subordinates were invariably slaves, even in such posts as "bank manager." However, the numbers were small.

In the domestic field, finally, we can take it as a rule that any free man who

11 Xenophon, Poroi 4.14.

12 See [Siegfried] Lauffer, [Die Bergwerkssklaven von Laureion (2 vols., Akad. Wiss. Mainz, Abh. Geistes- u. Sozialwiss. K1. 1955, no. 12; 1956, no. 11)], II 904–16.

13 Dem. 27.19,26; 28.12; see Finley, Studies in Land and Credit in Ancient Athens (New Brunswick 1952), 67. For another decisive text, see Xen. Memorab. 2.7.6.

possibly could afford one, owned a slave attendant who accompanied him when he walked abroad in the town or when he travelled (including his military service), and also a slave woman for the household chores. There is no conceivable way of estimating how many such free men there were, or how many owned numbers of domestics, but the fact is taken for granted so completely and so often in the literature that I strongly believe that many owned slaves even when they could not afford them. (Modern parallels will come to mind readily.) I stress this for two reasons. First, the need for domestic slaves, often an unproductive element, should serve as a cautionary sign when one examines such questions as the efficiency and cost of slave labour. Second, domestic slavery was by no means entirely unproductive. In the countryside in particular, but also in the towns, two important industries would often be in their hands in the larger households, on a straight production for household consumption basis. I refer to baking and textile making, and every medievalist, at least, will at once grasp the significance of the withdrawal of the latter from market production, even if the withdrawal was far from complete.[14] . . .

III.

The impression one gets is clearly that the majority of the slaves were foreigners. In a sense, they were all foreigners. That is to say, it was the rule (apart from debt bondage) that Athenians were never kept as slaves in Athens, or Corinthians in Corinth. However, I am referring to the more basic sense, that the majority were not Greeks at all, but men and women from the races living outside the Greek world. It is idle to speculate about proportions here, but there cannot be any reasonable doubt about the majority. In some places, such as the Laurium silver mines in Attica, this meant relatively large concentrations in a small area. The number of Thracian slaves in Laurium in Xenophon's time, for example, was greater than the total population of some of the smaller Greek city-states.

No wonder some Greeks came to identify slaves and barbarians (a synonym for all non-Greeks). . . .

The Greek world was one of endless debate and challenge. Among the intellectuals, no belief or idea was self-evident: every conception and every institution sooner or later came under attack—religious beliefs, ethical values, political systems, aspects of the economy, even such bedrock institutions as the family and private property. Slavery, too, up to a point, but that point was invariably a good distance short of abolitionist proposals. Plato, who criticized society more radically than any other thinker, did not concern himself much with the question

---

14 On the importance of the domestic slave as nursemaid and pedagogue, see Joseph Vogt's rectoral address, "Wege zur Menschlichkeit in der antiken Sklaverei," Univ. Tübingen Reden XLVII (1958), 19-38. (Dr. V. Ehrenberg kindly called my attention to this publication.)

in the *Republic*, but even there he assumed the continuance of slavery. And in the *Laws*, "the number of passages . . . that deal with slavery is surprisingly large" and the tenor of the legislation is generally more severe than the actual law of Athens at that time. "Their effect, on the one hand, is to give greater authority to masters in the exercise of rule over slaves, and on the other hand to accentuate the distinction between slave and free man."[15] Paradoxically, neither were the believers in the brotherhood of man (whether Cynic, Stoic, or early Christian) opponents of slavery. In their eyes, all material concerns, including status, were a matter of essential indifference. Diogenes, it is said, was once seized by pirates and taken to Crete to be sold. At the auction, he pointed to a certain Corinthian among the buyers and said: "Sell me to him: he needs a master."[16]

The question must then be faced, how much relevance has all this for the majority of Greeks, for those who were neither philosophers nor wealthy men of leisure? What did the little man think about slavery? It is no answer to argue that we must not take "the political theorists of the philosophical schools too seriously as having established 'the main line of Greek thought concerning slavery.'"[17] No one pretends that Plato and Aristotle speak for all Greeks. But, equally, no one should pretend that lower-class Greeks necessarily rejected everything which we read in Greek literature and philosophy, simply because, with virtually no exceptions, the poets and philosophers were men of the leisure class. The history of ideology and belief is not so simple. It is a commonplace that the little man shares the ideals and aspirations of his betters—in his dreams if not in the hard reality of his daily life. By and large, the vast majority in all periods of history have always taken the basic institutions of society for granted. Men do not, as a rule, ask themselves whether monogamous marriage or a police force or machine production is necessary to their way of life. They accept them as facts, as self-evident. Only when there is a challenge from one source or another—from outside or from catastrophic famine or plague—do such facts become questions. . . .

Obviously the attitude of one city to the slaves of another lies largely outside our problem. Athens agreed to help suppress helots when she and Sparta were allies; she encouraged helot revolts when they were at war. That reflects elementary tactics, not a judgment about slavery. Much the same kind of distinction must be made in the instances, recurring in Spartan history, when helots were freed as pawns in an internal power struggle. So, too, of the instances which

---

15 Glenn R. Morrow, Plato's Law of Slavery in Its Relation to Greek Law (Univ. of Illinois Press 1939), 11 and 127. Morrow effectively disproves the view that "Plato at heart disapproved of slavery and in introducing it into the *Laws* was simply accommodating himself to his age" (pp. 129-30). Cf. G. Vlastos, "Slavery in Plato's Thought," Philos. Rev. L (1941), 293: "There is not the slightest indication, either in the *Republic*, or anywhere else, that Plato means to obliterate or relax in any way" the distinction between slave and free labour.

16 Diogenes Laertius 6.74. On the Cynics, Stoics, and Christians, see Westermann, op. cit., pp. 24-25, 39-40, 116-17, 149-59.

17 Westermann, op. cit., p. 14 n. 48.

were apparently not uncommon in fourth-century Greece, but about which nothing concrete is known other than the clause in the agreement between Alexander and the Hellenic League, binding the members to guarantee that "there shall be no killing or banishment contrary to the laws of each city, no confiscation of property, no redistribution of land, no cancellation of debts, no freeing of slaves for purposes of revolution."[18] These were mere tactics again. Slaves were resources, and they could be useful in a particular situation. But only a number of specific slaves, those who were available at the precise moment; not slaves in general, or all slaves, and surely not slaves in the future. Some slaves were freed, but slavery remained untouched. Exactly the same behaviour can be found in the reverse case, when a state (or ruling class) called upon its slaves to help protect it. Often enough in a military crisis, slaves were freed, conscripted into the army or navy, and called upon to fight.[19] And again the result was that some slaves were freed while the institution continued exactly as before.

In sum, under certain conditions of crisis and tension the society (or a sector of it) was faced with a conflict within its system of values and beliefs. It was sometimes necessary, in the interest of national safety or of a political programme, to surrender the normal use of, and approach to, slaves. When this happened, the institution itself survived without any noticeable weakening. The fact that it happened is not without significance; it suggests that among the Greeks, even in Sparta, there was not that deep-rooted and often neurotic horror of the slaves known in some other societies, which would have made the freeing and arming of slaves en masse, for whatever purpose, a virtual impossibility. It suggests, further, something about the slaves themselves. Some did fight for their masters, and that is not unimportant.

Nothing is more elusive than the psychology of the slave. Even when, as in the American South, there seems to be a lot of material—autobiographies of ex-slaves, impressions of travellers from non-slaveholding societies, and the like—no reliable picture emerges.[20] For antiquity there is scarcely any evidence at all, and the bits are indirect and tangential, and far from easy to interpret. Thus, a favorite apology is to invoke the fact that, apart from very special instances as in Sparta, the record shows neither revolts of slaves nor a fear of uprisings. Even if the facts are granted—and the nature of our sources warrants a little scepticism—the rosy conclusion does not follow. Slaves have scarcely ever

18 Ps.-Demosthenes 17.15. For earlier periods, cf. Herod. 7.155 on Syracuse and Thuc. 3.73 on Corcyra (and note that Thucydides does not return to the point or generalize about it in his final peroration on *stasis* and its evils).

19 See the material assembled by Louis Robert, Etudes épigraphiques et philologiques (Bibl. Éc. Hautes Ét. 272, Paris 1938), 118–26. Xenophon, Poroi 4.42, uses the potential value of slaves as military and naval manpower as an argument in favour of his proposal to have the state buy thousands of slaves to be hired out in the mines. Cf. Hypereides' proposal after Chaeronea to free all the Athenian slaves and arm them (see fragments of his speech against Aristogeiton, Blass no. 18, and Ps.-Plut., Hyper. 848F–849A).

20 See [Kenneth M.] Stampp, [The Peculiar Institution: Slavery in the Ante-Bellum South (New York 1956)], 86–88.

revolted, even in the southern states.[21] A large-scale rebellion is impossible to organise and carry through except under very unusual circumstances. The right combination appeared but once in ancient history, during two generations of the late Roman Republic, when there were great concentrations of slaves in Italy and Sicily, many of them almost completely unattended and unguarded, many others professional fighters (gladiators), and when the whole society was in turmoil, with a very marked breakdown of social and moral values.[22]

At this point it is necessary to recall that helots differed in certain key respects from chattel slaves. First, they had the necessary ties of solidarity that come from kinship and nationhood, intensified by the fact, not to be underestimated, that they were not foreigners but a subject people working their own lands in a state of servitude. This complex was lacking among the slaves of the Greek world. The Peripatetic author of the *Oeconomica* made the sensible recommendation that neither an individual nor a city should have many slaves of the same nationality.[23] Second, the helots had property rights of a kind: the law, at least, permitted them to retain everything they produced beyond the fixed deliveries to their masters. Third, they outnumbered the free population on a scale without parallel in other Greek communities. These are the peculiar factors, in my opinion, which explain the revolts of the helots and the persistent Spartan concern with the question, more than Spartan cruelty.[24] It is a fallacy to think that the threat of rebellion increases automatically with an increase in misery and oppression. Hunger and torture destroy the spirit; at most they stimulate efforts at flight or other forms of purely individual behavior (including betrayal of fellow-victims), whereas revolt requires organisation and courage and persistence. Frederick Douglass, who in 1855 wrote the most penetrating analysis to come from an ex-slave, summed up the psychology in these words:

"Beat and cuff your slave, keep him hungry and spiritless, and he will follow the chain of his master like a dog; but feed and clothe him well,—work him moderately—surround him with physical comfort,—and dreams of freedom intrude. Give him a *bad* master, and he aspires to a *good* master; give him a good master, and he wishes to become his *own* master."[25]

There are many ways, other than revolt, in which slaves can protest.[26] In particular they can flee, and though we have no figures whatsoever, it seems safe to say that the fugitive slave was a chronic and sufficiently numerous

---

21   Ibid, pp. 132–40.

22   [Joseph] Vogt, [Structur der antiken] Sklavenkriege [(Mainz Abh. 1957, no. 1)]

23   Ps.-Arist., Oec. 1.5, 1344b18; cf. Plato, Laws 6.777C–D; Arist., Pol. 7.9.9, 133oa 25–28.

24   Note that Thucydides 8.40.2 makes the disproportionately large number of Chian slaves the key to their ill-treatment and their readiness to desert to the Athenians.

25   My Bondage and My Freedom (New York 1855), 263–64, quoted from Stampp, op. cit., p. 89.

26   Stampp, op. cit., ch. III: "A Troublesome Property," should be required reading on this subject.

phenomenon in the Greek cities.[27] Thucydides estimated that more than twenty thousand Athenian slaves fled in the final decade of the Peloponnesian War. In this they were openly encouraged by the Spartan garrison established in Decelea, and Thucydides makes quite a point of the operation. Obviously he thought the harm to Athens was serious, intensified by the fact that many were skilled workers.[28] My immediate concern is with the slaves themselves, not with Athens, and I should stress very heavily that so many skilled slaves (who must be presumed to have been, on the average, among the best treated) took the risk and tried to flee. The risk was no light one, at least for the barbarians among them: no Thracian or Carian wandering about the Greek countryside without credentials could be sure of what lay ahead in Boeotia or Thessaly. Indeed, there is a hint that these particular twenty thousand and more may have been very badly treated after escaping under Spartan promise. A reliable fourth-century historian attributed the great Theban prosperity at the end of the fifth century to their having purchased very cheaply the slaves and other booty seized from the Athenians during the Spartan occupation of Decelea.[29] Although there is no way to determine whether this is a reference to the twenty thousand, the suspicion is obvious. Ethics aside, there was no power, within or without the law, which could have prevented the reenslavement of fugitive slaves even if they had been promised their freedom.

The *Oeconomica* sums up the life of the slave as consisting of three elements: work, punishment, and food.[30] And there are more than enough floggings and even tortures in Greek literature from one end to the other. Apart from psychological quirks (sadism and the like), flogging means simply that the slave, as slave, must be goaded into performing the function assigned to him. So, too, do the various incentive plans which were frequently adopted. The efficient, skilled, reliable slave could look forward to managerial status. In the cities, in particular, he could often achieve a curious sort of quasi independence, living and working on his own, paying a kind of rental to his owner, and accumulating earnings with which, ultimately, to purchase his freedom. Manumission was, of course, the greatest incentive of all. Again we are baffled by the absence of numbers, but it is undisputed that manumission was a common phenomenon in most of the Greek world. This is an important difference between the Greek slave on the one hand, and the helot or American slave on the other. It is also important evidence about the degree of the slave's alleged "acceptance" of his status.[31]

27   I am prepared to say this despite the fact that the evidence is scrappy and has not, to my knowledge, been properly assembled. For mass flights in time of war, see e.g., Thuc. 7.75.5; 8.40.2.

28   Note how Thucydides stressed the loss in anticipation (1.142.4; 6.91.7) before actually reporting it in 7.27.5.

29   Hellenica Oxyrhynchia 12.4.

30   Ps.-Arist., Oec. 1.5,1344ª35.

31   The technical and aesthetic excellence of much work performed by slaves is, of course, visible in innumerable museums and archaeological sites. This is part of the complexity

IV.

It is now time to try to add all this up and form some judgment about the institution. This would be difficult enough to do under ordinary circumstances. It has become almost impossible because of two extraneous factors imposed by modern society. The first is the confusion of the historical study with moral judgments about slavery. We condemn slavery, and we are embarrassed for the Greeks, whom we admire so much; therefore we tend either to underestimate its role in their life, or we ignore it altogether, hoping that somehow it will quietly go away. The second factor is more political, and it goes back at least to 1848, when the *Communist Manifesto* declared that ''The history of all hitherto existing society is the history of class struggles. Free man and slave, patrician and plebeian, lord and serf, guild-master and journeyman, in a word oppressor and oppressed, stood in constant opposition to one another. . . .'' Ever since, ancient slavery has been a battleground between Marxists and non-Marxists, a political issue rather than a historical phenomenon.

Now we observe that a sizable fraction of the population of the Greek world consisted of slaves, or other kinds of dependent labour, many of them barbarians; that by and large the elite in each city-state were men of leisure, completely free from any preoccupation with economic matters, thanks to a labour force which they bought and sold, over whom they had extensive property rights, and, equally important, what we may call physical rights; that the condition of servitude was one which no man, woman, or child, regardless of status or wealth, could be sure to escape in case of war or some other unpredictable and uncontrollable emergency. It seems to me that, seeing all this, if we could emancipate ourselves from the despotism of extraneous moral, intellectual, and political pressures, we would conclude, without hesitation, that slavery was a basic element in Greek civilisation.

Such a conclusion, however, should be the starting-point of analysis, not the end of an argument, as it is so often at present. Perhaps it would be best to avoid the word ''basic'' altogether, because it has been preempted as a technical term by the Marxist theory of history. Anyone else who uses it in such a question as the one which is the title of this paper, is compelled, by the intellectual (and political) situation in which we work, to qualify the term at once, to distinguish between *a* basic institution and *the* basic institution. In effect what has happened is that, in the guise of a discussion of ancient slavery, there has been a desultory discussion of Marxist theory, none of it, on either side, particularly illuminating about either Marxism or slavery. Neither our understanding of the historical process nor our knowledge of ancient society is significantly advanced by these repeated statements and counter-statements, affirmations and denials of the proposition, ''Ancient society was based on slave labour.'' Nor have we gained much from the persistent debate about causes. Was slavery the cause of the

---

and ambiguity of the institution (discussed in the following section), which extended to the slaves themselves as well as to their masters.

decline of Greek science? or of loose sexual morality? or of the widespread contempt for gainful employment? These are essentially false questions, imposed by a naive kind of pseudo-scientific thinking.

The most fruitful approach, I suggest, is to think in terms of purpose, in Immanuel Kant's sense, or of function, as the social anthropologists use that concept. The question which is most promising for systematic investigation is not whether slavery was the basic element, or whether it caused this or that, but how it functioned.[32] This eliminates the sterile attempts to decide which was historically prior, slavery or something else; it avoids imposing moral judgments on, and prior to, the historical analysis; and it should avoid the trap which I shall call the free-will error. There is a maxim of Emile Durkheim's that "The voluntary character of a practise or an institution should never be assumed beforehand."[33] Given the existence of slavery—and it is given, for our sources do not permit us to go back to a stage in Greek history when it did not exist—the choice facing individual Greeks was socially and psychologically imposed. In the *Memorabilia* Xenophon says that "those who can do so buy slaves so that they may have fellow workers."[34] That sentence is often quoted to prove that some Greeks owned no slaves, which needs no proof. It is much better cited to prove *those who can,* buy slaves—Xenophon clearly places this whole phenomenon squarely in the realm of necessity. . . .

32 Cf. Vogt, "Wege zur Menschlichkeit," pp. 19–20: "What we lack is a clear picture of the functions maintained by slavery in the organism of ancient society, and a critical evaluation of its role in the rise, development, and decline of the culture."

33 E. Durkheim, The Rules of Sociological Method, transl. from 8th ed. (repr. Glencoe, Ill., 1950), 28.

34 Xen., Mem. 2.3.3.

WORK AND SLAVERY IN ROME

Agriculture was the chief source of income and the chief occupation in all ages and lands of the ancient world. Trade and industry were by modern standards little developed. For this there were many reasons. Technology was backward and fuel scarce. Legal and social institutions did not favor the accumulation of liquid capital. Above all, transportation was slow and costly. Under Diocletian's tariff of maximum prices the cost of moving a bushel of grain fifty miles by wagon would have absorbed two-fifths of the permitted retail price. It was less expensive to move goods by sea or inland waterway. But ships were small and slow, there were few navigational aids, and voyages were normally suspended in the winter. Italy, in particular, has few good harbours or navigable rivers. As most people lived near the subsistence level, there was no effective demand for most goods that had to travel a long distance. Some indispensable raw materials like iron might have to be imported despite the costs, but consumer goods could not have found a world-wide market, as Lancashire cottons did in the nineteenth century, and this alone can explain why there were no large factories. Industry catered for local needs or for the production of high-class goods which could stand the costs of transport. Trade was chiefly in luxuries or semi-luxuries. One great exception must be noted. The large population of Rome and later of Constantinople was fed with grain imported from overseas, especially from Africa and Egypt. But much of it was paid for by the Imperial treasury out of provincial revenues. Other cities without similar resources could not rely on imports of food. In general each community, indeed each large estate, aimed at self-sufficiency, and the result of a local failure of crops was famine.

Even by ancient standards Italy was not important for industry, nor, except for a short period, for commerce. Rome itself was never a manufacturing centre; it was only some Campanian, Etruscan and north Italian towns that were noted for armaments and certain fine products. Thus in the time of Augustus the ware of Arretium in Etruria was the most prized in the Mediterranean world; but it was soon imitated elsewhere, and lost its imperial market. In the first century B.C. Italian business men were dominant in the east. As a result of the great conquests Rome had made, enormous capital flowed into Italy, and Italians became the financiers of the Greek cities. They also traded in grain which the Italian tax-

From Peter A. Brunt, "Work and Slavery," in *The Romans,* ed. J.P.V.D. Balsdon (New York: Basic Books, Inc., 1965), pp. 177–91, by permission of Sir Isaac Pitman and Sons, Ltd., London.

farmers had collected in kind. These were temporary advantages which faded when Rome ceased to exploit her subjects so ruthlessly; Syrians or Gauls replaced Italians in imperial commerce. Italy herself had little to export except wine and oil; her available surplus of timber had vanished with deforestation, and she had virtually no mineral wealth. It is for the fertility of her land that the highest praises are heaped upon her by ancient writers. . . .

The old-style peasant had just enough land on which to raise and support a family; he was not producing for the market, except to the extent that he needed to buy tools and a few other things he could not make for himself. The women spun and weaved; even great ladies in later times are commended for their wool-making, and the Emperor Antoninus Pius was proud to wear home-spun clothes.

Of course there were also skilled craftsmen. The second of the Roman Kings, Numa, is said to have organised guilds of flute-players, goldsmiths, carpenters, dyers, cobblers, tanners, copper-workers and potters, and of the 193 centuries into which the Roman people in arms were divided (the Comitia Centuriata) two were appointed for the makers of arms, who enjoyed, it seems, a position of some honour. In the early period such craftsmen in Rome were evidently for the most part free citizens, and presumably this was true elsewhere.

The great majority of Romans and of other Italians, however, must have lived on the land. Their life was never easy. In a bad year they had to borrow, and if they could not repay, their creditors could reduce them to a form of bondage. Roman conquests in Italy probably did more than remedial legislation to improve the position of the small man. Rome confiscated part of the territory of the Italian cities she subdued and used it to settle her own citizens, a policy which at once increased her population and military strength and provided the poor with lands. But from the beginning of the second century B.C. onwards wars overseas contributed to ruin the peasantry. While the ploughman was doing military service, perhaps for six years on end, in Spain, his farm was neglected. Other factors helped to promote the concentration of landed property in the hands of a few rich men who sought to accumulate it because it was both the safest and the most honourable investment and who did not scruple to secure it even by force or fraud. Pasturage, which required relatively little labour, was often the most lucrative way of exploiting their lands, and they often preferred slaves to free workers.

Thus the old yeomanry gradually diminished. Many displaced farmers sought shelter in the city of Rome. We must not exaggerate the extent or speed of the process. At the lowest and probably correct estimate the free population of Italy under Augustus did not exceed five millions, and probably under one million lived in Rome. In 37 B.C. Varro spoke of large numbers of the poor who tilled their lands with the help of their children, smaller owners, or, perhaps, tenants of the great proprietors, who were recommended by the experts to lease farms, if they could not supervise them closely or if they were situated on unhealthy land, where slaves would suffer heavy mortality. It was also uneconomic to maintain enough slaves for seasonal operations, harvest or vintage for which gangs of free labourers were employed, probably men who eked out subsistence at other times on their own little plots or by casual work in the towns. In the late Republic some two hundred thousand free Italians were often under arms; these soldiers came from the country and sought allotments of land as a reward for their service. But numerous assignations of land to the rural poor seem to have done no more than retard the concentration of property. The process went on, and in the late Empire we hear of enormous estates in Italy called *massae*.

It is indeed generally held that under the Augustan peace the supply of slaves dwindled and that the large proprietors had to rely more on free labour and, in particular, on leasing farms to tenants. This is dubious. Certainly fewer slaves were made by war, piracy and brigandage, but we cannot be sure that Italian slaveowners did not then breed them in large numbers, like the owners of plantations in the Southern states. Even tenants often worked their farms with the help of slaves, who might be supplied to them along with other expensive equipment by the landlords. Nor were the tenants themselves prosperous; they were often in debt, and by the time of Constantine they had come to be tied to their lands and were little better than serfs. Probably, in most periods of Roman history, there must have been perennial under-employment and near starvation among the agricultural poor.

Driven from the land, what could the Roman peasant do? Unlike his successor in the England of the industrial revolution, he could not readily find alternative employment in the towns. This was not merely due to the absence of a large-scale industry; there was also slave competition. The freeborn poor in the towns had to depend in large part on public corn doles and on the bounty of the great houses. There were also casual earnings, especially in the building trade, where the operations were not sufficiently continuous to warrant the employment of slaves who had to be fed and clothed, whether they were working or not. The Emperor Vespasian was a lavish builder; once when an engineer came to him with a labour-saving device, he was rewarded—but Vespasian refused to adopt his invention. "You must let me feed my poor commons" he said. The Colosseum and his other great monuments were evidently constructed by free labour.

One result of the impoverishment of the masses from the second century B.C. onwards was decline in the birth rate. Many of the poor were unable to raise children. This was a source of concern to many statesmen from Tiberius Gracchus to Trajan. That Emperor made public funds available to feed poor children under a scheme which endured for a century. Its success is uncertain; plague, endemic malaria and famine helped to reduce the population, and in Marcus Aurelius' reign parts of Italy were desolate and could be used for settling barbarians.

What has already been said indicates the importance of slavery in Roman society. As in all other ancient lands it was an institution of immemorial antiquity, which no one ever proposed to abolish. Greeks who were accustomed to question everything had challenged its legitimacy and evoked a powerful defence from Aristotle; the slave was in his view a man who had only enough rationality to understand and obey orders, and it was as much in his own interest as the master's that he should be subject to rational government. (Slightly modified, this argument is familiar today from the writings of imperialist apologists.) But this controversy was in the realm of theory. Even when slaves rebelled, they did not object to slavery as such: they merely wanted to be free themselves. A Roman jurist said that by natural law all men are born free, but he hastened to add that slavery existed by the law of nations. The Stoics, who were influential at Rome, taught that all men were brothers, including slaves; but in their philosophy man's welfare is purely spiritual, and material conditions irrelevant to it; true misery lies in being a slave to one's own passions, and legal servitude does not stop a man from being master of himself in the moral sense. The Christian attitude was much the same. Slaves, according to Paul, are not to worry about the condition in which they were called; and he did not recommend Philemon to liberate Onesimus. Hence it is no surprise that when Christianity became the official religion, the Church did not advocate abolition: on the contrary, it acquired slaves of its own. In the breakup of the Empire slavery gradually dwindled, for reasons that are not clear; but as great numbers of free men were reduced to serfdom, from which it was often harder to escape, the net gain to human freedom was not large. . . .

The enormous importance of slavery in the economy of ancient Italy raises a large historical question. Obviously if the technical advances of even the early modern period of European history had been anticipated in the Graeco-Roman world, the Empire must have been too strong for the barbarians, whose invasions were at least the proximate cause and the necessary condition for its disruption. Can the extensive use of slavery be held responsible for technological backwardness and economic stagnation?

It has been argued that because slave labour was abundant and cheap the ancient world had no incentive to technological invention and that slavery so far abased the dignity of labour that the best minds turned away in disgust from everything connected with manual tasks; hence the backwardness of the Greeks and Romans in all scientific investigations which, unlike mathematics, demanded any approach other than that of abstract thinking. At the same time, to quote Cairnes' famous judgement on American slavery, slave labour "is given reluctantly; it is unskillful; it is wanting in versatility"; it must therefore be assumed that it was inefficient.

Even on these premises slavery cannot have been a prime cause of Rome's decline. After Augustus the Empire drew its strength increasingly and in the end exclusively from the provinces, where slavery was not predominant as it was in

Italy. Not only did the provinces furnish soldiers; some of them, notably Gaul and Egypt, were economically more prosperous, and it is certain of Egypt and probable of Gaul that slavery there was on a small scale. Yet these regions were no more inventive or progressive than Italy. We must therefore look elsewhere for reasons that will explain scientific or technological stagnation. Some have already been given; and we must add that progress was to depend on the formulation of fertile scientific hypotheses or on crucial inventions like optical glass; it is perhaps no more easy to understand why these happen in one age and not in another than to account for the flowering of poetical genius.

And was slave labour so inefficient? Roman experts on agriculture assumed that on good land and adequately supervised it brought in higher profits than free labour. We lack ancient evidence to test this assumption, and modern analogies yield no clear conclusion; the latest analyses of the economy of the Old South seem to show that its backwardness compared with the North cannot be certainly ascribed to slavery. In trade and industry the slaves were skilled workers spurred on by the hope of freedom; they are actually credited with minor inventions (like American negro slaves) and, if other factors had permitted mechanization, they were clearly capable of minding machines; indeed negroes too were used successfully in factories, although they were at a lower cultural level and lacked such strong incentives. (Similarly in the last world war German productivity actually increased with the extended use of what was in all but name slave labour.) However cheap Roman slaves were, and we do not know just how cheap, the owners still had no motive to be indifferent to devices that might have increased their output.

It is thus on moral rather than on economic grounds that Roman slavery merits opprobrium. And many Roman slaves were no worse off than the mass of the peasantry who, though free in name, found it hard to assert their rights or defend their interests and never lived far from starvation. In a preindustrial and poor society, of course, the poverty of the masses is the price to be paid if even a few are to enjoy leisure and civilisation and the opportunity of promoting further progress. But in the Roman world such inevitable inequality was carried too far, further, for instance, than in democratic Greek communities. Hence, in the first century B.C. agrarian discontent in Italy helped to bring the Republic down, and in and after the third century A.D. the peasantry, unconscious of the benefits that accrued even to them from the Roman peace, often showed themselves indifferent and sometimes hostile to an empire in which the interests of the wealthy, *beati possidentes,* were always preponderant. This was no doubt one reason why despite its immensely superior resources the Empire succumbed to the inroads of barbarians.

EXPLOITATION BEGINS
AT HOME

Family life is a special concern of social historians. The rules and procedures concerning marriage and divorce, birth and death, tell us much
about a society. Specifically, we can learn from such a study about the fate
of women, who make up slightly more than half of the world's population.
The readings in this section provide many interesting details but few real
surprises about the status of women in Greece and Rome.

Robert Flacelière contends that outside of their own home most Greek
women enjoyed only a few more political and legal rights than slaves. To
be sure there were differences from city to city, and obviously class distinctions made the daily condition of women far from uniform. Still, the social
behavior, personal freedom, and potential accomplishments of women
were largely dependent on the station of their husbands. The French
scholar adds, however, that the highest-born were not necessarily the freest
of women.

Sarah B. Pomeroy shows that marital customs were little changed in
Rome. If there was a difference from Greece, it was the greater emphasis
on family planning, which sometimes took the grim form of exposing (that
is abandoning) infants—especially girls—to death. Contraception and abortion were also practiced, mainly by the upper classes. The poor were more
often condemned to combine childbearing with a life of hard work or prostitution.

J.P.V.D. Balsdon raises a number of intriguing questions about the com-
portment of women in Rome. How did they deal with men before and after

marriage? How did they behave in public and in private? To what standards of morality did they conform or not conform? To what extent, in short, were they emancipated? The answers, of course, varied considerably from class to class. But in general, insofar as we know, the Roman woman's place was in the home, whether supervising or participating in the work that was done there. They also found time to talk and even to drink, albeit preferably not to excess. Above all, they were expected to bear children and to stay out of public life. Only the spread of Christianity under the late Roman Empire brought a hint of change in attitudes and values.

Clearly, classical times were a man's world. Not only does the available evidence indicate that the legal status of women was narrowly circumscribed, it is striking how little evidence about women can be gathered from classical sources. That they were so frequently ignored by writers and legislators is probably the best indication of their true social position.

———ROBERT FLACELIÈRE————————————————

WOMEN, MARRIAGE, AND THE FAMILY IN ATHENS

THE STATUS OF WOMEN

In Athens, the wives of citizens enjoyed no more political or legal rights than did their slaves. Women had lost the important role they formerly played in Minoan society,[1] and which, as it seems, they had at least partially preserved during the Homeric period.[2] Yet though a married Athenian woman might be confined to her house, here at least she enjoyed absolute authority—subject always to the consent of her lord and master: to her slave-girls she was the *despoina*, the mistress. In any case, her husband was so busy with other matters—in the country, hunting or farming; in the city, his profession, and political or legal

Reprinted with permission of Macmillan Publishing Co., Inc., from *Daily Life in Greece at the Time of Pericles*, by Robert Flacelière, trans. Peter Green (New York: Macmillan, 1965).

1 See G. Glotz, *La Civilisation égéenne*, pp. 166–70.
2 See E. Mireaux, *La Vie Quotidienne au temps d'Homère*, pp. 204–27.

affairs of state—that he was compelled, more often than not, to leave his wife to run their home as she pleased.

The dependent and subordinate position of Athenian women can be deduced, first, from the life led by young girls, and the way in which they came to be married. There was no question of a girl being free to meet other young people, since she scarcely ever left the women's apartments, the *gynaikeion*. Whereas married women seldom crossed the thresholds of their own front door, adolescent girls were lucky if they were allowed as far as the inner courtyard, since they had to stay where they could not be seen—well away, even, from the male members of their own family. There is nothing in fifth-century Athens corresponding to the "school" for well-connected girls which the poetess Sappho conducted, at the beginning of the sixth century, on the island of Lesbos. Nor do we find anything in Athens resembling the physical training given to young Spartan girls, in short tunics which "exposed their thighs," and concerning which Euripides wrote:

> Spartan maidens, allowed out of doors with the young men, running and wrestling in their company, with naked thighs and girt-up tunics.[3]

In this respect, and this alone, disciplinarian Sparta was more tolerant than Athens; and Euripides chooses just this aspect of Lacedaemonian *mores* to criticize as scandalous, for the simple reason that here he has a direct contrast with accepted Athenian custom.

Everything a young Athenian girl learnt—which meant, basically, domestic skills such as cooking, spinning, and weaving, with perhaps a little reading, music and arithmetic thrown in—she would be taught by her mother, or her grandmother, or some family slave-girl. The only occasions on which girls normally went out were during certain religious festivals, when they assisted at the sacrifice and took part in the procession, as we learn from the Panathenaic frieze on the Parthenon. Still, some of them must have been trained to sing and dance, in order to join the festival choir—though in such choirs boys and girls were always kept strictly apart.

In Xenophon's *Oeconomica* Ischomachus says of his young bride:

> What can she have known about life when I married her, my dear Socrates? She was not yet quite fifteen at the time she crossed my threshold; and till that moment she had lived under the most cramping restrictions, trained from childhood to see and hear as little as possible, and ask an absolute minimum of questions.[4]

This was, indeed, the ideal aimed at when giving girls a good education.

Here is another statement on the subject by Ischomachus. This time it is his wife he is addressing:

---

3 Euripides, *Andromache* 597–598.
4 Xenophon, *Oeconomica* 7.5.

Do you now understand why it was I married you, and why your parents bethrothed you to me? There would have been no difficulty in finding another girl to share my bed: I am quite sure you realize *that*. No; the decision was only taken after a great deal of thought—both by me on my own account and by your parents on yours—as to the best helpmeet each of us could find for the care of our home and future children. Eventually I picked on you, just as your parents settled for me—probably after considering various other potential husbands.

It was, in fact, the girl's *Kyrios* (that is, her father, or, failing him, a blood-brother, or a grandfather, or, in the last resort, her legal guardian) who chose a husband for her and decided when she was to be married. Doubtless in many cases her own wishes were ascertained; but we have no evidence to suggest this, and her consent was not in the slightest degree necessary. Herodotus, it is true, tells a very strange anecdote about one sixth-century Athenian: "His treatment of his three daughters was as follows: when they reached marriageable age, he gave them the most magnificent dowry, and then let each of them choose—from the whole body of Athenian citizens—the man she desired for a husband; to whom, in due course, he married her off."[5]

Herodotus, who was himself a product of the fifth century, appears to find this paterfamilias' behaviour admirable, and certainly quotes it in an approving manner. But he also makes it clear that it was the exception rather than the rule. The rule was that formulated in verse by a much later author: "Girl, wed the man your parents wish you to."[6]

An Athenian citizen married, primarily, to have children: he expected them not only to care for him in his old age, but also—more important—to bury him with the full appropriate rites and keep up the family cult after he was gone. The first and foremost reason for marriage was thus a religious one, and on this point the conclusions of Fustel de Coulanges, in his *Cité antique,* have lost none of their validity. A man married, above all, in order to have male children: one son at least, to perpetuate the line and guarantee him the cult-honors which he, the father, performed for *his* ancestors, and which were regarded as indispensable for the well-being of the dead in the nether world.

At Sparta, confirmed bachelors were liable to legal sanctions; there was no such law of enforcement in Athens, but the pressure of public opinion was strong, and any unmarried male found himself subjected to much scornful censure. Despite this, a man whose elder brother had married and produced children found it somewhat more socially permissible to remain single himself.

It looks very much as though the majority of Athenians married for religious and social convenience rather than from personal choice. According to the poet Menander, writing at the end of the fourth century, they regarded marriage as a

5 Herodotus, 6. 122.

6 Naumachius *ap.* Stobaeus Vol. 3 pp. 22, 68, 234 [ed. Gaisford]: his poem *Advice to the Married* 12.

"necessary evil."[7] At any rate, we have no evidence of love between the engaged couple prior to the New Comedy. Besides, how could an Athenian have conceived a passion for a girl whom, in most cases, he had never so much as set eyes on? We know that the Greeks of the fifth and fourth centuries used the word *erôs* (love) in the first instance to describe the passion linking an *erastés* with his *erômenos*—in other words, just that type of relationship which we mean when we talk of "Greek love." . . .

All this, of course, does not mean that love could not subsequently come about between husband and wife. Xenophon makes Socrates say, in his *Symposium:* "Niceratus, from what I hear, is passionately in love with his wife, and she with him."[8] The poet Euripides, though he was commonly regarded as a misogynist, made a play out of the sublime self-sacrifice and devotion of Alcestis, who gave up her own life for love of her husband; and even Plato, the theorist of ideal pederasty, once wrote: "Only those who love can ever be willing to die for another's sake: and this applies to women no less than men." He cites the instance of Alcestis, "whose case impressed the gods so much that they allowed her to return from Hades and behold the light of heaven once more."[9] The works of Aristotle, who had married the niece of his friend Hermias, and found his wife eminently satisfactory, are full of passages in which marriage is regarded, not as a mere alliance, the sole function of which is to perpetuate one's line, but as a relationship full of affection and mutual tenderness, capable of satisfying all the moral and emotional demands that life may make on it. Nevertheless, it was only through late Stoicism—probably under the influence of Roman *mores*—that conjugal love was to be finally rehabilitated in Greece. The philosophical tradition favoring all-male love was strong and persistent: even at the beginning of the second century A.D. Plutarch, before embarking on the apologia for marriage, feels constrained to demonstrate that young girls are just as capable of arousing the passions as young boys![10]

Incest was not legally forbidden in Athens, but unions between parent and child were regarded as an abomination that called down the wrath of the gods: Sophocles' *Oedipus Rex* is ample demonstration of this. The same religious taboo was extended to unions between brother and sister born of the same mother, but a half-brother could marry his sister if the common strain came through their father. For instance, a daughter of Themistocles named Mnesiptolema, born to the great statesman by his second wife, married her own brother Archeptolis, he being the child of a different mother.[11] Similarly we find a plaintiff referring to his grandfather's marriage—the old man wed his sister, but they had different

7   Menander, *The Arbitration* 490 ff., and fr. 651.

8   Xenophon, *Symposium* 8.3.

9   Plato, *Symposium* 179 b-c.

10   Cf. Plutarch, *Amatorius, passium,* and R. Flacelière, *Les Epicuriens et l'amour,* in *Rev. Et. Gr.* Vol. 67 (1954), pp. 69-81.

11   Plutarch, *Life of Themistocles* 32.

mothers.[12] The principle of endogamy, that is to say marriage within a limited social group, results in unions between close relatives being not only tolerated but actively encouraged. We find one Athenian admitting, in the course of a lawsuit, that he married his daughter off to his nephew rather than to some stranger, so as to preserve and reinforce family ties. Marriages between first cousins, or even uncle and niece, are by no means rare: in the latter case the bridegroom's brother would also become his father-in-law. An *epikléros,* that is, a daughter who inherited her defunct father's estate in the absence of any male heir, was obliged to marry her father's closest relative who would agree to the match. Here we have an unmistakable instance of the primitive urge to ensure the continuity of race and family cult alike. . . .

THE GYNAIKEIA

Marriage did not put an end to the confined and sedentary existence that women led before it. In Athens, it is true, the *gynaikeia* were not locked up (except at night) and did not have barred windows; but customary usage sufficed to keep women within doors. This rule was strictly enforced, and gave rise to various categorical aphorisms such as: "Respectable women should stay at home: the street is for worthless hussies."[13] Even those who lingered on their doorsteps, out of sheer curiosity, were treated as suspect. It was husbands or slaves who normally went to market and did the daily shopping.

Nevertheless, it is important to distinguish, in this respect, between the various social classes. Poor Athenians, with nothing but cramped lodgings at their disposal, were more inclined to allow their wives out. In any case, the wives often had to take a job in order to make ends meet: we know, for instance, that many of them worked as stallkeepers in the market. Athenians of the middle class, on the other hand, and those with large incomes, seem to have been far more strict in the seclusion of their women; but then the wives of such citizens possessed a far more ample *gynaikeion,* often provided with an inner courtyard where they could take the air, safe from the inquisitive eyes of the multitude.

Still, every woman, even one from the ranks of the bourgeoisie, on occasion needed to do some essentially personal shopping, e.g., for clothes or shoes, which meant that she had to go out. On such occasions she was obliged to take one of her attendants with her—that is, one of her slaves. But the main occasions on which women were allowed away from their homes were during the various city festivals, or for special family events. Athens was remarkable in having one festival specially reserved for married women, the Thesmophoria.[14] We find a deceived husband, who has killed his wife's lover, telling the court: "To begin

12 Demosthenes, *Against Eubulides* 20–1.
13 Menander, fr. 546.
14 Eg Aristophanes in the *Thesmophoriazusae.*

with, my wife was a paragon of marital virture—she ran the house efficiently and economically, in short she was a first-class domestic manager. But then I lost my mother, and her death was the cause of all my subsequent misfortune. You see, it was while walking in her funeral procession that my wife was first spotted by Eratosthenes, who managed, in course of time, to seduce her: he lay in wait for the slave-girl who did her shopping, used this girl as a go-between to make contact with her mistress, and finally achieved the latter's ruin.'' The same plaintiff later reveals how he was tipped off about his wife's infidelity by the slave of yet another married woman who had succumbed to Eratosthenes' advances, and how, by means of threats, he made his own wife's maid tell him the whole truth: "She told me how he had accosted her after the funeral . . . and finally how, at the time of the Thesmophoria, when I was away in the country, she had gone to the sanctuary with his mother.''[15]

Women were not even supposed to take any interest in what went on outside the house: that was strictly the men's business. Nor did they have much opportunity for talking at any great length to their own husbands, since the latter were nearly always out, and do not seem to have been in the habit of taking meals with their wives. "Is there anyone of your acquaintance with whom you have less conversation than your wife?" Socrates asks Critobulus, and the latter replies: "Hardly anyone, I think.''[16] When an Athenian invited friends to his home, his wife never appeared in *andrón,* the banqueting-chamber, except perhaps to supervise the slaves waiting at table; nor did she accompany her husband out when he was a guest in his turn. It was only at family festivals that men and women mingled.

Yet it was the wife who held supreme authority within the home, where she was responsible for everything: Xenophon's *Oeconomica* acquaints us in detail with the duties that developed on the mistress of the house. These instructions, laid down for his wife by Ischomachus, will suffice to give us some idea of her responsibilities:

> You are to stay in the house, and ensure that all those servants whose work takes them out of doors leave at the same time. You are also responsible for supervising those who remain, and who perform their duties in the house itself. You must personally take charge of all goods brought into the house, and issue what is needed for necessary outgoings—budgeting in advance for a reserve, and taking care not to squander in a month what should last a full year. When your slaves bring you spun wool, you must see to it that this wool is used to make clothes for those who need them. You must keep a constant eye on the grain in the store-room, and make sure it remains fit to eat . . . When a servant falls ill, you must always ensure that he is receiving proper care and attention.[17]

15   Lysias, *On The Murder of Eratosthenes* 7–8, 20.
16   Xenophon, *Oeconomica* 3.12
17   *Ibid.* 7.35–7.

The wife did not bake bread herself except in the very poorest families. When Alexander's envoys accompanied the Athenian Phocion to his home, Plutarch tells us, "they found his domestic arrangements austere indeed: his wife was busy kneading dough, and Phocion himself took a bucket off to the well to get water for washing his own and his guests' feet."[18] Normally such tasks were performed by slaves, under the supervision of the *despoina*—as in Homeric times, when Eurycleia washed the feet of Odysseus.[19]

A wife's badge of authority consisted of the keys she carried about with her, in particular those to storeroom and cellar. Theophrastus' picture of the Distrustful Man contains these words: "When he is in bed he will ask his wife if she has locked up the big chest and the silver cabinet, and whether the back door is properly bolted."[20] Gluttony, drunkenness, or prodigality in a wife might lead her husband to withdraw the keys from her.

It is hard to evaluate Aristophanes' evidence on the social life of women, since we can never be quite sure where realism ends and caricature begins. Yet the overall impression one gets from his comedies is that by the end of the fifth century the traditional seclusion of women was giving rise to numerous exceptions, and it is not hard to understand why. The Peloponnesian War meant that Athenian menfolk, whether serving in some expeditionary force or manning the ramparts of Attica, were absent from their homes for even longer periods than in peacetime. The chorus of women in the *Lysistrata*—free women, certainly, and Athenians—observe: "At crack of dawn I went and filled my water-pot from the fountain—and what a business it was! All that crowd, and the noise, and jars banging against each other, and a mob of servants and branded slaves elbowing past you . . ."[21]

According to Aristophanes, women went not only to the fountain, but down to the market as well, to do their shopping and sell their own produce: like Euripides' mother, who was, it seems, some sort of green grocer.[22] We also hear, in a plaintiff's brief, of one Athenian woman who was in turn a ribbon-seller and a paid nurse;[23] but whereas freeborn Athenian women only took jobs in the last resort, as a matter of extreme necessity, the wives of metics were often wool-weavers, shoemakers, dressmakers, and so on. Some of them seem to have been genuine "businesswomen."[24]

18 Plutarch, *Life of Phocion* 18.

19 Homer, *Odyssey* 19. 350–94.

20 Theophrastus, *Characters* 18.

21 Aristophanes, *Lysistrata* 327.

22 Aristophanes, *Wasps* 497; *Thesmophoriazusae* 387.

23 Demosthenes, *Against Eubulides* 34, 35.

24 See M. Clerc, *Les Métèques athéniens* (1893) p. 395, and G. Glotz, *Le Travail dans la Grèce ancienne,* pp. 218, 221.

CONJUGAL AND FAMILY LOVE

It seems fairly clear, then, that there was little intimacy, intellectual contact, or even real love between husband and wife in classical Athens. Men constantly met and entertained one another: in their homes, in the Agora or the law courts of the Assembly, about their business affairs. Women, by contrast, lived a wholly secluded life. The *gynaikeion* was always kept well away from the *andrôn*. Many Athenians must have held opinions on marriage such as Montaigne was later to express: "In this discreete match, appetites are not commonly so fondling; but drowsie and more sluggish . . . A man doth not marry for himselfe, whatsoever he aleageth; but as much or more for his posteritie and familie . . . Nor is it other than a kinde of incest, in this reverent alliance and sacred bond, to employ the efforts and extravagant humor of an amorous licentiousnes . . . A good marriage (if any there be) refuseth the company and conditions of love."[25]

But these carnal or emotional needs that the Athenian did not satisfy at home (since he saw his wife as the mistress of his house and the mother of his children) he tended to find an outlet for elsewhere, in the company of boys or courtesans. Here we must make a distinction between the fifth and the fourth centuries. The Athenian family, as a social unit, seems to have stood firm throughout the greater part of the fifth century; but the Peloponnesian War, a savagely fought conflict which lasted for thirty long years, brought about fundamental changes in Athenian *mores*. The terrible Plague of 430–429, which claimed Pericles among its victims, was directly attributable to the war, and Thucydides thus describes its effect upon public morality:

> These sudden changes of fortune which people witnessed—the wealthy struck dead overnight, paupers inheriting their riches—made them the more willing to indulge openly in such pleasures as they would before have taken care to conceal. They sought quick returns for their money, and saw immediate self-gratification as the one reasonable pursuit in a world where they, and their wealth, were liable to perish at any moment.[26]

Many women acquired more free and easy habits, following the example of Spartan wives, who lived a far less secluded life than did their Athenian counterparts, and spent a good deal more time in men's company. The resultant disorder led to the appointment of a special magistrate, whose job it was to control the behaviour and, in particular, the extravagance of women—a problem to which Solon, too, had already bent his mind. This magistrate was known as the *gynaikonomos*.[27] To read the *Lysistrata,* which dates from 411 B.C., and the *Women in Parliament,* performed as late as 392, one might be forgiven for inferring that

---

25   Montaigne, *Essays,* Vol. 3 Ch. 5 (Florio's translation).

26   Thucydides, 2. 53.

27   Aristole, *Politics* 6. 15 [p. 1299 a].

many Athenian women, having seen an exclusively masculine government carry the city headlong to disaster, were convinced that things might go a little better if *they* expressed their views and gave their husbands advice, but these two plays by Aristophanes are wildly exaggerated fantasy-farces, which afford us no evidence that there existed what today we would term a "feminist movement"— something quite inconceivable in ancient Athens. . . .

In the fourth century, it would appear, many Athenians kept a concubine without considering this a reason to dismiss their legitimate wives. But did these concubines (who might equally well be Athenians, slaves, or freeborn foreigners) enjoy any legal, publicly recognized status? From the advocates' speeches in which allusions to them occur, we might well doubt it.[28] But custom, if not the law, looked on them with remarkable tolerance, and a large number of Athenians seem to have been, to all intents and purposes, bigamous. Socrates is supposed to have had a second wife called Mytro, as well as the acidulous Xanthippe; but this story may well be pure fiction. The misogynist streak which Euripides reveals in several of his plays was explained by the assertion that he, too, was bigamously married, and therefore had twice as much opportunity as most men to study feminine malice! Some authorities—late ones, it must be said—also inform us that during the Peloponnesian War, as a measure designed to counter the slump in population, every male Athenian was authorized to have another woman, over and above his legally married wife, to bear him children: the woman might be a foreigner, and all offspring of such a union were treated as legitimate.

But long before this we find the case of Themistocles, whose father, it is true, was an Athenian citizen but whose mother was a Thracian slave, one Abrotonon: his illegitimacy had proved no bar to a successful career. "When one's legal wife becomes intolerable," Plutarch wrote, "is not the best solution to take a companion like Abrotonon of Thrace or Bacchis of Miletus, without any *engyésis*—just buy them outright, and scatter a few nuts over their head?"[29] But if the concubine was an Athenian, how could one make a distinction between her and one's legal wife, especially if the children she bore were likewise considered Athenian citizens? Isaeus informs us that "even those parents who give their own daughters into concubinage negotiate a fixed sum, payable to the concubine."[30] We may well suppose that some poor Athenians, who could not provide a dowry for their daughters, made them contract an alternative union of this nature instead, asking nothing on their behalf except some financial recompense in case of a separation. A legally married wife, on the other hand, normally brought her husband a dowry.

---

28   E.g. in particular Demosthenes, *Against Boeotus,* I and II, and Isaeus, *On the Succession of Phyrrhus.*

29   Plutarch, *Amatorius* 753 D.

30   Isaeus, *op. cit.* 28.

As for the *hetairai,* or courtesans, they were for the most part slaves. Many of them were content with the modest enough fee of one obol, though some—the top-grade *hetairai*—cost their lovers a pretty penny. During the Hellenistic epoch certain courtesans even managed to marry reigning princes, and thus become queens: "Flute-girls, dancers from Samos, an Aristonica or an Agathocleia or an Oenanthe with her tambourine—all these have trodden a royal diadem under-foot."[31] Even as early as the fourth century the celebrated Phryne, a Boeotian from Thespiae, had managed to make a really rich killing. Her actual name was Mnesarete, which means "mindful of virtue"; "Phryne" was a nickname, given her on account of her yellowish complexion (the word in fact means "toad"; though this, apparently, did not make her any the less beautiful). It is well known what methods the orator Hyperides, himself one of her lovers, is supposed to have employed in order to secure her acquittal on an impiety charge that had been brought against her; but this anecdote is highly suspect.[32] [Hyperides is said to have made her bare her bosom before the court, an argument which proved irresistible. (Trs.)] She was also Praxiteles' mistress, and served as the model for several statues he made of Aphrodite. Her personal fortune was so immense that it enabled her to set up her own statue, in gold, in the sanctuary at Delphi, amongst those of generals and kings. Plutarch, himself a priest of Pythian Apollo, was to take great exception to this centuries later: he described the statue as "a trophy won from the lechery of the Greeks."[33]

Brothels had existed in Athens at least since Solon's day, in the Ceramicus and, particularly, the Piraeus;[34] a percentage of the profits had gone to build the temple of Aphrodite Pandemos.[35]

Were these courtesans (whether freelance or institutionalized) really, as is sometimes claimed, better educated and more culturally aware than respectable Athenian matrons? To judge from those whom we can observe in conflict with legitimate wives, during various court hearings, the matter is at least open to doubt. Consider Alcé the brothel-madam, who gobbled up poor old Euctémon,[36] or Neaera, who lived with Stephanus, or her daughter Phano, who managed to hook an Athenian holding the office of King-archon, and later took part with him in various highly sacred rituals:[37] none of these women would appear to have received a refined education. Neaera was reared by a procuress "who was highly skilled in picking out future beauties on the strength of their appearance in infancy"; but her education seems to have consisted, first and foremost, in

31 Plutarch, *op. cit. ibid.*
32 See G. Colin's introduction to his edition of Hyperides (Coll. G. Budé) pp. 10–12.
33 Plutarch, *On the Pythian Oracles* 401 A.
34 Cf. Aristophanes, *Peace* 165.
35 Athenaeus, 13. 569 d.
36 Isaeus, *On the Succession of Philoctemon* 19–20.
37 Ps-Demosthenes, *Against Neaera, passim.*

learning the secrets of dressing and make-up, and other aids to physical seduction. We hear that Phryne was beautiful; no one suggests that she was clever or cultivated, like Aspasia. It was by their compliant ways and willingness to please that these *hetairai* kept their lovers. As one comic poet put it: "Is not a mistress always more loving than a wife? Indeed she is, and for a very good reason. However unpleasant your wife may be, you are legally bound to keep her. A mistress, on the other hand, knows that a lover can only be kept by constant attentiveness, failing which he will turn elsewhere."[38]

It is quite likely, however, that many courtesans received a somewhat freer and wider education than the middle-class ladies of Athens, especially in such fields as music, singing, and dancing: numbers of them had been trained to perform on the flute (*aulos*), and were employed to play, sing, and dance at banquets. . . .

38   Amphis, *ap.* Athenaeus, 13. 559 a.

—SARAH B. POMEROY————————————————

MARRIAGE AND MOTHERHOOD IN ROME

Marriage and motherhood were the traditional expectation of well-to-do women in Rome, as they had been in Greece. The rarity of spinsters indicates that most women married at least once, although afterward a number chose to remain divorcées or widows.

Augustus established the minimum age for marriage at twelve for girls and fourteen for boys. The first marriage of most girls took place between the ages of twelve and fifteen. Since menarche typically occurred at thirteen or fourteen, prepubescent marriages took place.[1] Moreover, sometimes the future bride lived with the groom before she had reached the legal minimum for marriage, and it

1   See Amundsen and Diers, "Age of Menarche," [*Human Biology* 41(1969): 125–132] and Keith Hopkins, "The Age of Roman Girls at Marriage."

was not unusual for these unions to be consummated. Marriages of young girls took place because of the desire of the families involved not to delay the profit from a political or financial alliance and, beginning with the reign of Augustus, so that the bride and groom could reap the rewards of the marital legislation, although some of the benefits could be anticipated during the engagement. Sometimes one motive outweighed another. Thus there are cases of dowerless daughters of the upper class who nevertheless found social-climbing men so eager to marry them that the husbands surreptitiously provided the dowry, to save the pride of the girl's family.[2] Another factor which we have traced back to Hesiod was the desire to find a bride who was still virginal.

Most upper-class Roman women were able to find husbands, not only for first marriages but for successive remarriages. One reason for this, apparently, was that there were fewer females than males among their social peers.[3] As in Greece, this disproportion was the result of the shorter lifespan of females, whose numbers fell off sharply once the childbearing years were reached. There were the additional factors of the selective infanticide and exposure of female infants and, probably more important, a subtle but pervasive attitude that gave preferential treatment to boys. This can be surmised from a law attributed to Romulus that required a father to raise all male children but only the first-born female. This so-called law of Romulus—while not to be accepted at face value as evidence that every father regularly raised only one daughter—is nevertheless indicative of offical policy and foreshadows later legislation favoring the rearing of boys over girls. The attitude may be criticized as short-sighted in face of the manpower shortage continually threatening Rome: the policy of Sparta, where potential childbearers were considered as valuable as warriors, should be compared.

The law of Romulus incidentally shows that it was not inconvenient for a daughter to be automatically called by the feminine form of her father's name (*nomen*). But it was awkward when the father decided to raise two daughters, who thus had the same name, like Cornelia and her sister Cornelia. The Romans solved the problem with the addition of "the elder" (*maior*) or "the younger" (*minor*). In families where several daughters were raised, numerals, which in earlier times may have been indicative of order of birth, were added (e.g., Claudia *Tertia* and Claudia *Quinta*).[4] A wealthy father might decide to dispose of an infant because of the desire not to divide the family property among too many offspring and thereby reduce the individual wealth of the members of the next generation. Christian authors such as Justin Martyr doubtless exaggerate the ex-

2 David Daube, *Roman Law,* pp. 102–12.

3 For a different viewpoint, see W. den Boer, "Demography in Roman History." Whether women are enumerated in the census figures at particular periods in Roman history remains unclear, despite the efforts of Joël Le Gall, "Un critère de différenciation sociale," and P. A. Brunt, *Italian Manpower 225* B.C.*–14* A.D.

4 On the names of Roman women, see Iiro Kajanto, "Women's Praenomina Reconsidered."

tent to which contemporary pagans engaged in infanticide,[5] but, on the other hand, it is clear that this method of family planning was practiced without much fanfare in antiquity. An infant of either sex who appeared weak might be exposed; in his *Gynecology* Soranus, a physician of the second century A.D., gives a list of criteria by which midwives were to recognize which newborns should be discarded and which were worth rearing. In deciding to expose a daughter, the provision of a dowry was an additional consideration. However, there was enough of a demand for brides, as we have mentioned, to make even the occasional dowerless bride acceptable.

Additional evidence for a dearth of females in the upper classes is that in the late Republic some men were marrying women of the lower classes. We know of no spinsters, yet upper-class women are not known to have taken husbands from the lower classes. Studies of tombstones generally show far more males than females.[6] This disproportion is usually explained away by the comment that males were deemed more deserving of commemoration.[7] Such a factor might discourage the erection of tombstones for those low on the social scale, but at least among the wealthier classes—the very group where small families were the trend—we could expect that, once having decided to raise a daughter, her parents would commemorate her death. In our present state of knowledge we cannot finally say that women were actually present in Rome in the numbers one expects in an average pre-industrial society, and that their lack of adequate representation in the sepulchral inscriptions is totally ascribable to their social invisibility; but it should be noted that the existence of masses of women who are not recorded by the inscriptions is, at most, hypothetical.

The traditional doctrine, enforced by Roman censors, was that men should marry, and that the purpose of marriage was the rearing of children.[8] The example of Hellenistic Greece, where men were refusing to marry and consequently children were not being raised, had a subversive influence on the ideal, although Stoicism affirmed it. A decrease in fecundity is discernible as early as the second century B.C., a time when the production of twelve children by Cornelia became a prodigy—probably because her son Gaius harped on it—although only three lived to adulthood. Metellus Macedonicus, censor in 131 B.C., made a speech urging men to marry and procreate, although he recognized that wives were troublesome creatures. The speech was read out to the Senate by Augustus as evidence that he was merely reviving Roman traditions with his legislation.[9]

Augustus' legislation was designed to keep as many women as possible in the

5 Justin Martyr, *Apology for the Christians*, "To Antoninus Pius," 27. I owe this reference to JoAnn McNamara.

6 Degrassi, "L'indicazione dell'età nelle iscrizioni sepolcrali latine," pp. 85–86.

7 In his sample Keith Hopkins found 149 sons and 100 daughters ("On the Probable Age Structure of the Roman Population," p. 262).

8 Watsen, *Roman Private Law Around 200* B.C., p. 22; Brunt, *op. cit.,* p. 559.

9 Suet. Aug. 89. 2; Livy Per. 59; Aul. Gell. 1. 6; H. Malcovati, *Oratorum Romanorum Fragmenta,* p. 107.

married state and bearing children. The penalties for nonmarriage and childlessness began for women at age twenty, for men at twenty-five. Divorce was not explicitly frowned upon, provided that each successive husband was recruited from the approved social class. Failure to remarry was penalized, all with a view to not wasting the childbearing years. Women were not able to escape the penalties of the Augustan legislation as easily as men. A man who was betrothed to a girl of ten could enjoy the political and economic privileges accorded to married men, but a woman was not permitted to betroth herself to a prepubescent male.[10]

But the low birth rate continued, and the Augustan legislation on marriage was reinforced by Domitian and reenacted in the second and third centuries A.D. It appears that women as well as men were rebelling against biologically determined roles. One reason for the low birth rate was the practice of contraception.

Not only infanticide and neglect of infants, but contraception and abortion were used by the married Romans to limit their families, and by unmarried and adulterous women to prevent or terminate illegitimate pregnancies.[11] Among the upper classes, the essential element in contraception—the wish not to have children—was present. Contraception was obviously preferable to abortion and infanticide, since the mother did not endure the burden and dangers of pregnancy and childbirth. There was a long tradition of medical and scientific writing on contraception and abortion, but most of our evidence comes from authors of the early Empire, who collected earlier knowledge and added their own recommendations.

Techniques for contraception were numerous; some were effective, more not. Among the ineffective were potions drunk for temporary or permanent sterility, which could, of course, be administered to unsuspecting parties to render them infertile. Amulets and magic were recommended. Pliny gives a recipe for fabricating an amulet by cutting open the head of a hairy spider, removing the two little worms which were believed to be inside and tying them in deerskin. Aëtius recommends wearing the liver of a cat in a tube on the left foot, or part of a lioness' womb in an ivory tube.[12] It was also thought possible to transfer the qualities of the sterile willow or of sterile iron for contraception.

The rhythm method was also practiced, but this was ineffective since the medical writers believed that the most fertile time was just when menstruation was ending, as that is when the appetite was said to be strongest. Conversely, it was thought that conception was not likely to occur when the woman did not have a desire for intercourse. Among other contraceptive techniques mentioned

10   Dio 54. 6. 7.

11   On contraception, see Hopkins, "Contraception in the Roman Empire," and John T. Noonan, Jr., *Contraception,* pp. 23–46. For the possibility of coitus interruptus in Archaic Greece, see the fragment of Archilochus, *P. Coloniensia* 7511.

12   Pliny, *H N* 29. 85; Aëtius 16. 17.

are for the woman to hold her breath at ejaculation, and post-coitally to squat, sneeze, and drink something cold.[13] Lucretius recommends that whores, but not wives, should wriggle their hips and so divert the plow and the seed.[14]

Mixed with ineffective techniques were effective methods, including the use of occlusive agents which blocked the os of the uterus. Oils, ointments, honey, and soft wool were employed.

Contraception was overwhelmingly left to women, but a few male techniques were recommended. Certain ointments smeared on the male genitals were thought to be effective as spermicides or as astringents to close the os of the uterus upon penetration. The bladder of a goat may have been used as an early version of a condom, although this item would have been costly.[15] Whether men practiced coitus interruptus is debatable. The sources do not mention this technique. Two explanations for this omission are equally plausible, but mutually inconsistent: coitus interruptus is not mentioned either because it was not used, or, more likely, because it was so much used and so obvious that it needed no description. . . .

It must be evident that lower-class women were always more numerous, but less notorious—the activities of celebrities tend to captivate the historical imagination. Nevertheless, it is essential to acknowledge a new trend in Roman historical studies that is directed at finding out about the lower classes and which integrates women in its purview. . . .

The Roman household (*familia*) included not only kinsmen legally dependent on the head of the family, but also slaves. The number of slaves of course varied according to the means of the family, but even humble families might own a few. There is more abundant documentation on the slaves of the wealthy, as is true of the wealthy themselves. Wealthy families owned thousands of slaves, living on their various holdings, and the household of the emperor (*familia Caesaris*) was probably the largest. Owners of slaves invested in human property with the expectation that certain services would be performed, and that their own wealth would thereby be increased and their personal comfort enhanced. The complexities of Roman slavery were such that a woman might gain more prestige by marrying a slave than a free person, and that slaves and ex-slaves might be more highly educated and enjoy greater economic security than the freeborn poor.

The variety of the jobs held by female slaves was more limited than those of the males. Some women were enslaved only in adulthood, either by kidnappers

---

13　Soranus 1. 61. The references to Soranus are to his *Gynecology*, translated by O. Temkin (Baltimore: Johns Hopkins University Press, 1956). Hopkins, "Contraception," p. 140, note 47.

14　Lucretius 4. 1269-78.

15　Hopkins, "Contraception," p. 135, note 30.

or pirates, or because they were camp followers or ordinary citizens where the Romans made a conquest. In a population of captive Greeks, the Romans would find male scholars, historians, poets, and men with valuable skills. Owing to the limitations of women's education, a freshly captured woman may have been at most a midwife, an actress, or a prostitute. Most women did not have any training beyond the traditional household skills. In slavery, as in freedom, they could work as spinners, weavers, clothesmakers, menders, wetnurses, child nurses, kitchen help, and general domestics. . . .

Most freedwomen, however, were not spectacularly wealthy, but rather comprised a large part of the Roman working class, serving as shopkeepers or artisans or continuing in domestic service. The occupations pursued by freedwomen were commonly those for which they had been trained as slaves, and are not notably more varied than the occupations of working women in Classical Athens. Nevertheless, women were the tastemakers of textile manufacture throughout classical antiquity.

Working in wool was traditionally a woman's task, in Rome as well as in Greece. Spinning was so sex-stereotyped that . . . even in Dark Age burials spindle whorls served to identify corpses as female. The reader will be reminded of earlier references to woolworking by women: the tablets from Pylos, Homeric epic (Hector's admonition to Andromache to return to her loom), Xenophon's descriptions in the *Memorabilia* and *Oeconomicus,* the weaving of the *peplos* for Athena Polias, Erinna's titling her poem "The Distaff," and the predominance of woolworkers in a list of women manumitted in Athens between 349 and 320 B.C.[16] We also recall that the Greek Plutarch noted Fulvia's masculinity, pointing out that "she did not care for spinning." The Phoenician queen Dido, who in many ways is modeled on Homeric queens, has a subtle blemish: Virgil never shows her spinning or weaving.

So among the Romans spinning was always a woman's task. The sepulchral inscription of the archetypal Roman matron Claudia makes this association clear:

> Stranger, what I have to say is short. Stop and read it through. This is the unlovely tomb of a lovely woman. Her parents named her Claudia. She loved her husband with her whole heart. She bore two sons, one of whom she leaves on earth; the other she has placed beneath the earth. She was charming in conversation, yet her conduct was appropriate. She kept house, she made wool.[17]

The old-fashioned Roman bride wreathed the doorposts of her new home with wool. When Augustus wished to instill respect for old-fashioned virtues among the sophisticated women of his household, he set them to work in wool

16   *IG* 2² 1553–78. Cf. M. Tod. "Epigraphical Notes on Freedmen's Professions," pp. 10–11.

17   *CIL* 1.2.1211. Cf. [Marcel] Durry, [ed.] *Eloge funèbre* [*d'une matrone romaine*], p. 9.

and wore their homespun results.[18] Many women of the lower classes, slave and freed, were also employed in working wool both at home and in small-scale industrial establishments where working-class men joined women as weavers and as weighers of balls of wool to be apportioned to weavers.[19] Spinning, however, continued to be solely women's work. But women were not restricted to spinning alone.

Laundry work was done by women and men, unlike the situation in Classical Athens, where this occupation was confined to women. That men worked as fullers and weavers is probably a result of the organization of this work into small-scale industries in the Roman period. At Pompeii, women worked at mills where grain was ground, and we find a landlady and a female moneylender.[20] Freedwomen, since they often came from the East, frequently sold luxury items or exotic merchandise, such as purple dye or perfumes. They also sold more mundane merchandise, such as clothing and food, and worked as butchers or even as fisherwomen—and afterward hawked their catch.

The occupations of women at Pompeii give a good sample of the types of economic activity open to women. Moreover, the sepulchral inscriptions of many women from the entire Roman world record how a woman had made her living. Métiers as lowly as "dealer in beans" or "seller of nails" and as lofty as "commercial entrepreneur" or "physician" are found. Women's names stamped on pipes and bricks also record their involvement with building activities—from the ownership of a brickmaking or stonecutting operation by an upper-class woman to actual participation in the making of building materials and construction work by working women of the lower classes.[21]

The best-known woman at Pompeii is Eumachia, a businesswoman whose family manufactured bricks. She was the patroness of the fullers, who set up her statue. She, in turn, donated to the town porticos, colonnades, and a crypt, and erected an imposing tomb for herself.

The selection of a woman as patroness (*patrona*) of a men's guild (*collegium*) was by no means unique. A few women are known to have served as patronesses of guilds, either by themselves or simultaneously with male patrons who frequently were their husbands: yet, women comprised less than five per cent of known patrons during the period of the Empire.[22] In return for the gratitude and

---

18   Suet, *Aug.* 73.

19   [Mima] Maxey, [*Occupations of the Lower Classes in Roman Society*], p. 31. The weighing of wool is the only supervisory job as yet attested for slave women in an upper-class household ([Susan] Treggiari, "Women in Domestic Service in the Early Roman Empire").

20   On Pompeii, see H. H. Tanzer, *The Common People of Pompeii,* and Michele D'Avino, *The Women of Pompeii.*

21   Helen Jefferson Loane, *Industry and Commerce of the City of Rome (50* B.C.*-200* A.D.*),* pp. 103–5, 110–11.

22   See J.-P. Waltzing, *Etude historique sur les corporations professionelles chez les romains jusqu'à la chute de l'empire d'occident,* 1: 348–49, and 4:254–57; Guido Clemente, "Il patronato nei collegia dell'impero romano."

praise awarded by the guild, the patrons and patronesses—who were wealthy and influential—were expected to bestow benefactions on their guilds. Women could belong to religious and burial guilds, and indeed a few held high office in them. At least two women were chosen as patronesses of synagogues. But there is no evidence that women were permitted to belong to the professional or craft guilds of men, even when they worked in the same occupation.

Many women worked as waitresses in taverns and at counters dispensing drinks and food. These women were selected, doubtless, for their ability to attract customers, and sometimes the taverns had rooms for prostitution upstairs. The names of waitresses and prostitutes are found scribbled on walls at Pompeii. The graffiti refer to the women's vices and attractions, and announce that some women can be had for two asses—the price of a loaf of bread. But these may be written as insults, rather than reflect a true price. The highest price of a woman is given as sixteen asses.[23]

Prostitutes came from a variety of ethnic origins. Foreign-born prostitutes would be attractive both to men of the native lands who happened to find themselves in Pompeii and to men who wanted to try out exotic women. It is impossible to determine the status of the women who worked in brothels from the information in graffiti, but it seems likely that they were slaves or freedwomen. Prostitution was recognized and taxed, and brothels were regarded by some as a respectable investment, but the Roman comedy shows that slave-dealers who traded in prostitutes were despised.[24] Relatively few respectable women wrote electoral graffiti, but women who mingled with the crowds—the waitresses and prostitutes—are responsible for numerous electoral endorsements (which incidentally indicate that they knew how to write): e.g., "Sucula [little sow]asks you to make Marcus Cerrinius aedile."

Many freedwomen continued working for their former owners after manumission. Within the household, there was a good chance that female slaves engaged in female-oriented activities—such as ladies' maids and midwives—would be freed by the mistress, and male slaves by the master. Freed slaves were legally obliged to provide service, so long as enough time remained to earn their own livelihood. Prostitutes were exempt from the obligation to continue service but often had no other way of making a living. Women of high status and those over the age of fifty were also exempt, and so, in practice, were women who had married with their master's consent.[25] Julia Phoebe, a freedwoman of Augustus' daughter Julia, remained close to her *patrona* and hanged herself when Julia was exiled.[26] Dorcas, the dresser (*ornatrix*) of Livia, was a

---

23   On the price of prostitutes, see Richard Duncan-Jones, *The Economy of the Roman Empire,* p. 246.

24   Ramsay MacMullen, *Roman Social Relations 50* B.C. *to* A.D. *284,* pp. 86–87.

25   Exemptions from *operae:* prostitutes, *Digest* 38. 1. 38; high status, 38. 1. 34; over fifty, 38. 1. 35; married to patron, *Code Iust.* 6. 39; married with patron's approval, *Digest* 38. 1. 48.

26   Suet, *Aug.* 65. 2.

freedwoman.[27] Freedwomen, particularly domestics or ladies' maids with no marketable skills, probably welcomed the opportunity to remain in the security of their patron's employ and to continue living in the house, for it was preferable to being released into the throngs of the poor.

The fate of very poor women can only be guessed at. They were probably worse off than slaves, for slaves at least were property, and were cared for in a manner commensurate with their value. Some freedwomen, as well, might have been able to count on the good will of their former owners. We assume that many unskilled poor women maintained themselves through prostitution. Some did not even have the security of a brothel but practiced their trade out-of-doors under archways.[28] Indeed, the word "fornicate" is derived from the Latin word for "arch."

27 *CIL* 6. 8958.
28 *Juvenal 11. 172–73. Hor. Epist.* 1. 14. 21; *Sat.* 1. 2. 30.

—J. P. V. D. BALSDON—

ROMAN WOMEN IN DAILY LIFE

History is not exclusively the history of government. There is the whole social history of the Roman people, and the history of Roman women is the history of woman through the centuries in all the different strata of Roman society. And here we are fortunate in the fact that from as early as the fifth century B.C. a continuous succession of foreigners—Greeks in the main—wrote about Rome; so that we know what appeared to a foreigner to be the idiosyncrasies of Roman women. Plutarch's *Roman Questions,* for instance, are largely concerned with Roman women and their habits. Why, in the remote past if a Roman was returning from the country, did he always send a messenger ahead, to warn his wife that he was coming? Why did Roman women always kiss their close male relations and, after marriage, also the close male relations of their husbands? How explain the innumerable complications of the Roman marriage rites? Most

From J. P. V. D. Balsdon, *Roman Women: Their History and Habits* (New York: The John Day Company, 1963), pp. 13–14, 270–73, 275–77, 282–83, 329–31. Reprinted by permission of Harold Ober Associates, Inc. Copyright © 1962 by J.P.V.D. Balsdon.

extraordinary of all to a Greek was the fact that in Rome you were liable to meet respectable women at dinner parties.

The importance of women in public and social life in Rome derived, as it derives in all early societies, from two causes.

First they had, as women, their own peculiar magic. At a high level, therefore, their correct performance of, in particular, their sacerdotal duties was something on which the good health of the community depended. The wives of certain priests were priestesses in their own right. The Vestal Virgins were the emblem of the State's morality and the guarantee of its economic well-being. Moral delinquency on the part of a Vestal Virgin was, therefore, a kind of high treason and, when it suited the politicians, an irresponsible prank (a man entering a house during the celebration of a cult which was reserved for women) could be treated as a public crime.

Secondly women bear children and are necessary for the survival of particular families and for the survival of society itself. Hence the political importance of arranged marriages among the Roman aristocracy; and, in a wider field, the Romans were obsessed from the second century B.C onwards with the problem of a falling birth-rate, a problem all the more serious on account of the high rate of infant mortality and, indeed, of deaths in childbirth. Well-intentioned statesmen in the second century B.C. led the way and in due course the Emperors followed their lead. When exhortations were unavailing, substantial rewards were offered under the Empire to married couples who gave Rome the children which the State—in particular its hungry legions—needed.

In a developing society, the history of women is the history of their increasing emancipation. A hundred years and more before the end of the Republic women were in rebellion against a marriage system under which they were fettered to their husbands, unable to throw off the chains. They rebelled, too, against a senseless austerity. The practice of divorce, rare at first, grew common and eventually tedious. Novel diversions spread from Greece to Rome; young women—and young men too—started to take singing and dancing lessons. History records the protests of the old men, the puritans and the prigs. But such change could not be arrested. Women emancipated themselves. . . .

The Romans being for the first centuries of their existence an agricultural people, their houses, large or small, were country houses, and while the husband took care of the land, his wife took care of the household. She held the keys of the store-cupboard, she brought up the children. The larger the establishment, the greater the number of slaves, both in the house and on the land.

In poorer families daughters went to school, like their brothers, and were taught by schoolmasters; in richer families they were generally educated at home. A part of their upbringing, spinning and weaving, they learnt working with the slave-girls under the supervision of their mother. This domestic manufacture of homespun, which never died out in poorer households, survived even in the houses of the great down to the early Empire. At the end of the

Republic, in 52 B.C., in the town house of M. Aemilius Lepidus (the later trium-vir) a loom on which cloth was being woven stood in the hall (*atrium*); and when a mob of ruffians broke in, they destroyed this as well as the couch on which, presumably, Lepidus' wife—that "lady whose integrity was a byword"—re-clined, to supervise the work. And, as has been seen, Augustus wore home-made cloth inside the house, and insisted that in his family the tradition of weaving should be observed.

There is evidence of a considerable staff of clothing specialists in the inscrip-tions of the *columbarium* in which the ashes of Livia's slaves and freedmen were placed; her household staff included five patchers, two supervisors, six women in charge of clothing, one cloak-maker, one tailor and two fullers. In similar fashion the vault of another family, the Statilii Tauri, contained the ashes of eight spinners, one supervisor of the wool, four patchers, four weavers, two dyers and four fullers.[1]

Writing in the middle of the first century A.D., Columella states that this style of living survived to his young days, but that a general change had taken place, anyhow in richer families, during his lifetime. In country houses the bailiff's wife had come to exercise what had once been the mistress's housekeep-ing responsibilities. It was no longer smart to wear homespun; instead clothes were bought, far more expensively, from shops.[2]

While in the modern world the furnishing and decorating of a house is either a wife's responsibility and interest, or a responsibility and interest which she shares with her husband, there is no evidence to show that furniture was a mat-ter of great interest to Roman women. Rooms in Roman houses were small and, by modern standards, very sparsely furnished. Cicero's letters give evidence of the purchase of busts for his library (a transaction in which it is unlikely that Terentia was consulted) and Pliny tells us that Cicero once spent half a million sesterces on a table. Tables, indeed, particularly of citrus wood (sometimes with ivory legs), and sofas inlaid with tortoise-shell or ornamented with precious metal were an extravagance of rich men. Women sometimes bought objects for the household; "one *materfamilias*, and not a particularly rich one," paid 150,000 sesterces for a wine-ladle. But, in general, if money was to be spent, a woman preferred to see it spent on jewels. Furniture was a male extravagance; and Pliny[3] tells us that when husbands protested against the sums which their wives spent on pearls, the wives were often able to retort, "What about you and your tables?"

What of the wall-paintings and the mosaics? When there was a question of

---

1 Asc., *In Milon.* 43C (for the identify of Lepidus' wife, *RE i*, 560 f.); Suet., *DA* 73, 1 (cf. *Vit.* 8, 1, "vestis domestica"); *CIL* vi, 3926–4326; 6213–640; Tenney Frank, *Econ. Survey of An-cient Rome* v (Baltimore, 1940), 201, n. 43.

2 Columella, *praef.* 1–3, 7–9.

3 Pliny, *NH* 37, 29; 13, 91.

artist, of subject, of design, of colour, how often had a wife the deciding vote? We have no means of knowing.

How much of a woman's day was taken up in household duties and in supervision of her slaves is, again, something which we do not know. From Aelius Aristeides' remark in his Roman Oration at the middle of the second century A.D. that "it is a pauper's household in which the same person has to do the cooking and the dusting and to make the beds," it is evident that you had to sink to a very low level indeed in society to find a *materfamilias* who was faced with what today are the ordinary housewife's chores.[4]

Down to the second century B.C. the mistress of the house had taken an active part in the housekeeping; indeed before 164 B.C. she is said to have baked the bread. After this, bakeries were started; large kitchen staffs were engaged by rich households, and "a chef became as expensive as a horse."

The mistress continued, presumably, to order and to supervise the ordinary family meals. Whether (apart from official banquets) she was also responsible for, or even attended, the gargantuan dinners which in the late Republic and early Empire were given from time to time in rich households, and which so deeply shocked men whose morals were as high and whose appetites were as poor as Seneca's, we cannot say. Seneca does not mention them; and it is extremely improbable that, in any but the most debauched households, respectable women and young children sampled the kind of after-dinner coarseness and indelicacy into which such parties sometimes degenerated.

In a household like Trimalchio's the mistress performed all the functions of an active housekeeper. Fortunata dashed in and out of the dining-room with the slaves during a dinner party, and when at the end of the meal the monumental mason Habinnas called and asked for her, Trimalchio told him that she never joined the guests until she had seen the silver locked up and given the slaves their supper.[5]

We must not be misled by the satirists and the moralists into thinking of banquets (whether or not they became debauches) as being, except in degenerate imperial society, anything but rare occasions. Dinner even in a rich household, whether or not there were guests, was in general a polite and restrained occasion, and at Rome the women of the family were present, as they had always been present, at the meal. Until the time of Augustus they sat (as in Etruscan funerary sculpture the wife sits, while her husband reclines); but after Augustus they reclined like the men—graciously in gracious circles, less graciously in the households of Trimalchio and his like.

There was a similar distinction in the matter of drinking. While Trimalchio's wife got drunk, the women of better-class families observed by instinct and upbringing the rules which Ovid laid down for his less impeccable

    4   71b.
    5   Pliny, *NH* 18, 107; 9, 67; Petr., *Sat.* 37; 67; L. Friedlander, *Roman Life and Manners under the early Empire* ii, 146–85.

young ladies; if they drank at all, they drank sparingly. No civilized society has ever liked the notion of an intoxicated woman; in the Roman tradition, dislike was an obsession.

That many women played an important part in conversation on social occasions, is certain. A woman's conversation—*sermo*—was often singled out for praise. Maecenas' wife Terentia talked amusingly. Debauched as Sempronia was, by Sallust's account, he admits that she was a good conversationalist. Macrobius remarks on the fact that Augustus' disappointing daughter Julia talked well. Juvenal describes the women who talked too much and talked too loudly; their existence implies as a corollary women who talked quietly and talked well. Here again Ovid's instructions are significant: not only to talk quietly and with restraint, but also to be well informed on the subjects about which men of culture liked to talk. . . .

Apart from the Vestal Virgins, the only Roman women who enjoyed absolute independence in the management of personal property were those who, after Augustus, had presented their husbands with three—in Italy (or in Rome, if they were freedwomen) four; outside Italy, five—children, or who, with their husbands, had been given the honorary status of productive parenthood. Women married under one or other of the primitive marriage ceremonies were dependents of their husbands (*in manu*) and, when married, held no possessions of their own. A woman married under the system of free marriage (unless, after Augustus, she was independent on account of the number of her children) was not independent of her father; she was *in patria potestate.* When her father died, she had a guardian ("tutor") who was a man appointed under her father's will; or, if the father had not appointed a guardian for her, a man who was either next of kin or a nominee of the magistrate in response to an application which she herself had made. A woman who had been *in manu* when married likewise had a "tutor" if she became a widow, a man appointed by her husband or, with his agreement, chosen by herself. A woman could not be appointed guardian even to her own children.[6]

Such in strict law was the position of a woman in the late Republic and in the Empire. But in fact she was all but independent, for her guardian took his duties very lightly; if he was tiresome, a woman had only to apply to the praetor, and he was replaced by someone more accommodating. If, on the other hand, she required substantial help in a difficult matter, she applied for the appointment of an administrator, a "curator."

A wife who owned property in her own right might either hand over its administration to her husband, who was accountable to her for the income, or she could administer it herself through her own agents and slaves. Such independence on a woman's part was naturally something of which the elder Cato disapproved. A woman's property of this sort, bequeathed in the main to her second husband, was the subject at issue in the case in which Cicero defended

6   See F. Schulz, chap. 5, "Guardianship."

Caecina in 69 B.C. And we have from the end of the first century A.D. an epigram of Martial warning a husband against a "curled spark" who was his wife's agent and, Martial suggested, her lover too. This, indeed, was one weakness of the smart young agent; dishonesty was another.[7]

The property of the wealthy ladies of the imperial family must have been very large indeed. We can gauge the size of Livia's personal staff from the number of inscriptions of her freedmen and slaves which have been recovered from the *columbarium* built to house their ashes on the Appian way. Burrus, who ended his life as Prefect of the Guard, had once been employed as her agent.[8]

Many women, without doubt, were engaged in business. Often they were widows who took over the control of their husbands' affairs. There were enough freedwomen or women living in Italy outside Rome with shipbuilding interests for Claudius to offer them special rewards if they co-operated in his shipbuilding programme. And inscriptions bear witness to a number of women—freedwomen, perhaps, in the main—who were lady doctors.

Apart from serious and commendable activities, there were, of course, innumerable foibles on which rich women, like rich men, could squander their wealth. Ummidia Quadratilla kept a private company of ballet-dancers, who performed in public and also privately in her house. When she died, just over eighty years old, in A.D. 107, they were inherited, with two-thirds of her property, by her prig of a grandson, who had lived in her house (since the age of twenty-four, with his wife), and who had ostentatiously refused ever to see them perform. After her death, they gave one public performance, and then he got rid of them. A shocking old lady: Pliny, too, was at his most priggish, sharing her grandson's opinion of her.[9] . . .

Complete equality of the sexes was never achieved in ancient Rome because of the survival, long after it was out of date, of a deep-rooted tradition that the exclusive sphere of a woman's activity was inside the house, the exclusive sphere of a man's outside it.[10] In the field of domestic economy, woman's power and *expertise* were unchallenged. She looked after the food, the clothes, the servants and the upbringing of the children in their infancy.

But for active participation in public affairs woman was considered, from the circumstances of her daily life, to lack the knowledge and experience which were needed. So women were never given the vote; and it was unthinkable that they should compete for public office. In the Empire, though nobody could doubt the political sagacity of such imperial women as Livia, Plotina or Julia

7 Cic., *Pro Caec.* 13-17; Mart. 5, 61, "Crispulus ille." Cf. "Procurator calamistratus" of Seneca, *De matrim.,* ed. Haase, p. 429, para. 51.

8 *CIL* vi, 2926-4326; *ILS* 1321.

9 Shipbuilding: Suet., *D. Cl.* 18, 2 and 19. Lady Doctors: ILS, 7802-6. Ummidia Quadratilla, Pliny, *EPP.* 7, 24.

10 See F. Schulz, *Classical Roman Law* (Oxford, 1951), part 2, chap. 3, "Husband and Wife" (pp. 103-41).

Maesa, they were barred from offical participation in government. The suggestion that a woman should be chosen to rule as Empress was never even mooted.

Similarly, in civil procedure women could not sit on juries; far less could they plead in court. They were not allowed, before Justinian, to be appointed legal guardians to their own children. They were not even allowed—unless, after Augustus, they produced the requisite number of children or were given the honorary status of a fruitful mother—the independent administration of their own affairs.

It suited a barrister often to refer to women as the weaker sex, and to suggest that they lacked the necessary toughness to compete in the rough and tumble of public life. "*Infirmitas consilii*" was a moving expression in a good orator's mouth.[11] But while the Romans were hypocritical enough to pretend that inexperience was an insuperable barrier to women's participation in public life, they were not so hypocritical as to pretend with any seriousness that woman's intelligence was of a lower order than man's.[12]

Not that women are known ever to have sought to enter the world of politics, administration or law. Indeed we have no knowledge of their even seeking an alteration in the law, so that they might have a legal claim for maintenance by their husbands. . . .

In marriage, despite the curb which Augustus' legislation placed on a husband's licensed immorality, a husband was never required to live the chaste life which was expected of his wife. In this matter, the conversion of the Roman world to Christianity was to bring a great change in woman's status. Reform, which Stoicism had long advocated, was introduced, and infidelity was punished with the same rigour in a husband as in a wife. And with Christianity the chaste unmarried woman, whom Augustus had punished, became an object of respect, even of veneration.

---

11   Cic., *Pro Murena* 27, "Mulieres omnes propter infirmitatem consilii maiores in tutorum potestate esse voluerunt."
12   Gaius i, 190 is honest about this.

MOMENTS OF LEISURE

Throughout history both rich and poor have found time for amusement. Sports, games, festivals, and religious holidays have always been a part of Everyman's existence. But not all people have participated in them to the same extent; often, it seems, one person's fun has proved to be another's hardship. The diversion of the wealthy meant only more work, and in some cases even death, for slaves and servants. Without dwelling on extreme cases, however, we can probably posit that the lower classes usually participated on the fringes and derived at least some vicarious pleasure from the spectacles that were presented.

Ludwig Drees describes the most famous sporting events in history, the Greek Olympic Games. Competition was open only to freemen, although a woman might in rare cases enter a team of horses. Slaves were altogether excluded, except perhaps as spectators. Otherwise, many of the elements of the games—the training, the intense rivalry among states, the problems of professionalism and deliberate cheating, the overflowing crowds, the pride of victory and the disappointment of defeat—should be quite familiar to us. Even some of the individual events were conducted then very much as they are now.

Peter D. Arnott shows that storytelling, especially reciting the exploits of the gods, was another favorite pastime of the ancients. Roman divinities differed somewhat from Greek ones. They were less exalted, more familiar, more approachable. They were so much a part of everyday life, in fact, that they were apparently often taken for granted or else exploited for the purpose of staging some public festival.

Roland Auguet acquaints us in painful detail with the most characteristic of Roman sports, the gladiatorial contest—which, curiously, had its origin in funeral games. The association of blood, magic, violence, and sport obviously exercised an immense fascination for the Roman crowds who flocked to their favorite arena. What they saw there would surely shock our own sensibilities. Yet any modern person whose holidays are regularly devoted to the brutal rituals of professional football can easily appreciate the ordinary Roman's fanaticism. At least in that regard, certain social customs have changed remarkably little in two thousand years.

If societies can be judged by their forms of leisure, then classical civilization would seem to be closer to our own than many of the societies of the intervening eras. The Greeks and Romans probably knew a degree of formalization in sports and public festivals not equaled again until the twentieth century. With them we share the reverence for the arena and the gymnasium, and the revival of the Olympic Games in our time may be symptomatic of the lessening significance that is now given to the focal institution of Christianized Europe: the Church.

—LUDWIG DREES————————

THE ANCIENT OLYMPICS

ELIGIBILITY FOR THE GAMES

Neither foreigners nor slaves were allowed to take part in the Olympic games. Only men—and later boys—of pure Greek descent were eligible. . . .

Initially this ban also applied to the Romans, but once Rome began to assert her power within the Greek world they were exempted.

. . . The competitors had to be free citizens. This rule also applied to the boys, whose lineage was checked with great care. Philostratus tells us that, quite

From Ludwig Drees, *Olympia: Gods, Artists and Athletes* (New York and Washington, D.C.: Frederick A. Praeger, Publishers, 1968), pp. 41–43, 52, 57, 72, 74–76, 169–72. Copyright © 1967 in Stuttgart by Verlag W. Kohlhamm GmbH. English translation © 1968 by Gerald Onn and © 1968 in London by Pall Mall Press. Reprinted by permission of Pall Mall Press.

apart from ascertaining that the contestants for the boys' events were not overage, the judges also had to establish that they were members of a settled tribe, that they had a father and a family, and that they were free-born and not simply the bastard sons of free-born fathers.[1] There were two principal reasons why the competitors had to be free-born citizens of Greek descent. In the first place, the Greeks despised foreigners and slaves; in the second, they wished to ensure that all the contestants approached the games in the same spirit. This has been well put by Ziehen, who points out that those who competed for the victor's crown in Olympia were free citizens of Greek communities who shared a common attitude to life. They were not men who practised sport for its own sake or for the sake of breaking a record. On the contrary, they used it as a means of pursuing the Greek ideal of physical perfection and military proficiency.[2]

It was felt that if the cream of Greek youth and manhood met in Olympia to compete with one another to this end, and if thousands of people from every part of Greece came to the festival to watch them, a sense of national unity and solidarity might well be engendered, which would bear fruit beyond the purely sporting sphere.[3] . . .

Although women were forbidden to take any part in the festival several of them were nonetheless associated with the contests in the hippodrome. In the equestrian events it was not the charioteers or horsemen who were proclaimed victors but the owners, and there was nothing to prevent a woman from owning horses. Cynisca, a daughter of King Archidamus of Sparta, was the first woman to enter a team at Olympia. Plutarch tells us that it was her brother Agesilaus who persuaded her to do so because he wished to impress on his fellow Greeks that victory in the equestrian events had nothing to do with ability but was simply a question of wealth.[4] And Cynisca's team won the chariot-race. But according to Pausanias Cynisca's one great ambition had been to win an Olympic prize; apparently she was the first woman ever to train horses. Subsequently, Pausanias tells us, many other women—chiefly Spartans—were victorious at the games but, of them all, Cynisca was the most famous.[5] She gained her victory between 390 and 380 B.C. She also made a votive offering in Olympia and this, too, has been described by Pausanias: "Near the statue of Troilus there is a basement of stone with a chariot and charioteer and also an effigy of Cynisca by Apelles. . . . There are also inscriptions to her."[6] In the course of the excavations a fragment of limestone was unearthed on which a number of characters were engraved which had once formed part of one of these inscriptions. According to the ancient tradition the full text read:

1   Philostratus, *Gymnasticus*, 25.
2   Plato, *Protagoras*, 312B.
3   Ziehen, RE XVIII, cols. 41–2.
4   Plutarch, *Agesilaus,* 20; and Xenophon, *Agesilaus,* IX 6.
5   Pausanias, III 8, 1.
6   Ibid., VI 1, 6.

Sparta's kings were fathers and brothers of mine,
But since with my chariot and storming horses I, Cynisca,
Have won the prize, I place my effigy here
And proudly proclaim
That of all Grecian women I first bore the crown.[7]

Another votive gift of Cynisca's, a team of brass horses smaller than life-size, stood in the antechamber of the temple of Zeus.[8]

We do not know whether the competitors at the games simply registered in Olympia or whether they first underwent a selection process in their native cities. What is quite certain, however, is that they were required to complete a course of preliminary training in Elis, where their proficiency was also tested.[9]

THE TRAINING PROGRAMME IN ELIS

The young Greek athletes trained very hard. Lucian's Anacharsis remarked on the fact to his friend Solon. He simply could not understand why the wrestlers and pankratiasts, who appeared to be on the best of terms and helped one another to prepare for their practice bouts, then proceeded to clash their heads together, throttle and throw each other and exchange the most fearsome blows.[10]

But if the general training in the Greek gymnasiums was hard, the more specialised training for the pan-Hellenic games was harder still. According to Antiphon, the price of victory at the Olympic, Pythian and other festivals was great hardship.[11] Of all the games, however, those at Olympia imposed the heaviest burden, for Lucian assures us that once a man had gained a victor's crown at Olympia none of the other stadia held any terrors for him.[12]

When they were in training the Olympic competitors lived extremely frugal lives; in the early days of the festival they even went without meat. Later, in the fifth century B.C., this diet was changed by Dromeus of Stymphalus, a famous long-distance runner, who won twice at Olympia, twice at Delphi, three times at the Isthmus and five times at Nemea. Pausanias tells us that he was thought to have been the first man ever to have eaten meat while preparing for the games, "for athletes in training before him used to eat only a particular kind of cheese."[13]

7   *Greek Anthology*, XIII 16.

8   Pausanias, V 12, 5.

9   Carl Diem, *Weltgeschichte des Sports und Der Leibeserziehune* (Stuttgart: 1960), pp. 240–41.

10   Carl Diem, *Ewiges Olympia* (Minden, Westphalia: 1948), pp. 31–32.

11   Antiphon, Fragment 128.

12   Lucian, *Harmonides* 4.

13   Pausanias, VI 7, 10.

During their period of preparation the Olympic competitors led a life that was far from enviable. Under the relentless supervision of the judges[14] they had to observe a strict diet, carry out set exercises and do exactly what their trainers told them. The Stoic philosopher Epictetus held up this harsh regime as an example to his followers, in order to impress on them that, before embarking on any undertaking, they should first consider what it involved.[15]

The athletes prepared for the games in the city of Elis. According to Philostratus they trained there for a period of one month,[16] according to Pausanias for a period of ten months. Certainly they had to swear on oath that they had "carefully trained for the space of ten months."[17] But since it is not clear from the wording of this oath whether the whole ten-month period had to be spent in Elis the most plausible explanation would seem to be that, while they were required to train for a total period of ten months, only one month, presumably the last, had to be spent in Elis. Incidentally, this must have been a relatively late innovation, for a ten-month training period could only have been prescribed for professional athletes, and although these were a common feature of Roman life, at the early Olympics the competitors had all been amateurs. Even a thirty-day period of residence would have posed problems in the early days since the sacred truce, which was subsequently extended to three months, had originally covered only one month, and that had included the journey to and from the sanctuary. Later of course, when the *pax romana* had been established throughout the whole of the *orbis terrarum,* there was no longer any need for a sacred truce.

In early times the competitors presumably arrived in Olympia accompanied by their trainers (or, in the case of the boys, by their fathers and brothers) just a few days before the beginning of the games in order to practise on the actual course. Subsequently rules would have been made fixing the length of the training period to ensure that all competitors enjoyed equal facilities. The training could, of course, only have taken place in Elis from 472 B.C. onwards, since it was in that year that the city was founded.

But once the thirty-day rule had been established all competitors were required to present themselves in Elis in good time. Great importance was attached to punctuality and any late arrivals were automatically disqualified unless they were able to prove *force majeure.* Pausanias describes one such case involving an Egyptian boxer from Alexandria, by the name of Apollonius, who arrived late for the 218th Olympiad in A.D. 107. He pleaded that his ship had been delayed by adverse winds near the Cyclades. But Heraclides, another Alexandrian boxer, was able to disprove his story and alleged that Apollonius had actually broken his journey to win prize money at the Ionian games. Apollonius

---

14 Philostratus, *Gymnasticus,* 11.

15 Epictetus, *Encheiridion,* 29.

16 Philostratus the Elder, *Apollonius of Tyana,* V 43.

17 Pausanias, V 24, 9.

was then disqualified and Heraclides, the only boxer to arrive on time, won by a walk-over.[18] . . .

CHEATING AT THE GAMES

In the solemn oath which they gave before the festival began the competitors had to swear that they would " not cheat at the Olympic games."[19] But there were some who violated their oath. The transgressions took three principal forms: breaking the rules, bribing opponents and competing on behalf of a foreign nation. In point of fact there was nothing in the regulations to prevent a competitor from representing a foreign nation, but those who did so were felt to have cast a slur on their motherland, which then brought its own punishment.

Breaking the Rules

Although our records of the ancient Olympics are incomplete, it seems that throughout the thousand and more years during which they were held there were very few infringements of the rules. Undoubtedly the rules in force then were less stringent than those applied today, which would of course offer a ready explanation for this phenomenon. Here too our knowledge is far from perfect. But there is one thing which we can say with certainty, namely that the competitors were not allowed to carry the contest to the point of endangering their opponent's life. Naturally this only applied to the more violent events such as the boxing and the pankration. The boxers were allowed to wound one another on the head and the face with blows of their heavily thonged fists, while the pankratiasts could apply strangleholds and even break their opponents' fingers and toes. An unlucky blow or excessive pressure on a stranglehold could easily prove fatal and some men actually were killed in Olympia: in 564 B.C. the Arcadian Arrhichion of Phigalia, who had already won the pankration at two previous Olympiads, lost his life when competing for the third time in this event. His opponent was disqualified and the crown was awarded to the dead man.[20] As far as we know disqualification was the only punishment inflicted on this occasion. In 492 B.C. the boxer Cleomedes of Astypalaea killed his opponent Iccus of Epidaurus. According to Pausanias, when the judges disqualified Cleomedes he "went out of his mind."[21] Here, too, disqualification appears to have been the only punishment imposed, for Pausanias makes no mention of anything else. But we know of one case in which the judges were far more severe. A boxer by the name of Diognetus of Crete, who appears to have been a rough fighter, killed his opponent Hercules in the heat of the contest, for which he was not only disqualified

18   Ibid., V 21, 12–14.
19   Pausanias, V 24, 9.
20   Ibid., VIII 40, 1–2.
21   Ibid., VI 9, 6.

but also expelled from Olympia.[22] This was an extremely harsh decision for, since victory at Olympia brought such great fame, expulsion brought absolute disgrace.[23]

But, even though our knowledge is admittedly imperfect, from the available evidence it would seem that the number of accidental or wilful deaths which occurred in the long history of Olympia was relatively small. This should not really surprise us if we consider that the games were dedicated to Zeus and the competitors were all required to swear a solemn oath that they would abide by the rules. During the early period of the festival at least, when the Olympian deities were still a very real force, this must have had considerable effect. . . .

THE PLEASURES AND HARDSHIPS OF A VISIT TO OLYMPIA

A visit to Olympia was not unmitigated joy. The journey there in the height of summer was a strenuous undertaking and so too was the actual period of the visit, for the sanctuary had been conceived as a residence for gods and not for men. From the middle of the fourth century B.C. onwards the guests of honour were accommodated in the Leonidaeum, which had been specially built by Leonidas of Naxos for this purpose. Subsequently, in late antiquity, it became a residence for the Roman praetors in Greece. But the remaining guests slept either in tents or beneath the stars, an arrangement which was, however, rendered tolerable if not indeed refreshing by the mild summer nights in that part of Greece. The competitors of course had their own special accommodation in the western colonnade of the gymnasium.

The pilgrims bought their food from itinerant merchants for, in view of the great crowds which flocked to the festival, it was only natural that a sort of trade fair should have developed in Olympia. Cicero once observed that many of those who travelled to the games were not inspired by a desire for fame and a victor's crown but by the prospect of profitable business.[24]

But how were these enormous crowds, who only came once every four years, to be provided with adequate supplies of drinking water in the midsummer drought? This was doubtless the most difficult of the tasks facing the organisers. Drinking water was supplied by nine fountains from a number of subterranean channels. But supplies were never really adequate until Roman times, when Herodes Atticus built a special conduit, from his own private resources, which carried a large volume of water from the hills along subterranean channels several kilometres long and delivered it to a central well, which was subsequently fashioned into the beautiful fountain known as the exedra of

22   Photius, Bibl. CXC; cf. Franz Mezö, *Geschichte der Olympischen Spiele* (Munich: 1930), p. 189.

23   Dionysius of Halicarnassus, *Ars Rhetorica*, VI 6; cf. Mezö, *Geschichte*, p. 188.

24   Cicero, *Tusculan Disputations*, V 3, 9.

Herodes Atticus. A magnificent marble bull, which was one of the ornaments on this fountain, has survived and is inscribed with the name and Olympic title of the wife of Herodes: Regilla, priestess of Demeter.

Lucian tells an interesting story in this connection about a contemporary of his, a man by the name of Peregrinus, who was always making speeches in order to attract attention. Eventually, when his oratory no longer drew the crowds, he announced that he intended to burn himself to death, which he actually did on a pyre not far from Olympia. But in one of the speeches which he gave in Olympia, Peregrinus inveighed against Herodes Atticus for supplying the crowds at the festival with abundant supplies of water. This was turning the Greeks into women, he said, arguing that it would be far better for them to suffer from thirst, even if it meant succumbing to the epidemics which ravaged the sanctuary during the festival period. In the course of this speech Peregrinus did not hesitate to drink from the self-same water to which he was taking such violent exception. In the end, when the crowd turned ugly and was about to stone him, our bold orator sought refuge in the altis at the statue of Zeus. This alone saved him.[25]

But it was not just a question of accommodation being difficult, of food and drink being hard to come by: life was altogether hectic at Olympia. . . .

THE PENTATHLON

On the afternoon of the second day the pentathlon was staged, the sequence of events being discus, jumping, javelin, running and wrestling.[26] Since running and wrestling were also contests in their own right, only the discus, javelin and jumping were regarded as "disciplines specific to the pentathlon."[27] The order of events had been well thought out, for the first four tested the athletes' arms and legs in an alternating sequence while the last tested the whole body. The pentathlon was composed of both light and heavy events. Philostratus laid down the canon for it in his *Gymnasticus,* where he defined the stade-race, the dolichos, the race in armour and the diaulos as light events; the pankration, wrestling and boxing as heavy events, and the pentathlon as a combination of both. In this combination the heavy events were the wrestling and the discus.[28]

Aristotle considered the contestants in the pentathlon to be the most attractive athletes since they were both fleet of foot and strongly built. To succeed in the pentathlon therefore a man had to be an all-rounder and this called for a particular kind of physique, which has also been described for us by Philostratus,

25   Lucian, *Anacharsis, Hermotimus* and *Peregrinus,* in *Works of Lucian of Samosata,* German Trans. Theodor Fischer (Berlin and Stuttgart: 1855–1903).

26   Joachim Ebert, *Zum Pentathlon der Antike* (Berlin: 1930), pp. 18–20. It would seem, however, that the stade-race was the first event in the Olympic pentathlon; see Xenophon, *Hellenica,* VII 4, 29.

27   Pollux, *Works,* III 151; see Ebert, *Pentathlon,* p. 20.

28   Philostratus, *Gymnasticus* 3.

who was the great authority on athletics in ancient times. In his view the ideal type was a tall, slim, well-built man of medium weight, whose muscles were well-developed but not overdeveloped; his legs needed to be long rather than well-proportioned and his back supple and flexible, for this facilitated the back-swing in both the javelin and the discus and was a distinct advantage in the jump; he also needed long hands and slender fingers, for this would afford him a stronger purchase on the discus and enable him to handle the throwing thong of the javelin without straining.[29] . . .

JUMPING

The only kind of jump practised in Olympia was the long jump, although whether this was a standing jump or whether the competitors used a run-up is not entirely clear. A form of pole vaulting, in which the competitors used a lance as pole and vaulted over a horse, was also in vogue in Greece at that time but it was never introduced in Olympia. The use of springboards in the long jump was quite unknown to the ancients but they did employ a *bater,* a sort of sill or threshold which afforded additional purchase for the take-off. This sill marked the beginning of the *skamma, i.e.,* the landing pit, which was simply a piece of ground fifty feet long that had been broken up with picks and subsequently raked over to form a level surface of soft earth.[30]

The jumping events in the Olympic pentathlon were accompanied by the flute player. It seems that this custom was first established in honour of Apollo who, according to ancient legend, defeated Hermes in the stade-race and Ares in the boxing. Pausanias tells us that ''the Pythian flute playing was introduced in the leaping contest in the pentathlon because the flute was sacred to Apollo and also because Apollo was on several occasions the victor at Olympia.''[31]

The jumpers used jumping weights or *halteres* which were roughly semi-circular in shape and so constructed that the fingers could pass through them.[32] These dumbbells were made of lead, iron or stone. From the finds made in the course of the excavations it would seem that their length varied from 12 to 19 centimetres, and their weight from 1.48 to 4.629 kilogrammes.[33] Clearly, the lighter weights would have been used by the boys and the heavier ones by the men. There was also another type of dumbbell which, instead of being pierced, was provided with grooves. This type was simply gripped in the hand, the grooves affording a better purchase for the fingers.

29   Ibid., 31.

30   Ebert, op. cit., pp. 44–45..

31   Pausanias, V 7, 10.

32   Ibid., V 26, 3.

33   Mező, *Geschichte,* p. 112; and Julius Jüthner, *Über antike Turngeräte* (Vienna: 1896), pp. 3–18.

These jumping weights served two main purposes: they helped the jumper to keep his balance and also to make a good clean landing in the pit. Whereas at the moment of take-off the competitor swung his arms forwards with considerable force in order to gain greater momentum, at the moment of landing he swung them backwards with equal force in order to prevent himself from toppling over. For the jumper had to make a clean landing; if he slithered or fell the jump was not counted.[34] We know this from Philostratus, who tells us that if the imprint of the jumper's feet was imperfect his jump was not measured.[35]

The jumping weights would of course also have been designed with a view to improving performances. In fact, we know that this was the case for, in a comparison which he made between running and jumping, Aristotle pointed out that a runner will run faster if he uses his arms and a jumper will jump further if he uses his jumping weights.[36]

Recently experiments were carried out in which a number of modern athletes executed both the standing and the running jump using dumbbells weighing 2.5 kilogrammes. In the running jump the weights proved a hindrance, reducing normal performances by more than a metre. In the standing jump, however, performances were improved by fifteen to twenty centimetres. The best standing jump achieved measured 2.84 metres. In this connection Ebert has observed that a standing jump of three metres must be regarded as a very good performance.[37]

We know of two quite extraordinary performances in the long jump in ancient times. At the 29th Olympiad in 664 B.C. Chionis of Sparta jumped 52 feet while in Delphi Phayllus of Croton jumped 55 feet. Since the Olympic foot measured 0.32047 metres and the Delphic foot 0.296 metres Chionis actually jumped further than Phayllus (16.66 metres as opposed to 16.28 metres.)[38] But neither of these performances appears at all credible if we regard them as single jumps. Consequently, unless the texts in which these figures were quoted are corrupt, we can only assume that the long jump in the pentathlon actually consisted of a sequence of jumps. Themistius seems to imply as much in his commentary on Aristotle's *De Physica,* where he argues that only those phenomena may be said tυ be continuous which "omit nothing either from the time or from the activity through which they move." The jumpers in the pentathlon, he suggests, do not move continuously because they "omit part of the space through which they move." Now if the jumpers "omit part of the space through which they move" this could mean that they do not cover the whole distance in one leap because they come into contact with the ground in the course of that leap.[39]

34   Adolf Boetticher, *Olympia: Das Fest und seine Stätte,* 2nd ed. (Berlin: 1886), p. 107.
35   Philostratus, *Gymnasticus,* 55.
36   Aristotle, *Problemata,* 5, 8; 881, a39–b6.
37   Ebert, op. cit., pp. 46–54.
38   Ibid., pp. 35–42.
39   Ibid., p. 58.

From this it would then follow that the jump in the pentathlon was a noncontinuous multiple jump, in other words a sequence of jumps.

But what are we to make of all this? The view advanced by Julius Jüthner and Carl Diem that the amazing performances of Chionis of Sparta and Phayllus of Croton were not set up in the long jump at all but in the hop-step-and-a-jump is scarcely tenable today. At first sight Ebert's hypothesis appears far more attractive. He argues that the jumping event in the pentathlon consisted of a sequence of standing jumps. In order to explain the fifty-foot-long pit and the tremendous distances put up by our two famous contestants he is of course obliged to assume a sequence of five jumps. Five jumps of three metres each would be about fifty feet. So far so good. But when Ebert tries to substantiate his theory of the quintuple jump by suggesting that the figure five also played a part in the other events in the pentathlon[40] his argument is far less convincing. In the discus and the javelin each competitor had three throws, in the wrestling victory went to the contestant who succeeded in throwing his opponent three times, and to become overall winner of the pentathlon a man had to win three separate events. Consequently Ebert's hypothesis of the quintuple jump receives no support from the procedures adopted in the other events.

THROWING THE JAVELIN

The Greek competition javelin was about six feet long. It was both shorter and lighter than the military javelin, although it had the same metal point. Before making his throw the contestant fitted an *amentum*, or throwing loop, to the shaft just behind the point of balance, in which he placed the index and perhaps also the middle finger of his right hand while the actual shaft rested on his thumb. The effect of the throwing loop was to increase the carry and perhaps also to impart a rotary movement to the javelin, which would have stabilised its flight and controlled its direction.

The old controversy as to whether the contestants in the javelin event at Olympia had to aim at a target or simply throw for distance, or both, is not at all easy to resolve, for none of the sources provides any firm evidence to go by. We might perhaps feel inclined to assume that, since the contestants had already demonstrated their ability to throw for distance in the discus, the judges would have been more likely to have tested their accuracy with the javelin. A wooden post, a suspended shield or a circle painted on the ground could have served as a target. The javelin was thrown from a horizontal position above the right shoulder with the left leg serving as fulcrum.[41]

40   Ibid., pp. 13 and 62.

41   Eugen Thiemann, "Die Olympischen Spiele im Altertum," in *Olympia in der Antike,* pp. 61–71.

Although we have no proof that the competitors at Olympia were each allowed three throws we may reasonably assume that this was the case. On the island of Cos it was customary to give the victor in this event three javelins as a prize; this we know from an ancient inscription. There are also ancient Greek monuments on which athletes are represented holding three javelins in their hands.[42] It is not, unfortunately, possible to give any precise information about the actual performances in this event since there are no reliable records.

THE FOOT-RACE

Although we do not know the precise length of the foot-race in the pentathlon the widely held belief that it was a stade-race, in which the competitors covered a single length of the stadium, is almost certainly justified.[43] The stade-race was the most convenient distance for a sprint event and for this reason alone it was likely to have been adopted for the pentathlon.

WRESTLING

Wrestling was the last contest in the pentathlon; it was also the most difficult and the most exacting. The rules were the same as for the independent wrestling event although the type of wrestling was very different. The pentathlon wrestlers were basically light-athletics men, which meant that they depended far more on the correct application of strength and on general expertise than on brute force. The fact that wrestling remained a highly intricate and attractive sport, which could justly be called an art, was largely due to its inclusion in the pentathlon. "All the enthusiastic and laudatory assessments of wrestling . . . which are to be found in virtually every account of Greek sport were really inspired by the wrestling contests in the pentathlon."[44] As in the individual contest, so too in the pentathlon only upright wrestling was allowed. In order to win, a contestant had to throw his opponent three times.

42 For sources, see Mezö, *Geschichte,* p. 129.

43 Ebert (*Pentathlon,* pp. 10–13) assumes a length of five stades for the pentathlon foot-race, and bases this assumption on an inscription discovered in Anazarbus in Cilicia, which he renders as follows: " . . . at the festival games of the provincial diet of Asia, Demetrius gained the victory on the fifth straight after making Optatus his pace-maker for the first four." (For original inscription, see Gough, *Anatolian Studies,* III, 1952, 127 ff., No. 1, lines 12 to 14. Even if this rendering is correct—and there are other interpretations of this particular passage—it is by no means certain that this account refers to a foot-race held within the framework of the pentathlon. Nor is there any other reference to a five-stade race in the source material.

44 Werner Rudolph, *Olympischer Kampfsport in der Antike* (Berlin: 1965), p. 58.

——PETER D. ARNOTT——————————————————————

ROMAN RELIGION

The vitality of Greek religion is seen in its mythology. The Greeks made up wonderful stories about the gods and their intervention in human affairs—stories which, in spite of the unifying effect of the Homeric poems, continued to survive in numerous local variants and were constantly being added to. The major myths, particularly in the hands of the dramatists, served as a basis for creative reinterpretation, and old stories became a vehicle for new truths. This ready flow of imagination has proved a continuous delight and inspiration to artists, but an embarrassment to scholars. It is often hard to disentangle the various accretions to a story and trace the myth back to the nuclear belief or ritual observance that started it on its snowball course. In Roman religion, less difficulty exists. The Romans, more prosaically, borrowed stories, as they borrowed gods, from others. Mythologically speaking, their divinities are barren. It is comparatively easy to distinguish the various strata in Roman religion and trace its development from primitive beliefs to a cosmopolitan system whose supreme tolerance betrays its fundamental lack of conviction.

Any religion, in its formative stages, reflects the most pressing needs of its society. The early Romans, like the early Greeks, were bound up with the soil. They saw spirits at work in the vital functions of the earth and sky; they believed that growing things were inhabited by forces which had to be placated if the work was to go well and the life of the community be assured. The Romans, however, developed very early in their society a fondness for system and particularity which the Greeks lacked. Where the Greek deities were often vaguely defined and overlapping in their functions, the Romans created a divine bureaucracy in which the major gods were surrounded by a number of smaller figures, precisely distinguished in function but not in character. This tendency may have been innate in them; it was certainly encouraged by their association with the Etruscans, whose own religious practices show the same insistence on precision. One of the most interesting Etruscan finds is a model liver, perhaps used to instruct initiate diviners. It is marked with the names of many deities, each located in his exact region in the sky. On the same principle, the Romans imagined the gods of the corn and crops as attended by a host of subordinates, each in charge of his own department: the breaker-up of fallow land, the renewer of the soil, the maker of furrows, the grafter, the plougher, the harrower, the

From Peter D. Arnott, *The Romans and their World* (New York: St. Martin's Press, 1970), pp. 98–104, 106–9, 132, by permission of the publisher.

weeder, the reaper, the gatherer, the storer, the taker of corn from the store-place to the mill.

A few of these rustic deities have minimally distinct personalities. Priapus was a fertility god originally worshipped in Asia Minor, passing to Italy by way of Greece. He was considered to be the son of Aphrodite, or of a nymph, and had a lustfulness appropriate to his parentage and function. He disliked asses, because one had once brayed and alarmed a nymph he was stealthily pursuing; his image, grossly obscene, stood in fields and gardens. Poets amused themselves by celebrating him in verse, such as the trifle attributed to Virgil:

> They bring me roses in the spring
> And apples in the fall;
> In summer, corn; but winter's rough
> And brings no joy at all.
> I hate the cold; and I'm afraid,
> Although I am a god,
> I'll end on some dull peasant's fire—
> My statue's made of wood.[1]

Priapus has his direct descendants in the gnomes still used to decorate gardens. A slightly more sinister figure was Silvanus, the god of the untilled land. His domain thus began where the civilized community ended, and he represented the spirit of wild nature, who had to be propitiated. He is thus somewhat akin to the Greek satyrs whose mythological buffoonery conceals a more dangerous quality.

Similar spirits watched over the hearth and home. When a child was born, a multiplicity of spirits attended him—one to watch over his first cries, another over his first teeth, another over his first steps. The household god, or Lar, was originally the spirit of a departed ancestor. He had his niche in the family dwelling, where it was customary to leave small offerings. Plautus sums up his attributes in the prologue to *The Pot of Gold*:

> In case somebody's wondering, I'll briefly
> Introduce myself. I am the Household God
> Belonging to the family you saw me leaving.
> I've kept a watchful and proprietary eye
> On this establishment for many years now,
> For the father of the present occupant
> And his before him. . . .
> He has one daughter. Every day she comes
> To pay her respects, and always has
> A pinch of incense for me, or some wine—
> Something, anyway—and hangs me round with garlands.[2]

The Lar was the guardian of the home in the widest sense—of the comings and

---

1   *Appendix Vergiliana*, Priapea, 1.
2   Plautus, *Aulularia*, 1-5, 23-5.

goings of its inhabitants, of the surrounding property, of relations with the neighbours. He could also preside over crossroads, including those of city streets; thus cities, as well as individual households, could have their Lares. A small temple to the Lares of Pompeii may be seen in the forum, erected to propitiate the guardian powers after the earthquake which foreshadowed the eruption of Vesuvius in A.D. 79. There is a similar structure at Ostia, in the form of a courtyard containing several niches arranged around a central fountain. The individual home also recognized the Penates, who were the guardians of the larder and watched over the food supply of the household.

The life of the average man was beset by such spirits, whose favour he had to preserve to ensure his own success. Roman religion is prolific in spells. We know of one to rid the house of ghosts, to be performed on three nights in May. The householder put nine black beans in his mouth and walked round the house spitting them out one by one. The ghosts were supposed to follow to pick them up. This done, the householder washed his hands and spoke the formula, "Good folk, get you gone." He addressed them as good in the same way that the Greeks gave propitiatory titles to the night, the Furies, and other powers they dreaded, not because they were good, but in the hope that they might be. Such euphemisms are part and parcel of early magical and religious observance.

The official gods of the state had more personality. Their chief was Jupiter, who like his Greek counterpart Zeus was primarily associated with the sky and its phenomena. Their names are related—Jupiter means simply "god the father"—and derive from a common Indo-European root. The sky god was worshipped by the early migrants from the north who imposed their religion, as well as their racial characteristics, on the first inhabitants of the Mediterranean basin. Zeus is regularly "the cloud-gatherer" in Homer, and presides over the daylight in opposition to his brother Hades, who rules the darkness of the underworld. In the same way, Jupiter is the god of thunder, lightning and weather in general; of light as a potent force; of the full moon. His priest enjoyed particular sanctity, and was restricted to a carefully prescribed range of activities. He was not permitted to see men at work; an attendant walked in front of him to clear the way and ensure that the people were standing idle. He was allowed no contact with war, or with elections. This was not because the Roman elections were violent (though in fact they often were) but because the voting system followed the lines of the military organization. He was not allowed to look on death, for fear of pollution. There was a whole list of unlucky things that had to be avoided.

Jupiter was worshipped on the Capitoline Hill together with the goddesses Juno and Minerva. Juno, the consort of Jupiter, may be equated with the Greek Hera; like her she was primarily a fertility goddess, and in one of her functions, as Juno Lucina, presided over childbirth. Minerva was the goddess of handicrafts. She was regularly identified with the Greek Athena, and had similar functions. Some scholars have argued that she is in fact Athena, imported to

Rome through Etruria, but it is more probable that she was of native Italian origin. She had another important temple on the Aventine Hill, which served as the headquarters of a guild of writers and actors during the second war with Carthage. Ennius was one of its members.

Another important native god was Mars, popular all over Italy under various names—Mavors, Marmar, or, in Etruria, Maris. He was the god of fertility and of war. Scholars have argued endlessly over which function came first. It is an unprofitable discussion; the two things had equal importance in the life of the early peoples. He was particularly associated with horses, which were made to race in his honour. He, Jupiter and Quirinus (the deified Romulus) were worshipped by the Salii, a group of priests who performed a war-dance of great antiquity, wearing Bronze Age armour. The shields they carried were supposed to be patterned after an original which had fallen from heaven. Their song, fragments of which have been preserved, was almost totally unintelligible, even to the priests of the Republic.

The god Janus was, like many Roman deities, a personification—in this case of the gate or door (*ianua*). He presided over entrances and exits, coming and goings; since to enter a house one must first go through the door, he became the god of beginnings. As such his name regularly occurs first in the list of deities, taking precedence even over that of Jupiter. The month named after him was first in the reformed calendar, and he was recognized as god of the new year. He was represented with two faces looking in opposite directions. A monument to Janus stood in the Forum, its gates closed in time of peace, and open for war.

With the other gods there is considerable confusion. The rapid spread of Roman contacts with other races led to the adoption of their deities, or at least the names of those deities. It is often impossible to say whether any given god is a native Italian deity or a foreign importation. Several times the functions associated with one deity in Greece reappear in Italy associated with another name. Are we to say that there were originally two gods, one Italian and one Greek, with exactly identical functions, or that the Greek god has been taken over into the Roman system and given a Latin name? Sometimes the transformation is obvious. The Greek name is retained, or slightly altered in transliteration. Roman tongues found occasional difficulty with Greek sounds.

Certainly the idea of the gods as a family derives from Greek influence. In the earliest period the Romans did not attempt to relate the gods to one another. But the family concept, once acquired, had an obvious appeal for a people so much concerned with family unity. The Greek pattern was reduplicated in the Roman religion, with the same general division of functions.

We have already seen Jupiter as the father of the gods and Juno as his wife. Ceres, the corn goddess, was the Roman equivalent of Demeter, the earth-mother, though her primal importance to an agricultural community suggests that she may originally have been an independent figure. Flora, her attendant, is essentially the same goddess in another aspect. Venus, originally an Italian goddess, was identified with Aphrodite. She therefore came to have a special connection with Rome, as the mother of Aeneas by a mortal father; in Virgil she appears as his guide and protector.

Hestia, goddess of the hearth, was a nebulous figure in the Greek pantheon in spite of the fact that she presided over the social centre of the community. Her Roman equivalent, Vesta (the names come from the same root, the Indo-European *wes*), had more prestige. Her shrine in the Forum contained a fire that was never allowed to go out. Tending this fire was one of the chief duties of the Vestal Virgins, a college of six priestesses selected under rigid conditions at an early age, and compelled to renounce marriage for their term of office. On retirement—at about forty—they were at liberty to seek a husband. Few did; Plutarch reports the superstition that it was unlucky. Though they enjoyed considerable power and prestige, and were in frequent attendance at festivals and processions, their life was an onerous one. If a girl let the sacred fire go out, she was whipped. If found unchaste, she was buried alive for the crime of incest, for the Vestals were the daughters of the state. On several occasions they were made the scapegoats for political and military disasters. When Hannibal defeated the Roman army at Cannae in 216 B.C., it was decided that two of the priestesses were to blame. . . .

The Roman religion thus absorbed most of the major and minor figures of the Greek pantheon. This ready acceptance of foreign deities betrayed a fundamental spiritual dissatisfaction. The Romans, as we have seen, were not a readily imaginative people. Their native deities were humdrum, workaday figures compared to the vivid personalities with which the Greeks invested their gods, nor were they able to use the traditional divine framework as a frame of reference, as the Greeks had done, within which to conduct philosophical investigations. The Roman religion was spiritually barren, and the greater part of it came at second hand. Why, then, did it have such importance in Roman society? To what extent did the average Roman believe in it? It is important to clarify what we mean by belief in this context. Obviously, few Romans believed in their gods as a Christian believes in Jesus Christ and sees him as a saviour and redeemer. Equally few, on the other hand, dismissed their religion as a hollow sham perpetuated by the upper classes for political purposes—though this argument is occasionally raised. The state religion can most usefully be seen as an emanation of the principles of social order and moral restraint that guided the people in their everyday lives. The temples and their attendant ceremonies were visible manifestations of the spirit of republican Rome. Religion, morality and political well-being were intimately connected. It is for this reason that most educated Romans gave the gods their willing adherence; it is for this reason, too, that the Emperor Augustus was able to conceive of social and moral legislation as parts of the same programme, and couple both with a religious revival.

Roman religion was largely a matter of propriety and state-ordained observance. The priestly offices were sought, like political appointments, as a means of social advancement. In the increasingly elaborate apparatus of the state religion the presiding body was composed of the *pontifices*—originally three, but increased to sixteen by the time of Julius Caesar—under the leadership of the *pontifex maximus.* In historical times the latter was an elected official who also controlled the fifteen *flamines,* each responsible for the cult of one god, the Vestals, and the *rex sacrorum,* who had inherited some of the religious functions of the early kings. These functionaries were chiefly concerned with the complex ritual which proliferated as any genuine religious feeling waned.

Most Romans would have been conscious of religion mainly as a social function. The number of festivals expanded alarmingly. As Ovid was later to remark, ''It is expedient that there should be gods.'' The authorities undoubtedly found it expedient to use the gods' festivals to boost public morale. Celebrations could take various forms. They usually involved processions. One example, interesting because it shows how elements of primitive folk ritual remained embedded in the elaborate state system, is the familiar *lustratio* or ceremony of purification, which involved a rite rather like the ''beating the bounds'' occasionally surviving in Christian usage. Cato gives the formula for purifying farmland. A sacrificial pig, ram and bull were led around the desired area, and various prayers offered, including one to Mars:

> Mars, our father, I pray and beseech you, look kindly on me, my home and all that dwell herein: for which purpose I have bidden these animals to be led around my land, my ground, my farm, that you may ward off, avert and keep away sickness visible and invisible, barrenness, devastation, and all malign and untimely influences; that you may permit my harvests, my grain, my vines and plantations to grow and bring forth fruit, preserve the well-being of my shepherds and my flocks, and give good health and strength to me, my house and all that dwell herein. To this intent, to the intent of purifying my land, my farm, my ground, and of making expiation, as I have said, for my wrongdoings, deign to accept the offering of these sucklings, who are given to you.[3]

On a public level, the same ceremony could be used to purify a people, a city, an army: every five years the censors conducted such a *lustratio* of the city of Rome.

The favourite public festivals were those which, in the Greek manner, involved athletic contests or the performance of plays. One may catch something of their flavour in the garrulous prologues of Plautus, addressed to a jolly holiday crowd, or in Terence's complaints about the events with which he had to compete. The Romans added the less desirable attraction of gladiatorial games, which were borrowed from the Etruscans. They appear first in a religious association, as part of a funeral ceremony in 264 B.C., and may have originated in memory of the custom of human sacrifice. Acquiring rapid popularity, they

3   Cato, *On Farming,* 141.

soon lost, like many of the other elements of Roman festivals, all traces of religious usage, and survived as an all too familiar blood sport.

In its public manifestations, therefore, the Roman religion tended to lavish ceremony which had a mass appeal, and could, in the wrong hands, easily be manipulated for political purposes. . . .

—ROLAND AUGUET————————————————————

GLADIATORS AND SPECTATORS

The gladiatorial combats first appeared in Rome long after the Circus games, in 264 B.C., as a funerary rite reserved to the aristocracy. That year, indeed, the sons of Junius Brutus, descendants of the great Brutus, decided to honour the memory of their father by matching three pairs of slaves against one another, according to a custom which was not of Roman origin. Though these first gladiators—known as *bustuarii*—derived their name from *bustum,* a word meaning the tomb or the funeral pyre, it does not seem that these combats formed part of the many ceremonies of the funeral itself or that the gladiators fought to the death "before the tomb" of the dead man, as has sometimes been assumed by a simplification of language. They took place in the days that followed, on a date difficult to state precisely but doubtless, at least at first, on the ninth day after the obsequies, the day which marked the end of the period of mourning after the solemn funeral ceremonies reserved for persons of importance, and on which the funeral games were traditionally celebrated.

The first combat of which we will speak took place in the *forum boarium,* that is to say the cattle-market, but the custom of using the Forum for this kind of display was rapidly established. It had long since ceased to be the "field of willows and barren reeds" sung by Ovid, or the necropolis watered by a brook which the archaeologists have revealed to us. The stalls of butchers and market-gardeners which at one time bordered the site were no longer there; they had been replaced by those of more noble trades whose façades were decorated with shields captured from the Samnites. These shops, ranged in two ranks, took up one side and the temple of Concord on the other marked off a roughly rec-

From Roland Auguet, *Cruelty and Civilization: The Roman Games* (London: George Allen and Unwin Ltd., 1972), pp. 19-25, 46-51, 195, by permission of the publisher and Humanities Press, Inc.

tangular arena. The site by this time was embellished by several monuments, whose red-tiled roofs tempered their severity. A sundial brought from Catania was placed near the Rostra, and for another century was destined to show the Romans a slightly incorrect time of day.

Though the setting in which these combats took place had, as we have seen, nothing wild about it, there must have been something rude and primitive about the combats themselves, since there was no preparation, no complicated stage management, to diminish or refine their brutality. Later, someone had the idea of placing seats for hire all round the Forum; but at the beginning the spectators—women were excluded—perched here and there wherever they could find a place, especially on the galleries which had been built above the stalls situated along the edges of the longer sides. Standing upright, and bareheaded since they had the feeling that they were taking part in a ceremony rather than attending an entertainment, they watched the blood flow among the flagstones of the Forum. The lack of distance conferred a violent and strongly emotional character on the bloodshed—"magic," if you will.

The gladiators fought in couples. At the time they were all armed in the same way, in the "Samnite" fashion: long, rectangular shield, straight sword, helmet and greaves. We lack, however, any details of the organization of these combats. The historians have only handed down to us the number of pairs summoned to take part; they increase steadily, from three to twenty-five, then from twenty-five to sixty in less than a century. These figures, however, should not make us lose sight of the fact that at this time the gladiatorial combats were totally exceptional in character. Moreover, they were frequently followed by a banquet which was held in the Forum. But it was not because they constituted a munificence in which the populace was invited to share, that these games were known as *munera;* the reason was, according to a tradition handed down to us by Tertullian, that they represented above all an "obligation" to the dead.

THE BLOOD OF THE SHADES

Thus, before becoming a spectacle applauded by the dense crowds of the Colosseum, the gladiatorial combats were a rite carried out in recollection of sacred ceremonies. What religious feeling drove the Romans to adopt these macabre games? What savage, archaic rite were they resuscitating, reviving or replacing? They themselves had forgotten—and, moreover, the question no longer preoccupied them. The origin of the combats is obscure. They probably came from Etruria by way of Campania, where, according to Jacques Heurgon, they found "their full development and classic form" before taking root in Rome. Their exact significance is no less obscure. It has been held that the blood shed by the gladiators was a tribute exacted by those gods, devourers of men, who still dwelt on some of the shores of the Mediterranean. But the texts cited to support this thesis appear to have been dictated, as the late Georges Ville has shown, by Christian propagandists seeking to discredit paganism.

It is wiser to credit the laconic details handed down to us by Festus. "It was the custom," he writes, "to sacrifice prisoners on the tombs of valorous warriors; when the cruelty of this custom became evident, it was decided to make gladiators fight before the tomb." Thus the origin of the combats lay in a softening of customs by which a people still half enslaved to old superstitions gave, if one may so put it, an orderly form to human sacrifice. The gladiators who took the place of the bound victim played a role similar to that of the reed manikins which were thrown, hands and feet bound, over the Pontus Sublicius on 14 May as a later substitute, no doubt, for living victims. But in the gladiatorial games the effect of this substitution were dramatic rather than symbolic.

The blood of the gladiators was thus shed for the dead. The object was "to appease their spirits," a convenient, even if ambiguous, formula. It was not intended, it seems, to guard against hostile acts by the dead man or, more specifically, against his always dreaded intrusion into the world of the living. Fear of the dead was undoubtedly far from being alien to Roman religion; in certain circumstances unsatisfied spirits could unchain calamities, of which the worst was to drag the living with them into the other world. But this fear was exorcised by a very exact jurisdiction which limited the return of the *manes* to earth to certain days and defined a host of public and private ceremonies aimed at rendering them inoffensive. The minute detail which in Rome governed the relations of the living and the dead makes it very improbable that the aim of a rite originally reserved to certain privileged persons, and as exceptional as the gladiatorial combats, was to guard against the maleficence of the dead. Above all, the dead man is not by nature an aggressive being who must at all costs be propitiated; the hostility which he harbours is latent and does not become manifest unless the obligatory duties have been neglected—if, for example, he has not been mourned or buried according to the rites. The dead man is, in essence, a shadow emptied of his substance, "a head without force," indistinct, anonymous. His condition may be defined as a "lack," a deaf and listless but tenacious quest for a feeling of reality. . . .

Luckily for us, it is not in religious history that we must seek the reasons for the exceptional success which the gladiatorial combats were to know. Very soon, even before the end of the Republic, they came to lose their significance as a rite and we can really speak of "secularization." Henceforth, in the political life of Rome, they played a precise and specific role for which two factors predestined them.

The first of these was their popularity, which from the very earliest times was great. There was no spectacle that the Romans would not have abandoned in order to attend a gladiatorial combat, except perhaps the chariot races, and even that is not certain; for these, though far more frequent, did not have the prestige conferred upon the *munera* by their comparative rarity. Terence, in any case, proved to his own cost that the public did not hesitate a moment between the cross-talk of his comedies and the sword-play of the gladiators.

The other factor was their private character. This requires some explanation. In the time of the Republic, the state—or the Senate—exercised, at least until the day when its authority became irremediably weakened, a rigorous control over all forms of spectacle. It was the Senate which, within the framework of the religious festivals, fixed the details of a ''calendar of spectacles'' whose enforcement was entrusted to the magistrates. A Roman spectacle was a ''public affair,'' originally at least, for the situation rapidly became more complicated, and the magistrate entrusted with providing entertainment for his fellow citizens was only an executive held in check by strict regulations. The gladiatorial combats alone escaped this control. Until 105 B.C. when it seems they were included among the official spectacles, they were given only by individuals. In theory, anyone could give a spectacle, though it goes without saying that the only people who did so were members of the great families, if only for purely financial reasons; for, even though in second-century Rome the *munera* were of interest to the entire city, the expenses which they involved, and those of the banquet offered to the populace which very frequently followed them, were naturally sustained by the individual who provided them.

Thus left to the initiative of anybody or everybody, these spectacles, by their very popularity, became an ideal instrument of propaganda and publicity for those who dreamed of exceptional careers or striking electoral successes; they afforded an easy method of winning over the plebeians. The Senate, however, was well aware of this. Even at the time when no personal ambition threatened its authority, it was reserved towards the *munera* which flattered the tastes of the ''populace.'' Not daring to forbid them or to attack them openly, it did nothing to assure the spectators even the minimum of comfort; we have already seen in what precarious conditions the combats often took place. On several occasions the Senate even took measures to maintain this discomfort. In fact, and this is significant, it was 20 B.C. before Rome was provided with a permanent amphitheatre, in store, built by Statilius Taurus. Despite these reservations, an innovation destined to have a great future soon made its appearance: a *munus* of exceptional magnificence, the first of a long series, was given not at Rome but at Cartagena by Scipio in honour of his father and his uncle who had been killed in Spain in the struggle against the Carthaginians. . . .

The first gladiators took their stand in the middle of the stretch of sand ninety-two yards by fifty-seven which formed the arena, frail silhouettes overwhelmed by the enormous surging crowd swarming on the tiers. Their helmets, which entirely covered their faces, first caught the eye; they rivalled each other in excessive weight and complexity. But other than that the two men differed completely in appearance: one, whose body apart from his chest was covered with pieces of metal and leather, carried a small shield in his left hand; the other, almost naked, held a rounded, oblong shield which, seen from the front, completely covered him so that only his head and feet were visible. The first belonged to the class of gladiators known as Thracians, whose appearance at Rome dated from the time of Sulla. He wore a red *subligaculum,* a sort of loin-cloth supported at the waist by a sword-belt (*balteus*). Both legs were protected by metal half-cylinders (*ocreae*) fixed against the tibia and covering a small portion of the hip. His left arm was covered by a *manica,* a sort of leathern sleeve reinforced by metal scales, of which one, at the lower end, protected the upper part of his hand, leaving only the fingers uncovered. His offensive weapon was not one of those strange swords bent almost at right angles in the centre with which the Thracian sometimes fought. It was a fairly short sabre known as a *sica,* curved in the manner of a scythe.

The other gladiator was one of those known in the days of Augustus as Samnites and later as *hoplomachi,* either because it might have seemed insulting to apply to gladiators the name of a people which had for a long time formed part of the Latin community, or because this class had practically disappeared, becoming split into two more specialized types of gladiator: the *secutor,* the usual adversary of the *retiarius,* and the *hoplomachus,* who was matched with the Thracian. It was indeed rare for two gladiators of similar class to fight each other. Each man had his own means of defence and his own technique, differing from that of his adversary, and it was this that partly provided the interest of a combat whose principle consisted just as much in matching two types of weapon as in matching two men. Thus the *hoplomachus* was deprived of those complicated trappings which his adversary wore, since the exceptional height of his shield—which differentiated him from his predecessor, the Samnite, whose shield was not so large—already assured him sufficient protection; other than the loin-cloth, he wore only an *ocrea* on the left leg and leather bands (*fasciae*) on the wrists, the knee and the ankle of the other, unprotected, leg.

Solidly planted on his legs, his body a little tensed, the *hoplomachus* watched; awaiting a favourable moment, he kept his shield close to his chest with such force that his movements seemed more aggressive than protective. His right hand was pressed against the hilt of his sword whose point was flush with the edge of his shield so that his body offered to his adversary only a single line, and when the Thracian, carrying his shield horizontally at the level of his chin and holding his *sica* against his hip, rushed at him, he avoided the attack by a slight sideways movement of his whole body. The crowd, fascinated, murmured in appreciation and, remembering that the small shield men were not usually the victors, already foresaw the defeat of the Thracian by the mastery of this parry.

But this was no more than a prelude; the arms now clashed in longer encounters, in the course of which each of the men parried and attacked several times. Feints, attacks, skilful withdrawals followed one another; it was the left side of the body which was the most frequently exposed for, because of the shield, it was more open to attack, as in fencing, which was why the gladiator with only one greave wore it on his left leg. But despite the fierceness of the combat the two gladiators scarcely moved from their pitch; both had many times been victors and experience had taught them to avoid unnecessary movement. The *hoplomachus* could be seen to crouch, flex his arm and place his sword ready to thrust on the rim of his shield wedged against his left knee; or with his shield hugging his body from chin to feet like an apron fall upon his adversary with drawn sword. Such regular movements did not characterize the Thracian. In the words of the Greek writer Artemidorus of Ephesus, he skimmed into the attack, sometimes throwing his whole body to the right as if to mow down the *hoplomachus* with his curved weapon, sometimes lifting his shield far in front of him on a level with his eyes so as to leave his weapon free for an upward thrust. At these times his blade flitted in short zig-zags while his shield see-sawed until it covered his arms almost horizontally, so much so that its inner face, with its fastening strap, became visible for several moments. It sometimes also happened that the two men confronted each other in an absolutely symmetrical position like two cats face to face.

But however great the part played by skill and technique, there was also the question of endurance which enabled a man "to last out the day and resist the scorching sun in the midst of the burning dust, drenched all the while with his own blood," or prevented him from doing so. Owing to excessive weariness, or possibly because he stumbled against something, or because the blow struck by his adversary had thrown him off balance or seriously injured him, the Thracian fell. In earlier days this would not have been pardoned. The emperor Claudius, in fact, hurriedly turning down his thumb before the crowd was able to show its feelings, used to have the throats cut even of those gladiators who had fallen by accident.

As soon as he tottered there was a unanimous shout from the tiers: "*Habet! Hoc habet!*" ("He's had it!") among which could be heard soon afterwards a very few cries of "*Mitte!*" ("Send him back!"), for the Thracian, whose fall had not been a bad one, continued to fight one hand behind him on the ground to hold himself up, his body arched to keep his enemy at a distance. This courageous attitude aroused the pity of some of the spectators who had thought him already beaten, a view he did not share. He was back on his feet with a bound, making a sign of vigorous denial to the crowd to show that he had not yet "had it" or scorn of the pity shown him. The combat was renewed but with a different rhythm. The *hoplomachus*, encouraged by the crowd, pressed his adversary, who no longer seemed so sure on his feet and was soon driven back against the wall of the *podium* where he restricted himself to parrying blows.

Suddenly the Thracian broke away, threw aside his shield, raised one finger of his left hand towards the spectators, in token of his inability to continue the combat, and begged for their clemency. His outstretched arm streamed with blood which dripped on to his greave, making furrows which mingled with the arabesques that decorated it; above his left breast another wound, which had till then been masked by his shield, spouted blood. The *hoplomachus,* his sword still threatening, stood motionless and turned towards the box of the *editor*, the president of the games, who happened to be the emperor himself; it was the *editor* who, in principle, decided whether the beaten man would be sent back safe and sound (*missus*) or put to death on the spot.

To be sure, certain emperors, when they gave the games, did not scruple to abuse this right. One could cite many examples resulting from cruelty; Claudius, for instance, had every defeated *retiarius* systematically killed because as they did not wear helmets they died with their faces exposed; and the course of their death agony could be followed; or from partisan passions in favour of one or other of the factions of the great or little shields, or from a kind of macabre humour, as when Caracalla once replied to the gladiator who was appealing for his life: "Go and ask your adversary." But most frequently the *editor* would share the views of the crowd and accept its verdict. While this brief consultation was taking place, the Thracian threw himself to the ground (*decumbere*), sat back on one heel and bowed towards the earth. He no longer had the right to touch his arms; if (like that *retiarius* mentioned by Suetonius, who in mass combat recovered his trident and after raising his thumb massacred his adversaries) he violated this law by the slightest gesture he would draw upon himself the curses of the spectators.

However, the spectators were not of one mind; some raised their hands and asked for mercy, others with downward-pointing thumb (*pollice verso*) demanded the execution of the vanquished. Generally speaking, the verdict was not the product of arbitrary cruelty; it was dictated by a very rough sort of justice, a sort of "sporting" equity, if you like. Had the gladiator shown himself cowardly, or had he let the combat drag on ignobly, the crowd, deprived of its pleasure, would assuredly have demanded his condemnation. But if he had fought well for a long time or shown exceptionally fine swordsmanship, or if luck had played a great part in his defeat, the loser had a good chance of being "sent back."

Perhaps the Thracian had been wrong to arouse hope of a longer and more violent combat by his haughty denial. In doubtful cases the slightest circumstance could tip the scales to one side or the other. In the first combats of an afternoon the crowd was avid for blood and was harsher than it was later on. With a final gesture the *editor*, noting that the cries for condemnation prevailed, turned down his thumb and shouted to the *hoplomachus: "Jugula!"* ("Cut his throat!"). From that moment a sort of collaboration was established between the movements of the two gladiators, like that which takes place in the fulfilment of a rite. As the victor, who had just put aside his shield, advanced sword in hand, the Thracian, who all this time had remained absolutely passive, half drew himself up, put one knee to the ground and gripped his executioner's thigh, just above the knee, to steady himself; the other, drawing back his free arm, placed his hand on his victim's helmet so as to hold his head firmly, and plunged his sword just below the vizor into his unprotected neck.

Gladiators, indeed, learned how to die even as they learned how to fight. Nothing counted so much in the eyes of the public as the ability to show oneself master of the slightest movement when face to face with death; that a gladiator should not have it was a disgrace, not only to himself but to the whole community, which resented it as an affront and a degradation. "We hate those weak and suppliant gladiators," said Cicero, "who, hands outstretched, beseech us to let them live." Courage alone was not enough. As Cicero and Seneca have been at pains to point out, the gladiator, in order to win renown, must know above all else how to avoid the reflex which comes at the last moment; he must not try to ward off the sword or shrink away, contract his neck or try to draw back his head. He must know how to make his muscles obey the simple principles which the *lanista,* without humour, repeated on the training ground: to offer his throat to his adversary, should the need arise, to direct against it, the point of the sword, and to receive the blow, as Cicero says, "with his whole body." The gladiators died without removing their helmets; to take them off would have been to show another face, to falsify the games and, so far as the public was concerned, to break a complicity which was doubtless the indispensable spice to the emotions felt during the spectacle.

After the *coup de grâce* the loser fell back; he supported himself on his outstretched arm, his hand spread out, the other hand clamped to his right thigh. He remained half-seated on his defeated arms. His chest thrust out, and leaning to the right, his head drooping, he died in the position of a traveller seated on the grass, prevented from rising by great weariness. . . .

At these spectacles, to be sure, the people wanted to be entertained, not to be morally uplifted by suitable contact with a world of heroes or fired by example. They were taken, like children, to "historical performances." In these they relived their own past in caricature, or found a cheap way of satisfying their lust for cruelty. For watching a struggle to the death between two men while sitting down in safety is surely a strange incitement to bravery; and sending someone to his death by means of a careless gesture, an even stranger one. The sophistry is gross: morally speaking, the habit of playing with impunity with the lives of others could only instil flabbiness; to use a famous phrase—which, from this point of view, so well characterizes the amphitheatre—"Many spectators and few men."

MANORS
AND MANNERS
IN MEDIEVAL TIMES

To discern medieval Europe, we need to run our eyes along the northern rim of the Roman Empire: from England, across France and Low Countries, into the Germanic regions, and on to the outer reaches inhabited by the Vikings, the Magyars, and the Slavs. It was in these territories that classical culture and the Christian church were received. As befitting a frontier, these were unsettled societies that only slowly began to achieve shape and stability after several centuries of commotion, during which the fringes of the Roman dominion disintegrated and the empire itself finally broke into fragments. That is the story of what has been called late antiquity. We are primarily concerned here with the time that followed.

A convenient date to remember is 800 A.D. On Christmas day of that year Charles the Great—Charlemagne—was crowned as the Holy Roman Emperor. Whatever else that act may have symbolized to those present in Rome at the moment, it was certainly significant that a northern European, the leader of a crude Frankish kingdom, should be present in the imperial city to become the titular ruler of the West. To be sure, the Mediterranean was far from losing its importance. Both Byzantium and Islam could indeed boast more brilliant and opulent cultures than Europe during much of the medieval age. Yet there was undeniably a new vigor in the northern borderlands of Europe, where a different civilization was slowly forming. We must now attempt to bring that society into focus.

The Europeans have not made our task easy, since they did not conveniently achieve political unification at a time when their society was perhaps sufficiently malleable to permit it. Charlemagne's empire failed to endure, and while the dream of a united Holy Roman Empire persisted, the reality proved to be otherwise. Even the theological and institutional mortar of Christianity was inadequate to hold Europe together and to prevent different peoples from developing their own social and political structures. To regard the medieval period merely as an age of incipient nationalism, however, would be seriously anachronistic. But neither should we suppose that the centuries after 800 were an epoch of bland uniformity and stagnation. To the contrary, for Europe these were years of active gestation and remarkable innovation. A society of great intrinsic complexity was emerging. The beginnings were usually modest and local. The horizon of most Europeans in the ninth century stretched no further than the edge of their village or the trees that outlined the plot of land where they labored day after day. Yet we need not romanticize the life of medieval peasants nor imagine that Europe altogether lacked the leavening of urban life. Walled towns were always a part of medieval society, as we shall see, and their importance for the rural culture that surrounded them should not be underestimated.

In seeking to establish a chronological framework, we have no reason to reject the conventional dating scheme according to which the terminus of medieval Europe was set in the fifteenth century. By then, the Islamic and Byzantine rivals had been eclipsed and Europe was prepared to face the challenge of Atlantic exploration. We should recall, however, that such sweeping notions as "the end of the Middle Ages" or "the discovery of the New World" had precious little immediate relevance to the daily existence of those average individuals whose lives we are attempting to study.

SERFS AND THEIR MASTERS

The slow dissolution of the Roman Empire and the steady incursion of Germanic peoples into the Mediterranean world brought important social changes. It is arguable, however, that social elites were far more affected than the common people. True, the institution of slavery as it had been known in previous times was shaken along with the rest but the confusion and conflict of early medieval Europe hastened the creation of serfdom. This was a protracted process of many centuries, and the conditions of manorial life were rarely identical from one plot of land to the next. Yet everywhere in Europe people labored in the fields, and everywhere their existence was narrowly circumscribed by custom, law, and religious practice.

Eileen Power has composed a classic account of a French peasant of the ninth century that is as charming as it is scrupulously documented. She gives a picture of daily life on an abbey estate near Paris: the physical setting, the toils and pleasures, the beliefs and superstitions of the serf. We also catch a glimpse of family life on the manor and of the many ways in which those two great abstractions, Church and State, actually impinged on the routine of ordinary people.

Lynn White, Jr., adds a crucial technological dimension to our understanding of peasant life. Specifically, the more widespread use of metal began to alter agricultural methods in the medieval period. The introduction of the heavy plow, as White shows, greatly increased the production of foodstuffs, especially in northern Europe. He also describes how an improved harness began to transform the way in which ordinary people worked, traveled, and lived.

John R. Hale rounds out this period of history by recording the wide variations in manorial organization from locale to locale and from territory to territory. Even within the same delimited area, such as medieval England, the experience of individual peasants could be quite different. Hale can only suggest how much more variety there was in other regions, such as the Iberian Peninsula, Scandinavia, and central and eastern Europe.

No three articles could possibly convey the entire variegated history of serfdom in every corner of Europe during a period of several centuries. Yet these selections are sufficient to put us on our guard against facile generalizations. Above all, it becomes clear that humankind's experience has not always been a steady advance toward some goal of freedom. Serfdom developed haltingly and unevenly, even in those places where individual peasants sometimes gained personal options that had not previously existed.

——EILEEN POWER——————————————————

THE PEASANT BODO

LIFE ON A COUNTRY ESTATE
IN THE TIME OF CHARLEMAGNE

Three slender things that best support the world: the slender stream of milk from the cow's dug into the pail; the slender blade of green corn upon the ground; the slender thread over the hand of a skilled woman.

Three sounds of increase: the lowing of a cow in milk; the din of a smithy; the swish of a plough.

—From *The Triads of Ireland* (9th century)

Economic history, as we know it, is the newest of all the branches of history. Up to the middle of the last century the chief interest of the historian and of the public alike lay in political and constitutional history, in political events, wars, dynasties, and in political institutions and their development. Substantially,

From Eileen Power, *Medieval People* (London: Methuen & Co Ltd, 1963), pp. 18–19, 24–33, 36–38, by permission of the publisher.

therefore, history concerned itself with the ruling classes. "Let us now praise famous men," was the historian's motto. He forgot to add "and our fathers that begat us." He did not care to probe the obscure lives and activities of the great mass of humanity, upon whose slow toil was built up the prosperity of the world and who were the hidden foundation of the political and constitutional edifice reared by the famous men he praised. To speak of ordinary people would have been beneath the dignity of history. Carlyle struck a significant note of revolt: "The thing I want to see," he said, "is not Red-book lists and Court Calendars and Parliamentary Registers, but the Life of Man in England: what men did, thought, suffered, enjoyed. . . . Mournful, in truth, it is to behold what the business called 'History' in these so enlightened and illuminated times still continues to be. Can you gather from it, read till your eyes go out, any dimmest shadow of an answer to that great question: How men lived and had their being; were it but economically, as, what wages they got and what they bought with these? Unhappy you cannot. . . . History, as it stands all bound up in gilt volumes, is but a shade more instructive than the wooden volumes of a backgammon-board."

Carlyle was a voice crying in the wilderness. Today the new history, whose way he prepared, has come. The present age differs from the centuries before it in its vivid realization of that much-neglected person the man in the street; or (as it was more often in the earliest ages) the man with the hoe. Today the historian is interested in the social life of the past and not only in the wars and intrigues of princes. To the modern writer, the fourteenth century, for instance, is not merely the century of the Hundred Years' War and of the Black Prince and Edward III; more significantly it is for him the era of the slow decay of villeinage in England, a fact more epoch-making, in the long run, than the struggle over French provinces. We still praise famous men, for he would be a poor historian who could spare one of the great figures who have shed glory or romance upon the page of history; but we praise them with due recognition of the fact that not only great individuals, but people as a whole, unnamed and undistinguished masses of people, now sleeping in unknown graves, have also been concerned in the story. Our fathers that begat us have come to their own at last. As Acton put it, "The great historian now takes his meals in the kitchen." . . .

. . . Let us try, now, to look at those estates [of Frankish landowners of the time of Charlemagne] from a more human point of view and see what life was like to a farmer who lived upon them. The abbey [of St. Germain des Prés] possessed a little estate called Villaris, near Paris, in the place now occupied by the park of Saint Cloud. When we turn up the pages in the estate book [of Abbot Irminon] dealing with Villaris, we find that there was a man called Bodo living there.[1] He had a wife called Ermentrude and three children called Wido and

---

1   "Habet Bodo colonus et uxor ejus colona, nomine Ermentrudis, homines sancti Germani, habent secum infantes III. Tenet mansum ingenuilem I, habentem de terre arabili bunuaria VIII et antsingas II, de vinea aripennos II, de prato aripennos VII. Solvit ad hostem

Gerbert and Hildegard; and he owned a little farm of arable and meadow land, with a few vines. And we know very nearly as much about Bodo's work as we know about that of a small-holder in France today. Let us try and imagine a day in his life. On a fine spring morning towards the end of Charlemagne's reign Bodo gets up early, because it is his day to go and work on the monks' farm, and he does not dare to be late, for fear of the steward. To be sure, he has probably given the steward a present of eggs and vegetables the week before, to keep him in a good temper; but the monks will not allow their stewards to take big bribes (as is sometimes done on other estates), and Bodo knows that he will not be allowed to go late to work. It is his day to plough, so he takes his big ox with him and little Wido to run by its side with a goad, and he joins his friends from some of the farms near by, who are going to work at the big house too. They all assemble, some with horses and oxen, some with mattocks and hoes and spades and axes and scythes, and go off in gangs to work upon the fields and meadows and woods of the seigniorial manse, according as the steward orders them. The manse next door to Bodo is held by a group of families: Frambert and Ermoin and Ragenold, with their wives and children. Bodo bids them good morning as he passes. Frambert is going to make a fence round the wood, to prevent the rabbits from coming out and eating the young crops; Ermoin has been told to cart a great load of firewood up to the house; and Ragenold is mending a hole in the roof of a barn. Bodo goes whistling off in the cold with his oxen and his little boy; and it is no use to follow him farther, because he ploughs all day and eats his meal under a tree with the other ploughmen, and it is very monotonous.

Let us go back and see what Bodo's wife, Ermentrude, is doing. She is busy too; it is the day on which the chicken-rent is due—a fat pullet and five eggs in all. She leaves her second son, aged nine, to look after the baby Hildegard and calls on one of her neighbors, who has to go up to the big house too. The neighbor is a serf and she has to take the steward a piece of woollen cloth, which will be sent away to St. Germain to make a habit for a monk. Her husband is working all day in the lord's vineyards, for on this estate the serfs generally tend the vines, while the freemen do most of the ploughing. Ermentrude and the serf's wife go together up to the house. There all is busy. In the men's workshop

---

de argento solidos II, de vino in pascione modios II; ad tertium annum sundolas C; de sepe perticas III. Arat ad hibernaticum perticas III, ad tramisem perticas II. In unaquaque ebdomada corvadas II, manuoperam I. Pullos III, ova XV; et caropera ibi injungitur. Et habet medietatem de farinarium, inde solvit de argento solidos II.'' [*Polyptique*], II p. 78. ''Bodo a *colonus* and his wife Ermentrude a *colona*, tenants of Saint-Germain, have with them three children. He holds one free manse, containing eight *bunuaria* and two *antsinga* of arable land, two *aripenni* of vines and seven *aripenni* of meadow. He pays two silver shillings to the army and two hogsheads of wine for the right to pasture his pigs in the woods. Every third year he pays a hundred planks and three poles for fences. He ploughs at the winter sowing four perches and at the spring sowing two perches. Every week he owes two labor services *(corvées)* and one handwork. He pays three fowls and fifteen eggs, and carrying service when it is enjoined upon him. And he owns the half of a windmill, for which he pays two silver shillings.''

are several clever workmen—a shoemaker, a carpenter, a blacksmith, and two silversmiths; there are not more, because the best artisans on the estates of St. Germain live by the walls of the abbey, so that they can work for the monks on the spot and save the labor of carriage. But there were always some craftsmen on every estate, either attached as serfs to the big house, or living on manses of their own, and good landowners tried to have as many clever craftsmen as possible. Charlemagne ordered his stewards each to have in his district "good workmen, namely, blacksmiths, goldsmiths, silversmiths, shoemakers, turners, carpenters, swordmakers, fishermen, foilers, soapmakers, men who know how to make beer, cider, perry and all other kinds of beverages, bakers to make pasty for our table, netmakers who know how to make nets for hunting, fishing and fowling, and others too many to be named."[2] And some of these workmen are to be found working for the monks in the estate of Villaris.

But Ermentrude does not stop at the men's workshop. She finds the steward, bobs her curtsy to him, and gives up her fowl and eggs, and then she hurries off to the women's part of the house, to gossip with the serfs there. The Franks used at this time to keep the women of their household in a separate quarter, where they did the work which was considered suitable for women, very much as the Greeks of antiquity used to do. If a Frankish noble had lived at the big house, his wife would have looked after their work, but as no one lived in the stone house at Villaris, the steward had to oversee the women. Their quarter consisted of a little group of houses, with a workroom, the whole surrounded by a thick hedge with a strong bolted gate, like a harem, so that no one could come in without leave. Their workrooms were comfortable places, warmed by stoves, and there Ermentrude (who, being a woman, was allowed to go in) found about a dozen servile women spinning and dyeing cloth and sewing garments. Every week the harassed steward brought them the raw material for their work and took away what they made. Charlemagne gives his stewards several instructions about the women attached to his manses, and we may be sure that the monks of St. Germain did the same on their model estates. "For our women's work," says Charlemagne, "they are to give at the proper time the materials, that is linen, wool, woad, vermilion, madder, wool combs, teasels, soap, grease, vessels, and other objects which are necessary. And let our women's quarters be well looked after, furnished with houses and rooms with stoves and cellars, and let them be surrounded by good hedge, and let the doors be strong, so that the women can do our work properly."[3] Ermentrude, however, has to hurry away after her gossip, and so must we. She goes back to her own farm and sets to work in the little vineyard; then after an hour or two goes back to get the children's meal and to spend the rest of the day in weaving warm woollen clothes for them. All her friends are either working in the fields on their husband's farms or else

2 *De Villis,* c. 45.
3 *Ibid.,* cc. 43, 49.

looking after the poultry, or the vegetables, or sewing at home; for the women have to work just as hard as the men on a country farm. In Charlemagne's time (for instance) they did nearly all the sheep shearing. Then at last Bodo comes back for his supper, and as soon as the sun goes down they go to bed; for their handmade candle gives only a flicker of light, and they both have to be up early in the morning. De Quincey once pointed out, in his inimitable manner, how the ancients everywhere went to bed, "like good boys, from seven to nine o'clock. Man went to bed early in those ages simply because his worthy mother earth could not afford him candles. She, good old lady . . . would certainly have shuddered to hear of any of her nations asking for candles. 'Candles, indeed!' she would have said; 'who ever heard of such a thing? and with so much excellent daylight running to waste, as I have provided *gratis!* What will the wretches want next?' "[4] Something of the same situation prevailed even in Bodo's time.

This, then, is how Bodo and Ermentrude usually passed their working day. But, it may be complained, this is all very well. We know about the estates on which these peasants lived and about the rents which they had to pay, and the services which they had to do. But how did they feel and think and amuse themselves when they were not working? Rents and services are only outside things; an estate book only describes routine. It would be idle to try to picture the life of a university from a study of its lecture list, and it is equally idle to try and describe the life of Bodo from the estate book of his masters. It is no good taking your meals in the kitchen if you never talk to the servants. This is true, and to arrive at Bodo's thoughts and feelings and holiday amusements we must bid good-bye to Abbot Irminon's estate book, and peer into some very dark corners indeed; for though by the aid of Chaucer and Langland and a few Court Rolls it is possible to know a great deal about the feelings of a peasant six centuries later, material is scarce in the ninth century, and it is all the more necessary to remember the secret of the invisible ink.

Bodo certainly *had* plenty of feelings, and very strong ones. When he got up in the frost on a cold morning to drive the plough over the abbot's acres, when his own were calling out for work, he often shivered and shook the rime from his beard, and wished that the big house and all its land were at the bottom of the sea (which, as a matter of fact, he had never seen and could not imagine). Or else he wished he were the abbot's huntsman, hunting in the forest; or a monk of St. Germain, singing sweetly in the abbey church; or a merchant, taking bales of cloaks and girdles along the high road to Paris; anything, in fact, but a poor ploughman ploughing other people's land. An Anglo-Saxon writer has imagined a dialogue with him:

4   From "The Casuistry of Roman Meals," in *The Collected Writings of Thomas De Quincey,* ed. D. Masson (1897), VII, p. 13.

"Well, ploughman, how do you do your work?" "Oh, sir, I work very hard. I go out in the dawning, driving the oxen to the field and I yoke them to the plough. Be the winter never so stark, I dare not stay at home for fear of my lord; but every day I must plough a full acre or more, after having yoked the oxen and fastened the share and coulter to the plough!" "Have you any mate?" "I have a boy, who drives the oxen with a goad, who is now hoarse from cold and shouting." (Poor little Wido!) "Well, well, it is very hard work?" "Yes, indeed it is very hard work."[5]

Nevertheless, hard as the work was, Bodo sang lustily to cheer himself and Wido; for is it not related that once, when a clerk was singing the "Allelulia" in the emperor's presence, Charles turned to one of the bishops saying, "My clerk is singing very well," whereat the rude bishop replied, "Any clown in our countryside drones as well as that to his oxen at their ploughing"?[6] It is certain too that Bodo agreed with the names which the great Charles gave to the months of the year in his own Frankish tongue; for he called January "Winter-month," February "Mud-month," March "Spring-month," April "Easter-month," May "Joy-month," June "Plough-month," July "Hay-month," August "Harvest-month," September "Wind-month," October "Vintage-month," November "Autumn-month," and December "Holy-month."[7]

And Bodo was a superstitious creature. The Franks had been Christian now for many years, but Christian though they were, the peasant clung to old beliefs and superstitions. On the estates of the holy monks of St. Germain you would have found the country people saying charms which were hoary with age, parts of the lay sung by the Frankish ploughman over his bewitched land long before he marched southwards into the Roman Empire, or parts of the spell which the bee-master performed when he swarmed his bees on the shores of the Baltic Sea. Christianity has colored these charms, but it has not effaced their heathen origin; and because the tilling of the soil is the oldest and most unchanging of human occupations, old beliefs and superstitions cling to it and the old gods stalk up and down the brown furrows, when they have long vanished from houses and roads. So on Abbot Irminon's estates the peasant-farmers muttered charms over their sick cattle (and over their sick children too) and said incantations over the fields to make them fertile. If you had followed behind Bodo when he broke his first furrow you would have probably seen him take out of his jerkin a little cake, baked for him by Ermentrude out of different kinds of meal, and you would have seen him stoop and lay it under the furrow and sing:

Earth, Earth, Earth! O Earth, our mother!
May the All-Wielder, Ever-Lord grant thee

5   Ælfric's *Colloquium* in [*The Welding of the Race*], p. 95.

6   The Monk of St. Gall's *Life* in *Early Lives of Charlemagne* [ed. A. J. Grant (1907)] pp. 87–8.

7   Einhard's *Life* in [Grant,] *op. cit.*, p. 45.

Acres a-waxing, upwards a-growing,
Pregnant with corn and plenteous in strength;
Hosts of grain shafts and of glittering plants!
Of broad barley the blossoms,
And of white wheat ears waxing,
Of the whole land the harvest. . . .

Acre, full-fed, bring forth fodder for men!
Blossoming brightly, blessed become!
And the God who wrought with earth grant us gift of growing
That each of all the corns may come unto our need.[8]

Then he would drive his plough through the acre.

The Church wisely did not interfere with these old rites. It taught Bodo to pray to the Ever-Lord instead of to Father Heaven, and to the Virgin Mary instead of to Mother Earth, and with these changes let the old spell he had learned from his ancestors serve him still. It taught him, for instance, to call on Christ and Mary in his charm for bees. When Ermentrude heard her bees swarming, she stood outside her cottage and said this little charm over them:

Christ, there is a swarm of bees outside,
Fly hither, my little cattle,
In blest peace, in God's protection,
Come home safe and sound.
Sit down, sit down, bee,
St. Mary commanded thee.
Thou shalt not have leave,
Thou shalt not fly to the wood.
Thou shalt not escape me,
Nor go away from me.
Sit very still,
Wait God's will![9]

And if Bodo on his way home saw one of his bees caught in a brier bush, he immediately stood still and wished—as some people wish today when they go under a ladder. It was the Church, too, which taught Bodo to add "So be it, Lord," to the end of his charm against pain. Now, his ancestors for generations behind him had believed that if you had a stitch in your side, or a bad pain anywhere, it came from a worm in the marrow of your bones, which was eating you up, and that the only way to get rid of that worm was to put a knife, or an arrow-head, or

8 Anglo-Saxon charms translated in Stopford Brook, *English Literature from the Beginning to the Norman Conquest* (1899), p. 43.

9 Old High German charm written in a tenth-century hand in a ninth-century codex containing sermons of St. Augustine, now in the Vatican Library. Brawne, *Althochdeutsches Lesebuch* (fifth edition, Halle, 1902), p. 83.

some other piece of metal to the sore place, and then wheedle the worm out on to the blade by saying a charm. And this was the charm which Bodo's heathen ancestors had always said and which Bodo went on saying when little Wido had a pain: "Come out, worm, with nine little worms, out from the marrow into the bone, from the bone into the flesh, from the flesh into the skin, from the skin into this arrow." And then (in obedience to the Church) he added "So be it, Lord."[10] But sometimes it was not possible to read a Christian meaning into Bodo's doings. Sometimes he paid visits to some man who was thought to have a wizard's powers, or superstitiously reverenced some twisted tree, about which there hung old stories never quite forgotten. Then the Church was stern. When he went to confession the priest would ask him: "Have you consulted magicians and enchanters, have you made vows to trees and fountains, have you drunk any magic philtre?"[11] And he would have to confess what he did last time his cow was sick. But the Church was kind as well as stern. "When serfs come to you," we find one bishop telling his priests, "you must not give them as many fasts to perform as rich men. Put upon them only half the penance."[12] The Church knew well enough that Bodo could not drive his plough all day upon an empty stomach. The hunting, drinking, feasting Frankish nobles could afford to lose a meal.

It was from this stern and yet kind Church that Bodo got his holidays. For the Church made the pious emperor decree that on Sundays and saints' days no servile or other work should be done. Charlemagne's son repeated his decree in 827. It runs thus:

> We ordain according to the law of God and to the command of our father of blessed memory in his edicts, that no servile works shall be done on Sundays, neither shall men perform their rustic labors, tending vines, ploughing fields, reaping corn and mowing hay, setting up hedges or fencing woods, cutting trees, or working in quarries or building houses; nor shall they work in the garden, nor come to the law courts, nor follow the chase. But three carrying-services it is lawful to do on Sunday, to wit carrying for the army, carrying food, or carrying (if need be) the body of a lord to its grave. Item, women shall not do their textile works, nor cut out clothes, nor stitch them together with the needle, nor card wool, nor beat hemp, nor wash clothes in public, nor shear sheep: so that there may be rest on the Lord's day. But let them come together from all sides to Mass in the Church and praise God for all the good things He did for us on that day![13]

10 Another Old High German charm preserved in a tenth-century codex now at Vienna. Brawne, *op. cit.,* p. 164.

11 From the ninth-century *Libellus de Ecclesiasticis Disciplinis,* art. 100, quoted in Ozanam, *La Civilisation Chrétienne chez les Francs* (1849), p. 312. The injunction, however, really refers to the recently conquered and still half-pagan Saxons.

12 *Penitential* of Halitgart, Bishop of Cambrai, quoted *ibid.,* p. 314.

13 *Documents relatifs à l'Histoire de l'Industrie et du Commerce en France,* ed. G. Faigniez, t. I, pp. 51–2.

Unfortunately, however, Bodo and Ermentrude and their friends were not content to go quietly to church on saints' days and quietly home again. They used to spend their holidays in dancing and singing and buffoonery, as country folk have always done until our own gloomier, more self-conscious age. They were very merry and not all refined, and the place they always chose for their dances was the churchyard; and unluckily the songs they sang as they danced in a ring were old pagan songs of their forefathers, left over from old Mayday festivities, which they could not forget, or ribald love-songs which the Church disliked. Over and over again we find the Church councils complaining that the peasants (and sometimes the priests too) were singing "wicked songs with a chorus of dancing women," or holding "ballads and dancings and evil and wanton songs and such-like lures of the devil";[14] over and over again the bishops forbade these songs and dances; but in vain. In every country in Europe, right through the Middle Ages to the time of the Reformation, and after it, country folk continued to sing and dance in the churchyard. Two hundred years after Charlemagne's death there grew up the legend of the dancers of Kölbigk, who danced on Christmas Eve in the churchyard, in spite of the warning of the priest, and all got rooted to the spot for a year, till the Archbishop of Cologne released them. Some men say that they were not rooted standing to the spot, but that they had to go on dancing for the whole year; and that before they were released they had danced themselves waist-deep into the ground. People used to repeat the little Latin verse which they were singing:

Equitabat Bovo per silvam frondosam
Ducebat sibi Merswindem formosam.
    Quid stamus? Cur non imus?[15]

Through the leafy forest, Bovo went a-riding
And his pretty Merswind trotted on beside him—
    Why are we standing still? Why can't we go away?

Another later story still is told about a priest in Worcestershire, who was kept awake all night by the people dancing in his churchyard and singing a song with the refrain "Sweetheart have pity," so that he could not get it out of his head, and the next morning at Mass, instead of saying "Dominus vobiscum," he said

---

14   See references in Chambers, *The Medieval Stage* (1913), I, pp. 161–3.

15   For the famous legend of the dancers of Kölbigk, see Gaston Paris, *Les Danseurs Maudits, Légende Allemande du XI' Siècle* (Paris 1900, reprinted from the *Journal des Savants,* Dec., 1899), which is a *compte rendu* of Schröder's study in *Zeitschrift für Kirchengeschichte* (1899). The poem occurs in a version of English origin, in which one of the dancers, Thierry, is cured of a perpetual trembling in all his limbs by a miracle of St. Edith at the nunnery of Wilton in 1065. See [Paris], pp. 10, 14.

"Sweetheart have pity," and there was a dreadful scandal which got into a chronicle.[16]

Sometimes our Bodo did not dance himself, but listened to the songs of wandering minstrels. The priests did not at all approve of these minstrels, who (they said) would certainly go to hell for singing profane secular songs, all about the great deeds of heathen heroes of the Frankish race, instead of Christian hymns. But Bodo loved them, and so did Bodo's betters; the Church councils had sometimes even to rebuke abbots and abbesses for listening to their songs. And the worst of it was that the great emperor himself, the good Charlemagne, loved them too. He would always listen to a minstrel, and his biographer, Einhard, tells us that "He wrote out the barbarous and ancient songs, in which the acts of the kings and their wars were sung, and committed them to memory";[17] and one at least of those old sagas, which he liked men to write down, has been preserved on the cover of a Latin manuscript, where a monk scribbled it in his spare time. His son, Louis the Pious, was very different; he rejected the national poems, which he had learnt in his youth, and would not have them read or recited or taught; he would not allow minstrels to have justice in the law courts, and he forbade idle dances and songs and tales in public places on Sundays; but then he also dragged down his father's kingdom into disgrace and ruin. The minstrels repaid Charlemagne for his kindness to them. They gave him everlasting fame; for all through the Middle Ages the legend of Charlemagne grew, and he shares with our King Arthur the honor of being the hero of one of the greatest romance-cycles of the Middle Ages. Every different century clad him anew in its own dress and sang new lays about him. What the monkish chroniclers in their cells could never do for Charlemagne, these despised and accursed minstrels did for him: they gave him what is perhaps more desirable and more lasting than a place in history—they gave him a place in legend. It is not every emperor who rules in those realms of gold of which Keats spoke, as well as in the kingdoms of the world; and in the realms of gold Charlemagne reigns with King Arthur, and his peers joust with the Knights of the Round Table. Bodo, at any rate, benefited by Charles's love of minstrels, and it is probable that he heard in the lifetime of the emperor himself the first beginnings of those legends which afterwards clung to the name of Charlemagne. One can imagine him round-eyed in the churchyard, listening to fabulous stories of Charles's Iron March to Pavia, such as a gossiping old monk of St. Gall afterwards wrote down in his chronicle.[18]

It is likely enough that such legends were the nearest Bodo ever came to see-

16 "Swete Lamman dhin are," in the original. The story is told by Giraldus Cambrensis in *Gemma Ecclesiastica*, pt. I, c. XLII. See *Selections from Giraldus Cambrensis*, ed. C. A. J. Skeel (S. P. C. K. *Texts for Students, No. XI), p. 48.*

17 Einhard's *Life* in [Grant], p. 45. See also *ibid.,* p. 168 (note).

18 The Monk of St. Gall's *Life* in [Grant]., pp. 144-7.

ing the Emperor, of whom even the poor serfs who never followed him to court or camp were proud. But Charles was a great traveler: like all the monarchs of the early Middle Ages he spent the time, when he was not warring, in trekking round his kingdom, staying at one of his estates, until he and his household had literally eaten their way through it, and then passing on to another. And sometimes he varied the procedure by paying a visit to the estates of his bishops or nobles, who entertained him royally. It may be that one day he came on a visit to Bodo's masters and stopped at the big house on his way to Paris, and then Bodo saw him plain; for Charlemagne would come riding along the road in his jerkin of otter skin, and his plain blue cloak (Einhard tells us that he hated grand clothes and on ordinary days dressed like the common people);[19] and after him would come his three sons and his bodyguard, and then his five daughters. Einhard has also told us that

> He had such care of the upbringing of his sons and daughters that he never dined without them when he was at home and never travelled without them. His sons rode along with him and his daughters followed in the rear. Some of his guards, chosen for this very purpose, watched the end of the line of march where his daughters travelled. They were very beautiful and much beloved by their father, and, therefore, it is strange that he would give them in marriage to no one, either among his own people or of a foreign state. But up to his death he kept them all at home saying he could not forgo their society.[20]

Then, with luck, Bodo, quaking at the knees, might even behold a portent new to his experience, the emperor's elephant. Haroun El Raschid, the great Sultan of the "Arabian Nights," had sent it to Charles, and it accompanied him on all his progresses. Its name was "Abu-Lubabah," which is an Arabic word and means "the father of intelligence," * and it died a hero's death on an expedition against the Danes in 810. It is certain that ever afterwards Ermentrude quelled little Gerbert, when he was naughty, with the threat, "Abu-Lubabah will come with his long nose and carry you off." But Wido, being aged eight and a bread-winner, professed to have felt no fear on being confronted with the elephant; but admitted when pressed, that he greatly preferred Haroun El Raschid's other present to the emperor, the friendly dog, who answered to the name of "Becerillo."[21]

Another treat Bodo had which happened once a year; for regularly on the ninth of October there began the great fair of St. Denys, which went on for a whole month, outside the gate of Paris.[22] Then for a week before the fair little

---

19   Einhard's *Life* in [Grant], p. 39.

20   *Ibid.*, p. 35.

*   *Abu-Lubabah.*—It is remarkable that the name should have suffered no corruption in the chronicles.

21   Beazley, *Dawn of Modern Geography* (1897), I, p. 325.

22   See Faigniez, *op. cit.*, pp. 43–4.

booths and sheds sprang up, with open fronts in which the merchants could display their wares, and the Abbey of St. Denys, which had the right to take a toll of all the merchants who came there to sell, saw to it that the fair was well enclosed with fences, and that all came in by the gates and paid their money, for wily merchants were sometimes known to burrow under fences or climb over them so as to avoid the toll. Then the streets of Paris were crowded with merchants bringing their goods, packed in carts and upon horses and oxen; and on the opening day all regular trade in Paris stopped for a month, and every Parisian shopkeeper was in a booth somewhere in the fair, exchanging the corn and wine and honey of the district for rarer goods from foreign parts. Bodo's abbey probably had a stall in the fair and sold some of those pieces of cloth woven by the serfs in the women's quarter, or cheeses and salted meat prepared on the estates, or wine paid in rent by Bodo and his fellow-farmers. Bodo would certainly take a holiday and go to the fair. In fact, the steward would probably have great difficulty in keeping his men at work during the month; Charlemagne had to give a special order to his stewards that they should ''be careful that our men do properly the work which it is lawful to exact from them, and that they do not waste their time in running about to markets and fairs.'' Bodo and Ermentrude and the three children, all attired in their best, did not consider it waste of time to go to the fair even twice or three times. They pretended that they wanted to buy salt to salt down their winter meat, or some vermilion dye to color a frock for the baby. What they really wanted was to wander along the little rows of booths and look at all the strange things assembled there; for merchants came to St. Denys to sell their rich goods from the distant East to Bodo's betters, and wealthy Frankish nobles bargained there for purple and silken robes with orange borders, stamped leather jerkins, peacock's feathers, and the scarlet plumage of flamingos (which they called ''phœnix skins''), scents and pearls and spices, almonds and raisins, and monkeys for their wives to play with.[23] Sometimes these merchants were Venetians, but more often they were Syrians or crafty Jews, and Bodo and his fellows laughed loudly over the story of how a Jewish merchant had tricked a certain bishop, who craved for all the latest novelties, by stuffing a mouse with spices and offering it for sale to him, saying that ''he had brought this most precious never-before-seen animal from Judea,'' and refusing

---

23 See the Monk of St. Gall's account of the finery of the Frankish nobles: ''It was a holiday and they had just come from Pavia, whither the Venetians had carried all the wealth of the East from their territories beyond the sea,—others, I say, strutted in robes made of pheasant-skins and silk; or of the necks, backs and tails of peacocks in their first plumage. Some were decorated with purple and lemon-coloured ribbons; some were wrapped round with blankets and some in ermine robes.'' [Grant], p. 149. The translation is a little loose: the ''phœnix robes'' of the original were more probably made out of the plumage, not of the pheasant but of the scarlet flamingo, as Hodgson thinks (*Early Hist. of Venice*, p. 155), or possibly silks woven or embroidered with figures of birds, as Heyd thinks (*Hist. du Commerce du Levant*, I, p. 111).

to take less than a whole measure of silver for it.[24] In exchange for their luxuries these merchants took away with them Frisian cloth, which was greatly esteemed, and corn and hunting dogs, and sometimes a piece of fine goldsmith's work, made in a monastic workshop. And Bodo would hear a hundred dialects and tongues, for men of Saxony and Frisia, Spain and Provence, Rouen and Lombardy, and perhaps an Englishman or two, jostled each other in the little streets; and from time to time there came also an Irish scholar with a manuscript to sell, and the strange, sweet songs of Ireland on his lips:

> A hedge of trees surrounds me,
> A blackbird's lay sings to me;
> Above my lined booklet
> The trilling birds chant to me.
>
> In a grey mantle from the top of bushes
> The cuckoo sings:
> Verily—may the Lord shield me!—
> Well do I write under the greenwood.[25]

Then there were always jugglers and tumblers, and men with performing bears, and minstrels to wheedle Bodo's few pence out of his pocket. And it would be a very tired and happy family that trundled home in the cart to bed. For it is not, after all, so dull in the kitchen, and when we have quite finished with the emperor, "Charlemagne and all his peerage," it is really worth while to spend a few moments with Bodo in his little manse. History is largely made up of Bodos.

FOOTNOTE SOURCES

1. The Roll of the Abbot Irminon, an estate book of the Abbey of St. Germain des Prés, near Paris, written between 811 and 826. See *Polyptyque de l'Abbaye de Saint-Germain des Prés*, pub. Auguste Longnon, t. I, *Introduction;* t. II, *Texte* (Soc. de l'Hist. de Paris, 1886–95).

2. Charlemagne's capitulary, *De Villis,* instructions to his stewards on the management of his estates. See Guerard, *Explication du Capitulaire "de Villis"*

24 The Monk of St. Gall's *Life* in [Grant], pp. 81–2.

25 This little poem was scribbled by an Irish scribe in the margin of a copy of Priscian in the monastery of St. Gall, in Switzerland, the same from which Charlemagne's highly imaginative biographer came. The original will be found in Stokes and Strachan, *Thesaurus Palæohibernicus* (1903) II, p. 290. It has often been translated and I quote the translation by Kuno Meyer, *Ancient Irish Poetry* (2nd ed., 1913), p. 99. The quotation from the *Triads of Ireland* at the head of this chapter is taken from Kuno Meyer also, *ibid.*, pp. 102–3.

(Acad. des Inscriptions et Belles-Lettres, *Mémoires,* t. XXI, 1857), pp. 165–309, containing the text, with a detailed commentary and a translation into French.

3. *Early Lives of Charlemagne,* ed. A. J. Grant (King's Classics, 1907). Contains the lives by Einhard and the Monk of St. Gall, on which see Halphen, cited below.

4. Various pieces of information about social life may be gleaned from the decrees of Church Councils, Old High German and Anglo-Saxon charms and poems, and Ælfric's *Colloquium,* extracts from which are translated in Bell's Eng. Hist. Source Books, *The Welding of the Race, 449–1066,* ed. J. E. W. Wallis (1913). For a general sketch of the period see Lavisse, *Hist. de France,* t. II, and for an elaborate critical study of certain aspects of Charlemagne's reign (including the *Polyptychum*) see Halphen, *Etudes critiques sur l'Histoire de Charlemagne* (1921); also A. Dopsch, *Wirtschaftsentwicklung der Karolingerzeit, vornehmlich in Deutschland,* 2 vols. (Weimar, 1912–13), which Halphen criticizes.

—LYNN WHITE, JR.—

PLOUGHS AND HARNESSES

From the Neolithic Age until about two centuries ago, agriculture was fundamental to most other human concerns. Before the late 1700's there was probably no settled community in which at least nine-tenths of the population were not directly engaged in tillage. Rulers and priests, craftsmen and merchants, scholars and artists, were a tiny minority of mankind standing on the shoulders of the peasants. Under such circumstances any lasting change in climate, soil fertility, technology, or the other conditions affecting agriculture would necessarily modify the whole of society: population, wealth, political relationships, leisure, and cultural expression.

Yet this has not been obvious to the world of scholars: nowhere are the ur-

From *Medieval Technology and Social Change* by Lynn White, Jr., © Oxford University Press 1962, pp. 39–44, 57, 66–68. Reprinted by permission of Oxford University Press.

ban roots of the word "civilization" more evident than in the neglect which historians have lavished upon the rustic and his works and days. While the peasant has normally been a lively and enterprising fellow, quite unlike the tragic caricature of combined brutishness and abused virtue presented in Millet's and Markham's "Man with the Hoe,"[1] he has seldom been literate. Not only histories but documents in general were produced by social groups which took the peasant and his labours largely for granted. Therefore while our libraries groan with data on the ownership of land, there is an astonishing dearth of information about the various, and often changing, methods of cultivation which made the land worth owning.[2]

To be sure, we have heard that in the late seventeenth and eighteenth centuries "Turnip" Townshend and a few other adventurous agronomists in Britain and on the continent developed root and fodder crops, reformed agriculture, and thus provided the surplus food which permitted labour to leave the fields and to man the factories of the so-called Industrial Revolution. Yet it is practically unknown that northern Europe from the sixth to the ninth century witnessed an earlier agricultural revolution which was equally decisive in its historical effects.

In the nature of things there is much which we do not know about these matters and perhaps can never know with certainty. For example, the habit among prehistorians of establishing an Iron Age in a region as soon as they turn up the earliest scrap of iron may distort our view of the actualities. Iron was long a rare and costly metal, used almost exclusively for arms and for cutting edges. While there was much iron in Pompeii, one's total impression of its remains is that in the later first century even so prosperous a Roman city was still living more in a Bronze than in an Iron Age. Northern Europe—Noricum especially—was far richer in iron resources than was the Mediterranean. It would seem, from the finds, that more iron was used in the Roman period for plough parts, spade-tips, sickles, and the like north of the Alps than to the south, despite the fact that we should expect the damper boreal climate to have destroyed the northern evidences of iron more often by corrosion.

One aspect of the rapid development of northern Europe in Carolingian times was the opening up of great new iron mines, which presumably made that

---

1   F. Martini, *Das Bauerntum im deutschen Schrifttum von den Anfängen bis zum 16. Jahrhundert* (Halle, 1944), esp. 390-3, analyses the very old elements entering into the modern stereotype of the peasant as they emerge in the works of medieval poets and preachers. On the one hand, the peasant is obtuse, grotesque, at times dangerous; on the other, he is hardworking, attached to the good old traditions, the supplier of food for all mankind, and loved of God for his humility. When the actualities rather than the fictions of rural life are examined, they appear as kaleidoscopic as those of any other form of human activity; cf. C. Parain, "La Notion de régime agraire," *Mois d'ethnographie française,* iv (1950), 99, and "Les Anciennes techniques agricoles," *Revue de synthèse, lxxviii* (1957), 326.

2   For example, A. Dopsch, "Die Herausgabe von Quellen zur Agrargeschichte des Mittelalters: ein Arbeitsprogram," in *Verfassungs-und Wirtschaftsgeschichte des Mittelalters* (Vienna, 1928), 516-42, is entirely legal and institutional in emphasis.

metal cheaper and therefore more available to common uses as well as to the military. Writing in the later ninth century, the Monk of St. Gall tells us how in 773 Charlemagne and his host mounted an assault against Pavia, the capital of the Lombard realm. Coming out upon his walls to view the enemy, King Desiderius was overwhelmed by the spectacle of the massed and glittering Frankish armour and weapons: "Oh, the iron! Alas, the iron!" he cried, and the captain with him fell fainting.[3] While the Monk of St. Gall is notoriously a novelist rather than an historian, nevertheless in this episode he symbolizes, even if he does not record, Europe's effective transition, under Charlemagne, to the Iron Age.

While no statistical proof is possible, it is the consensus among historians of agriculture that the medieval peasantry used an amount of iron which would have seemed inconceivable to any earlier rural population, and that the smithy became integral to every village.[4] What this meant for increased productivity cannot be demonstrated; it must be imagined.

In general the history of tools and implements is still rudimentary. For example, it is believed that a new type of felling axe, developed in the tenth century, does much to account for the great new extension of arable land beginning about that time.[5] But so few archaeologists or historians can view an axe with the eye of a professional woodsman judging the balance of the blade and the length and angle of the haft in terms of the job to be done, that the matter remains uncertain. A few tools, however, notably the plough, have been studied in much detail. . . .

The plough was the first application of non-human power to agriculture. The earliest plough was essentially an enlarged digging-stick dragged by a pair of oxen. This primitive scratch-plough is still widely used around the Mediterranean and in the arid lands to the east where it is reasonably effective in terms of soil and climate. Its conical or triangular share does not normally turn over the soil, and it leaves a wedge of undisturbed earth between each furrow. Thus cross-ploughing is necessary, with the result that, in regions where the scratch-plough is used, fields tend to be squarish in shape, roughly as wide as they are long. Cross-ploughing pulverizes the soil, and this both prevents undue evaporation of moisture in dry climates and helps to keep the fields fertile by bringing subsoil minerals to the surface by capillary attraction.

But this kind of plough and cultivation was not well suited to much of northern Europe, with its wet summers and generally heavier soils. As agriculture spread into the higher latitudes, inevitably it was largely confined to well-drained uplands with light soils, which were inherently less productive than the alluvial

---

3　"O ferrum! heu ferrum !", *Gesta Karoli, ii.* 17, ed. H. Pertz, in *MGH, Scriptores,* ii (1829), 760.

4　e.g. G. Duby, "La Révolution agricole mediévale," *Revue de géographie de Lyon,* xxix (1954), 361, 364; H. Mottek, *Wirtschaftsgeschichte Deutschlands* (Berlin, 1957), 68.

5　Duby, op. cit. 363.

lowlands: the scratch-plough could not cope with these richer terrains. Northern Europe had to develop a new agricultural technique and above all a new plough. . . .

For purposes of northern European agriculture, [the] advantages [of the subsequently developed heavy plow] were three.

First, the heavy plough handled the clods with such violence that there was no need for cross-ploughing. This saved the peasant's labour and thus increased the area of land which he might cultivate. The heavy plough was an agricultural engine which substituted animal-power for human energy and time.

Second, the new plough, by eliminating cross-ploughing, tended to change the shape of fields in northern Europe from squarish to long and narrow, with a slightly rounded vertical cross-section for each strip-field which had salutary effects on drainage in that moist climate. These strips were normally ploughed clockwise, with the sod turning over and inward to the right. As a result, with the passage of the years, each strip became a long low ridge, assuring a crop on the crest even in the wettest years, and in the intervening long depression, or furrow, in the driest seasons.

The third advantage of the heavy plough derived from the first two: without such a plough it was difficult to exploit the dense, rich, alluvial bottom lands which, if properly handled, would give the peasant far better crops than he could get from the light soils of the uplands. It was believed, for example, that the Anglo-Saxons had brought the heavy Germanic plough to Celtic Britain in the fifth century; thanks to it, the forests began to be cleared from the heavy soils, and the square, so-called "Celtic" fields, which had long been cultivated on the uplands with the scratch-plough, were abandoned, and generally remain deserted today.

The saving of peasant labour, then, together with the improvement of field drainage and the opening up of the most fertile soils, all of which were made possible by the heavy plough, combined to expand production and make possible that accumulation of surplus food which is the presupposition of population growth, specialization of function, urbanization, and the growth of leisure. . . .

The wide application of the heavy plough in northern Europe was only the first major element in the agricultural revolution of the early Middle Ages. The second step was to develop a harness which, together with the nailed horseshoe, would make the horse an economic as well as a military asset. . . .

Not only ploughing but the speed and expense of land transport were profoundly modified in the peasants' favour by the new harness and nailed shoes. In Roman times the overland haulage of bulky goods doubled the price about every hundred miles.[6] The result was that latifundia even close to Rome, but without water transport to compete with Egyptian, North African, and Sicilian

---

6 C. A. Yeo, "Land and sea transportation in Imperial Italy," *Transactions and Proceedings of the American Philological Society*, lxxvii (1946), 222.

shipments, could not afford to raise grain for the Roman market.[7] In contrast, in the thirteenth century the cost of grain seems to have increased only 30 per cent for each hundred miles of overland carriage[8]—still high, but more than three times better than the Roman situation. Now it was becoming possible for peasants not situated along navigable streams to think less in terms of subsistence and more about a surplus of cash crops.

We will know very little in detail about the improvement of wagons which followed the invention of modern harness—the development of pivoted front axles,[9] adequate brakes, whipple-trees,[10] and the like. Most Roman vehicles, except ceremonial equippages and post-chaises, seem to have been two-wheeled. But beginning with the first half of the twelfth century we find a large, horse-drawn, four-wheeled "longa caretta" capable of hauling heavy loads,[11] and by the middle of the thirteenth century a wagon normally had four wheels:[12] Friar Salimbene records that in 1248, at Hyères in Provence, Friar Peter of Apulia replied when asked what he thought of Joachim of Flora's teachings, "I care as little for Joachim as for the fifth wheel of a wagon."[13] Not only merchants but peasants were now able to get more goods to better markets.

In still another way the new harness affected the life of the northern peasants. When historical geographers began to study abandoned fields and settlements in Germany, they assumed that these had been deserted either during the Thirty Years War or after the Black Death of 1348–50. To their astonishment they found that abandonment of settlements, but not of fields, began in the eleventh century and occurred with great frequency in the thirteenth. Not only

7 Ibid. 224; cf. E. R. Grosser, "The significance of two new fragments of the Edict of Diocletian," ibid. lxxi (1940), 162.

8 R. J. Forbes, "Land transport and road-building (1000–1900)," *Fanus*, xlvi (1957), 109.

9 The fact that the front wheels in the Trier *Apocalypse* of *c*. 800 (*supra*, p. 61, n. 4 and Fig. 3) are smaller than the rear wheels indicates a pivoted front axle. For the later medieval evidence, see M. N. Boyer, "Medieval pivoted axles," *Technology and Culture*, i (1960), 128–38, and *infra*, n. 7.

10 I know of no whipple-tree earlier than those on the bronze doors of Novgorod Cathedral made at Magdeburg in Saxony in 1152–4; cf. A. Goldschmidt, *Die Bronzetüren von Novgorod und Gnesen* (Marburg a. L., 1932), 8, pl. 26.

11 Cf. A. L. Kellogg, "Langland and two scriptural texts," *Traditio*, xiv (1958), 392–6.

12 *A Book of Old Testament Illustrations of the Middle of the Thirteenth-Century sent by Cardinal Bernard Maciejowski to Shah Abbas the Great, King of Persia, now in the Pierpont Morgan Library*, ed. S. C. Cockerell, M. R. James, and C. J. ffoulkes (Cambridge, 1927), a manuscript of *c*. 1250, probably Parisian, which is very detailed in technical matters (showing, for example, fol. 21b, pivoted front axle, whipple-tree, and horn-harness for oxen), illustrates four-wheeled wagons on fols. 5*b*, 6*b*, 9*a*, 12*a*, 21*b*, 23*a*, 27*b*, 39*a*, and 44*b*, but no two-wheeled carts.

13 "Tantum curo de Ioachym quantum de quinta rota plaustri," *Cronica Fratris Salimbene de Adam*, ed. O. Holder-Egger, *MGH, Scriptores*, xxxii (1905–13), 239. P. Deffontaines, "Sur la répartition géographique des voitures à deux roues et à quatre roues," *Travaux du Ier Congrès International de Folklore, Paris, 1937* (Tours, 1938), 119, offers puzzling evidence of an early modern reversion to two-wheeled carts in certain areas of France which had used four-wheeled wagons during the later Middle Ages.

were peasants moving to neighbouring cities while still going out each day to their fields: villages were absorbing the inhabitants of the hamlets in their vicinity. In a period when the total population of Europe was increasing rapidly,[14] places long inhabited[15] were losing their identity because of a "balling" of peasants into larger and larger villages.

Despite the fact that one scholar has bewailed the resulting "spiritual urbanization" of the peasants of the thirteenth century,[16] the personal advantages of such concentration are evident: a hamlet with five to ten cottages led a restricted life. In a big village of two or three hundred families there would be not only better defence in emergency, but a tavern, a fine big church, maybe a school run by the priest in which the boys could learn their letters, certainly more suitors for your daughters, and not merely peddlers with packs but merchants with wagons and news of distant parts. But these virtues of a more "urban" life would always have attracted countrymen. How is it that, beginning in the eleventh century, so many of them were able to act upon their desires?

The answer seems to lie in the shift from ox to horse as the primary farm animal. The ox moved so slowly that peasants using oxen had to live close to their fields. With the employment of the horse both for ploughing and for hauling, the same amount of time spent going to and from the fields would enable the peasant to travel a much greater distance. The mathematical relation of the radius of a circle to its area governed the redistribution of settlement. Even a slight increase in the distance which it was convenient to travel from the village to the farthest field would greatly enlarge the total arable which could be exploited from that village. Thus extensive regions once scattered with tiny hamlets came to be cultivated wilderness dominated by huge villages which remained economically agrarian, for the most part, but which in architecture and even in mode of life became astonishingly urban.

14 L. Génicot, "Sur les témoignages d'accroissement de la population en occident du XI^c au XIII^c siècle," *Cahiers d'histoire mondiale,* i (1953), 446–62; J. C. Russell, "Late ancient and medieval population," *Transactions of the American Philosophical Society,* xlviii. iii (1958), 113.

15 É. Perroy, *La Terre et les paysans en France au XIIIème et XIIIème siècles* (Paris, 1953, mimeographed), 144–45, shows that by the 1280's, in France, some recently reclaimed land was proving unsuitable for agriculture, and was being abandoned. Evidently by that time assarting had reached the point of diminishing returns.

16 B. Huppertz, *Räume und Schichten bäuerlicher Kulturformen in Deutschland* (Bonn, 1939), 131–9. When H. Stoob, "Minderstädte: Formen der Stadtentstehung im Spätmittelalter," *Vierteljahrschrift für Sozial- und Wirtschaftsgeschichte,* xlvi (1959), 22, says of the myriad little cities which arose during the later Middle Ages, "bürgerliches Leben wird hier zur Miniatur, ja Karikatur," he is looking at the phenomenon from the standpoint of urban man, not with the eyes of the rising peasant.

VARIETIES OF RURAL LIFE

. . . The long medieval centuries had produced innumerable variations in peasant tenure and services, from the right-less slave, through the serf, able to catch the eye of the law of the land through the fence of his lord's control, to the prosperous freeholder. The nature of the land produced its own variety; the rancorous independence of the Breton peasant, walling off his thin-soiled patch from his neighbour, contrasting with the broad open fields south of the Loire with their corporate triumph of harvest-home. But some generalisation is possible. The essential social difference was between those with a plough and animals to tow it, and the majority who had only a spade or could contribute but one or two beasts to fill a richer man's team. Illiteracy was the rule. Physical tiredness; constant vigilance against incursions into strips or patches undefined by hedges or fences; isolation; these factors produced the "peasant mentality" and appeared to justify the stream of urban jest and abuse. Certainly they produced a conservatism in agricultural practise and a tenacious bloody-mindedness of which governments and would-be improving landlords had to take account. With no privacy—the majority had one- or two-roomed hovels which doubled as barn and stable—and few possessions, a table, a chest (for storage and to sit on), an iron pot and a kneading trough, with children who were set to scare birds as soon as they could toddle and a wife who worked as hard as he, the peasant was unfitted to become involved with changes in the superstructure of the civilisation of which he was the foundation. The voice with which he speaks from the written sources is violent, litigious, full of crude superstition. But this is because we hear him most clearly when he is up against government or being denounced from the pulpit. His endurance, his ability to work with others, his urge to collect land and stock of his own: these can best be seen in the land itself and the marks of his work in it, and for the rest we must turn to the peasants of modern Europe, of, for example, Montenegro or Sardinia or Ireland, to see how an ignorant conservatism can include generosity and humour.

A quick survey of Europe from west to east will show the regional variations against which these generalisations must be measured and how wide was the contrast between the reasonably prosperous peasantry of England and France and the declining status and living standards in Poland and Russia.

From John R. Hale, *Renaissance Europe: Individual and Society 1480–1520* (London: Collins Publishers, 1971) pp. 200–205, by permission of the publisher.

The variety in England was especially great. A gradually rising population meant that men with little or no land of their own, who relied on being employed by others, were meeting greater competition and being forced into reliance on charity. The same factor brought insecurity into the lives of the large number of cottagers, men who owned a house and a few acres of land but who looked to seasonal work for others to keep their families safely over the subsistence level. On the other hand, during the labour shortage after the Black Death significant numbers of peasants had bought or bargained their way into small farms of their own (or, if not absolutely their own in law, capable of being handed on without question to their heirs). The result was to increase the gap between the landless man and cottager and the smallholder who, while still working himself on the land, employed shepherds and labourers. Such a man might look forward to the time when his descendants could eschew labour with their hands and glide by the path to which no legal or universally recognised rules applied, but only local judgment and a reasonable prosperity, into the broad spectrum of the squirearchy or gentry; profits on farming were small and holdings could be built up only slowly, generation by generation. . . .

If the wealth of published material relating to English and French rural life makes generalisation hazardous, any conclusions about the position of the Spanish peasantry are temerarious for the opposite reason. A decree of the *cortes* held at Toledo in 1480 abolished servile tenure in Castile and feudal services were abolished for Catalonia in 1486 in return for a cash compensation. How far the peasantry actually benefited from these measures, in contrast to Aragon, where feudal relationships remained in force, it is impossible to say. There were enough prosperous peasant proprietors in Castile to be recognised as a social type in literature, but the possibility of a poor man's improving his status was severely inhibited by the massive support given by the government to the pasturage routes for the giant sheep flocks organised by the *Mesta*. In the peninsula as a whole it was further inhibited by the weight of seigneurial dues, state taxes and church tithes; for most peasants a life of desperate toil left their fortunes exactly as they had inherited them and provided no insurance against the indebtedness that followed a bad harvest. In Portugal rent, feudal dues and tithe could account for seventy percent of a peasant's produce.

Yet this was not, in Spain or Portugal, a time when peasant revolt, let alone peasant war, was feared. King John of Denmark (1481–1513) could safely refer to the peasants as men born to servitude (a condition into which, in contrast to Sweden, they were declining in his reign). The French proverb "Jacques Bonhomme has a strong back and will bear anything" took the peasant's passivity for granted, as did the German "a peasant is just like an ox, only he has no horns"—though peasant wars were to break out in southern and central Germany in 1524–25 and were preceded by clandestine associations like the *Bundschuh* movement of 1502–1517. For its size and the heterogeneity of its institutions, Germany was, of all European countries, the one about which it is most dangerous to generalise, but the status and prosperity of the peasant (and therefore the range between poor and well-to-do) seems to have been highest in the southwest and to have dwindled towards the northeast. Speaking of Alsace, Wimfeling wrote "I know peasants who spend as much at the marriage of their sons and daughters or the baptisms of their infants as would buy a small house and farm or vineyard." Moralists' evidence is always suspect; on the other hand, an ordinance issued in 1497 at Lindau forbad "the common peasant to wear cloth costing more than half a florin the yard, silk, velvet, pearls, gold, or slashed garments," evidence that the effects of the luxury trade routes through the Rhineland were not confined to the towns. Of greater concern to moralist and town council was the independence nurtured by the example of the neighbouring Swiss, who, by means of a largely peasant war, had not only thrown off the feudal dues which were still common (though no longer a badge of dependence) in southwest Germany but had created an independent community. It also reflects two crucial but at present immeasurable factors that bore on the position of the peasantry in western Europe as a whole: the mounting costs of bureaucratised administrations—state, civic and princely, which were passed on to the sector of society in which objection was least likely to be mobilised; and the professionalisation of war, which meant that landowners, denied profits from pay, loot and ransom, turned to the exploitation of their own properties. The *Junkers* of Prussia are a clear example of this second tendency; dormant feudal rights were reactivated in a movement to reduce peasant status to that of the numerous Slave bondmen whose labour was entirely at the disposal of their employers. . . .

A prime cause of this descent into serfdom was the declining importance of towns and of influential urban classes in eastern Europe. Noble resentment of the rival marketing activities of the towns, the high prices charged there for manufactured goods, the refuge they gave to runaway peasants and the consideration given them by rulers in need of cash subsidies; these factors led to a successful pressure on governments to reduce the independence and the commercial activity of the towns. And this pressure came at a time when the Hanseatic League, itself in decline and harassed in the Baltic by English and Dutch shipping, could no longer act as an example of urban energy in northeastern Europe, and when the westward overland trade routes virtually dried up when the Turks occupied the north coast of the Black Sea. In 1500 townsmen were excluded from representation in the Bohemian diet; they regained it in 1517, but the tendency was clear: nobles, with the support of government, confronted the peasants without the political and economic buffer of the towns.

—CHAPTER 5

WOMEN AND THEIR DUTIES

With very few exceptions the women of medieval Europe remained stylized figures: they were rarely allowed to become real people. For the most part this can be explained by a social ethos that assigned to men the roles of warrior and priest, the dominant idealized types of the time. If a woman was taught anything other than simple handicraft, she usually learned only to listen, to respond, to pray, to serve. To be sure there were important exceptions—one need only recall Eleanor of Aquitaine, the patroness of troubadours—but most medieval women, depending on their class, were left either on a pedestal or in the field.

Frances and Joseph Giess enumerate the factors that must be taken into account when appraising the condition of women in medieval society. They then undertake a comparison of the roles of the rich women in the lord's manor with those of the poor women in the peasant's cottage. We learn that marriage was an important social institution for both, and that it always provided for property and inheritance. Beyond these similarities, however, the differences between the fine lady and the dairymaid were so striking that generalizations applicable to all women do not come easily to mind.

David Herlihy attempts to employ statistical evidence to illuminate the position of women. He deduces that men had outlived and outnumbered women until the medieval period, when the survival rate of the latter increased markedly. Women also seem to have gained some political and financial power. At least they took a more active part in attempting to persuade men to make love instead of war, which may help to explain the growth of charitable institutions in Europe. But one may wish to retain a certain skepticism about the depth of such change, despite the optimistic note on which Herlihy concludes.

Friedrich Heer gives the outstanding women of medieval Europe their due. But he also notes a growing schism between the brilliance of a few and the drudgery of the many. There was often a wide gap between social theory and actuality. Heer's summation is necessarily pessimistic. If hopes were raised, he concludes, the reality of most women's lives was still far removed from the attainment of emancipation.

While some of the evidence indicates that women were not always and everywhere as helpless as the medieval stereotype would suggest, the general picture is nonetheless bleak. The extraordinary few were far from constituting a rule, and the theory of woman's dignity was hardly consonant with the social reality. The legacy of medieval Europe, in short, was singularly unpromising for the female.

—— FRANCES AND JOSEPH GIES ——————————

PEASANT WOMEN

What are the elements that affect a woman's life? Recent works in women's history have tended to focus on the status of women relative to men. But the first and most important consideration in evaluating the quality of life in the Middle Ages applies equally to men and women: the technological and economic level of a low-energy but expanding society, influencing work, housing, food, clothing, health, security, comfort, and self-fulfillment.

A second basic element, affecting only women, is the state of obstetrical practice. Throughout the ages, until antisepsis and improvements in obstetrical techniques arrived in the nineteenth century, childbirth was a mortal hazard. Rich or poor, women suffered and were injured in labor; often they died. A medieval gynecological treatise, *The Diseases of Women,* from the medical school at Salerno, reflects the problems and horrors of childbirth in the whole pre-industrial era, during which doctors and midwives had few aids other than potions and poultices. Nevertheless, amid prescriptions for rubbing the woman's flanks with oil of roses, feeding her vinegar and sugar, powdered ivory, or eagle's dung, placing a magnet in her hand or suspending coral around her neck, the Salernitan text also gives sound advice, for example on breech delivery: "If the child does not come forth in the order in which it should, that is, if the legs or arms should come out first, let the midwife with her small and gentle hand moistened with a decoction of flaxseed and chick peas, put the child back in its place in the proper position."[1]

Although abortion, with its own dangers, was practiced from very ancient times, contraception, by various methods—mechanical, medicinal, and magical—found limited use and even less effectiveness. Women had babies, successfully or otherwise.

Several other special criteria apply to the quality of a woman's life in any historical setting.

First, *simple survival:* in many times and on different continents, women have been victims of infanticide as a technique of selective population control. The reason, although usually rationalized in terms of the female's alleged weakness of physique, character, and intellect, is transparently economic: the contribution in work of a daughter was often outweighed by the cost of raising her and giving her a marriage portion: investment in a daughter went mainly to the profit of a future husband.

Second, *conditions of marriage:* the question of consent; the relative age of consent for men and women; monogamy versus polygamy, which emphasizes woman's biological role at the expense not only of her personal, but of her social and economic roles; the seclusion of women in harems or gynaeceums, or their "privatization" at home, where they were segregated from the male spheres of business, politics, and religion; attitudes toward adultery and divorce, where a double standard nearly always prevailed.

Property rights: a woman's competence to own land in her own right; to inherit, to bequeath and sell property; to conduct a business in her own name; to dispose of her own dowry or marriage portion—the money, land, or valuables contributed by her parents when she married.

Legal rights: the restrictions upon women in taking legal action, suing, pleading in court, giving evidence, witnessing wills.

Education: the relative level of literacy or cultivation of men and women.

Work: the distinction between men's work and women's work; of "outside" and "inside" jobs, the big jobs being outside, the little ones at home. Throughout most of history, activities within the house have been considered

---

1   Trotula of Salerno, *The Diseases of Women; a Translation of Passionibus Mulierum Curandorum,* by Elizabeth Mason-Hohl. Los Angeles, 1940, p. 23.

feminine, with a strong connotation of inferior importance, although they covered the whole process of textile manufacturing and almost every stage of food cultivation and preparation. In addition, women joined men in many of the "outside" jobs, working in the fields, in the shops, even in the mines, usually at lower wages.

Political roles: women's constitutional capacity to reign as queens, or in ceremonial and social functions as queen-consorts; their opportunity to hold office, serve on political councils, and occupy judgeships and posts of local leadership.

Religious roles: women's position relative to men as members of a congregation, as ministers, as officials in a church hierarchy. . . .

Most of our information about the Middle Ages, political, social, economic, is concerned with the tip of the iceberg, the perhaps one percent of the population—kings and queens, prelates, lords, ladies—that ruled the other ninety-nine percent. In addition, the developing (and literate) middle class of merchants, merchant-craftsmen, notaries, and officials contributed to the historical sources letters, accounts, cartularies, and diaries. But the bulk of the medieval population, the peasants whose surplus agricultural products supported the royalty, aristocracy, and clergy, the class that, in the words of an eleventh-century bishop of Laon, "owns nothing that it does not get by its own labor," and that provided the rest of the population with "money, clothing, and food. . . . Not one free man could live without them,"[2] remained illiterate and, for the historical record, largely inarticulate.

Yet the peasants did leave records: custom books, manor accounts, tax surveys, and manorial court rolls. The custom books tell us how much land was held by different tenants and what services they owed the lord of the manor at various seasons of the year. The accounts tell us what crops they raised, what were the average yields per acre, what uses the crops were put to—sold, paid out as wages, malted for ale—what servants and laborers were employed, by whom and for what pay. The tax surveys give us the value of land held by different tenants, as well as what livestock they owned. The rolls of the manorial courts—the lowest in the judicial hierarchy of the Middle Ages, and the only ones in which most of the peasants ever appeared—are the richest source of information, registering transfers of property and recording legislation as well as court cases that give us vivid if fleeting glimpses of village life. . . .

Villein or free, rich or poor, the peasant's wife was a partner to her husband in a way that the lady of the castle, whatever her responsibilities, was not. And, the obverse of the partnership, she fully shared her husband's day-in, day-out drudgery. Her "inside" work was not merely service, such as cooking and cleaning, but production and manufacture of the family's food and clothing. She milked the cows; soaked, beat, and combed out the flax; fed the chickens, ducks,

2 Adalbero, Bishop of Laon, cited in R. H. Hilton, *Bond Men Made Free.* New York, 1973, pp. 53-54.

and geese; sheared the sheep; made the cheese and butter; and cultivated the family vegetable patch. Sometimes she spun and wove to eke out a cash income. She also worked along with her husband "outside"—sowing, reaping, gleaning, binding, threshing, raking, winnowing, thatching. At times she even helped with the plowing, wielding the goad that drove the oxen while her husband gripped the handles of the plow.

Like the castle lady's, the peasant woman's life was intricately involved with landed property. The village holding, in an area like Cuxham where traditional open-field agriculture was practiced, usually passed to a single heir. There were two reasons for this arrangement: from the peasant's point of view, the holding could normally support only one family; from the lord's point of view , keeping the holding intact meant a stable arrangement for rents and labor services. If there were sons, the heir was usually the oldest son. Preference was given to male heirs, but daughters inherited if there were no sons—sometimes the eldest daughter, sometimes an unmarried daughter who had remained at home. In some places, the holding was divided among the daughters, but not at Cuxham; when Robert Benyt's widow Alice died in 1343, her daughters Matilda and Joan, who had married outside the manor, did not share in the inheritance, which passed intact to still unmarried Emma.

For both women and men, marriage on the peasant level remained closely connected to inheritance. The daughter who inherited became a matrimonial prize. In many villages she had to marry to take possession of the holding, on the theory that a woman could not work the land by herself. Sometimes she was fined if she did not marry, and the lord of the manor even chose her husband. But the male heir, too, was expected to marry, and a wife and family were regarded as indispensable to his operating the holding. Normally he alone was allowed to marry. His brothers could stay and work for him, but if they wished to marry they had to leave the village and seek their fortunes elsewhere.

This intimate connection between the land and the family bloodline was considered more important than male domination of inheritance. The feeling of right to land through blood was so strong that it triumphed even in periods when the competition for land was intense and the respect for law was weak. In spite of the fiction under which feudalism operated—that all land in England belonged to the king, who granted it to his barons, who in turn granted it to lesser lords, who granted it to the peasants—a pervasive sense of hereditary rights prevailed among the peasants, as among the barons. The man who married an heiress often took her family's name, so that it remained attached to the holding. If they had no children, the land reverted to her family on the wife's death; if there was an heir, the husband was allowed to hold the land for his lifetime, after which it went to the child, who was thus regarded as his wife's heir rather than his own, and kept the land in the family's name and bloodline. . . .

The marriage of the peasant woman was always arranged, but she had an advantage over the lady of the castle in that she at least knew the man she was to marry. Usually the groom's father initiated the proceedings, sometimes with the intervention of a go-between who negotiated with the girl's father. The two men discussed the girl's dowry—not land, but money or chattels, clothes, furniture, tools, utensils, livestock—and the lands with which the groom would endow her at the church door. Finally both fathers presented themselves at the manorial court. If the girl's parents were unfree, they had to obtain permission for her to marry, and pay a fine (merchet). If she married outside the manor, they had to pay an additional fine. Thus widow Alice Benyt, a villein, paid not only merchet but extra fines in 1328 and 1331 when her daughters, Matilda and Joan, married outside the village.

In contrast to the child marriages of royalty and nobility, peasant unions typically involved people in their twenties or older. The bride's age at marriage was determined by the availability of marriageable men; the groom often did not marry until his father died. A living father might turn over his holding to a son, who agreed to furnish his parents a room and a ration of food. This custom was immortalized in the medieval story "The Divided Horsecloth," which exists in several versions, the most common of which is: a peasant, whose elderly father has retired in his favor, grows tired of supporting him and decides to turn him out of the house, the peasant instructs his young son to fetch the old man a horse blanket and send him on his way. The boy cuts the blanket in two and gives his grandfather only half, explaining to his father, "I will keep the other half until I am a man, and then give it to you."

Most parents did not leave the arrangement to chance and children's gratitude, but took care to have the details spelled out in manorial court, with infractions punishable by fine. In the Ramsey Abbey manor of Ellington in 1278, William Koc admitted that he had not paid his father the grain, peas, and beans that he owed him for the year, as part of the arrangement by which the older man had surrendered his land; a new agreement was made, and William's two pledges, peasants who had vouched for him, were fined sixpence each (not as trifling a sum as it sounds at a time when pennies were silver).

In 1294 one family at Cranfield, another Ransey Abbey manor, even made allowance for the possibility that the old couple and the younger might not get along together. Elyas de Bretendon and his son John agreed that John would provide lodgings and "suitable food and drink" for Elyas and his wife Christine in his house, but in the event that "trouble and discord should in the future arise between the parties so that they are unable to live together, the above John will provide for Elyas and Christine, or whichever of them should outlive the other, a house and curtilage [yard] where they can decently reside," as well as specified amounts of grain, peas, and beans. In the event of a quarrel, the older couple would also retain all their furniture, tools, and other belongings.[3]

The marriage agreement was followed by betrothal, in which the couple

3 J. A. Raftis, *Tenure and Mobility.* Toronto, 1964, pp. 44–45.

joined hands, the man gave the women a ring, and they "plighted their troth." In the countryside, the distinction between the wedding ceremony and this rite, something more than an engagement and something less than a marriage, was even more ambiguous than in castle and city. The betrothal was often followed by a feast and by the couple's going to bed, the church ceremony postponed until the woman was pregnant, or sometimes until after she had had a baby—perhaps to assure the groom that she was not barren.

Many peasant women did not marry, thanks to the shortage of eligible land-holding partners. A girl might remain on her father's land and work for her brother in return for food and lodging; or she might leave, taking with her the dowry that would have been hers if she had married. She might become a servant in another village household. Peasants, and not necessarily the most impoverished, frequently put their daughters out to service in other peasant households in return for wages and clothes. Or she might become one of the *famuli*, the permanent workers on the manorial demesne, including house servants and farm laborers. At Cuxham, the *famuli* slept in rooms next to the kitchen of the curia and ate in the hall. Some were women—usually the dairy assistant and the woman who prepared the malt for ale. Women were also often among the hired laborers, forming a valuable reserve at harvest time, or when a sick tenant had to hire a substitute to perform his labor services for the lord. They did much the same work as the men: haymaking, weeding, thatching, mowing, reaping, and binding. Sometimes they lived in the village, in cottages, or as lodgers in other people's houses. Sometimes they formed part of the floating population that roamed the country at harvest time.

Wages for women were often lower than for men, particulary in the case of the *famuli*. Dairymaids were typically paid less than male plowmen, carters, and herdsmen. Women were also often paid less for the same work; but on the other hand there is evidence, at least in the late Middle Ages, that in many places independent female laborers gained the same wages as men for the same manual jobs.

One resource for single girls of the aristocracy and the wealthy merchant class—the convent—was not normally available to peasants. The demand for women's labor on the land fortunately made this outlet less necessary to peasant girls whose families could not afford the dowries which convents demanded, and whose low birth usually excluded them to begin with.

—DAVID HERLIHY—————————————————————————

ADVANTAGES AND DISADVANTAGES OF WOMEN

In our inquiry we shall try to enlist some of the new methods, largely quantitative in character, by which social historians today study the past. We shall then seek to lay upon our figures some interpretative comment, much of it frankly tentative, in keeping with the frequent deficiencies of our data and the inadequate research which has so far been devoted to women.

How can the position of women in medieval society be assessed? We shall rely upon three indicators—biological success, in the sense of female longevity; social position and prominence, or the position women could hold in the administration of property and power; and cultural importance, the influence they seem to have exerted in various fields of medieval cultural expression.

In the modern nations of the West, women characteristically live longer than men. But when in the history of Western civilization is that biological advantage first discernible? We cannot as yet give an entirely satisfactory answer, but some observations may be offered. Aristotle, perhaps the greatest biologist of the ancient world, affirmed that men live longer than women, as they were, in his estimation, warmer animals.[1] Longevity studies have been attempted for the period of late classical antiquity, on the basis of thousands of funeral inscriptions which state the age of death. If their conclusions can be trusted, Aristotle was correct: men could expect to outlive women by as much as 4, 5, 6 or 7 years.[2] Even among the upper levels of classical society, to which of course we owe most of these inscriptions, the life of women seems to have been harder and physically more taxing than that of men. And the situation seems also to have been slow in changing. From the early Middle Ages—beginning from the late eighth and ninth centuries—we have several, large surveys of the serfs resident on great estates, and characteristically men outnumber the women, suggesting that males survived more successfully than females under the harsh conditions of early medieval life. Upon the estates of St. Germain des Pres near Paris, among several thousand serfs recorded in a survey of the early ninth century, there seem

From David Herlihy, *The Social History of Italy and Western Europe, 700-1500* (London: Variorum Reprints, 1978), IX, pp. 4-14, by permission of the publisher.

1 De longitudine et brevitate vitae, cap. 5. "Natura tamen mares, atque ut in universum dixerim, vivaciores feminis sunt, cuius rei causa est quod mas femina calidior sit." The Latin translation cited is taken from his *Opera omnia* (Paris, 1887), p. 538. The same opinion is expressed in another tract, entitled "De iuventute et senectute, de vita et morte."

2 A. R. Burn, "Hic Breve Vivitur," *Past and Present,* IV (1953), p. 16.

to have been 132 males for every 100 females.[3] The serfs were of course the poorest and most exploited class in medieval society, but even among the privileged, there is indirect evidence that men significantly outnumbered, and presumably outlived, the women. According to the marriage customs of the barbarians, the groom usually paid a dowry to his bride. "The dowry," writes Tacitus of the Germans, "is brought by husband to wife, not by wife to husband."[4] Did young women command a higher price than young men in the marriage market, because there were fewer of them? According to the law of the Salian Franks, the young woman of child-bearing age was protected by a wergild—the penalty which had to be paid to her family if she was killed—three times that of the male freeman.[5] This extraordinary provision, together with the practice of the male dowry, suggests that women in their child-bearing years were in short supply and much valued among the barbarians and the semi-barbarized societies of the early Middle Ages.

It is interesting to note that the male dowry of the Germans fades everywhere in Europe, but gradually, over the course of the Middle Ages. In Italy, for example, the male dowry remained probably the usual arrangement in marriage until the twelfth century.[6] In the thirteenth century, the dowry given for the bride triumphed everywhere, and in the fourteenth, it entered upon an inflationary spiral, which evoked the comment and usually the condemnations of moralists.[7] By the early fifteenth century, St. Bernardine of Siena, who rigorously scrutinized the moral practices of his society, claimed that the great city of Milan contained no less than 20,000 young girls unable to marry, because of the shortage of men, their reluctance to take a wife, or the disastrously high dowries demanded.[8] The complete reversal of the flow of property and money in the making of the marriage suggests that there were more young women than young men competing for spouses. At some point in the course of medieval history, perhaps in the twelfth or thirteenth century, had the balance between the sexes shifted to favor women? Were women surviving in numbers unknown in previous epochs?

3 J. C. Russell, *Late Ancient and Medieval Populations* (Transactions of the American Philosophical Society, n.s. 48, pt. 3; Philadelphia, 1958), p. 14.

4 *On Britain and Germany. A Translation of the "Agricola" and the "Germania" of Tacitus,* transl. H. Mattingly (Baltimore: Penguin Books, 1964), p. 115.

5 If she was pregnant the wergild was six times greater. Free women not in the child-bearing years carried the same wergild as men. See Lehmann, *Le rôle de la femme,* p. 42.

6 Antonio Pertile, *Storia del diritto italiano dalla caduta dell' impero romano alla codificazione,* III: *Storia del diritto privato* (2nd ed.; Turin, 1894), p. 320.

7 Dante himself, in a famous passage (*Paridiso,* canto XV, vv. 103–105), had his ancestor Cacciaguida complain that the size of the dowries was exceeding all measure at Florence, and that the birth of a baby girl struck fear in the heart of her father.

8 *Le prediche volgari,* ed. C. Cannarozzi, O. F. M. (Florence, 1958), II, 107, " . . . in Milano, quando frate Bernardino tornò, li fu detto che venti milia fanciulle v'erano da maritare, senza le maritate. . . "

Sometime about 1250, a scholar named Vincent of Beauvais put together a vast encyclopedia of medieval science, called the *Speculum Naturale,* the "Mirror of Nature." In it he considered whether men live longer than women.[9] He replied that men live longer than women, because, as the Philosopher (meaning of course Aristotle) says, they are warmer. Then, sometime probably between 1258 and 1288, the Dominican scholar Albert the Great addressed himself to the same question: "Whether man or woman has a longer life?"[10] He replied that, as the Philosopher says, men live longer than women by nature (*naturaliter*). But he at once added that women live longer than men *per accidens,* that is, through the intervention of factors not determined by nature. He declared that menstruation purified the female system, and that sexual intercourse took less from females than from males: it is hard only to see what in these reasons could be regarded as accidental. But he also mentioned another, purely socio-cultural consideration—the sole support he could cite for asserting that women "accidentally" live longer than men. "They work less," he explained, "and for that reason are not so much consumed." We may doubt that Albert had conducted a statistical survey, but clearly he believed that Aristotle's words on the superior longevity of men had to be reconciled with his own, quite contrary impressions.

Unlike Albert, we can conduct statistical surveys, but only for certain favored periods and regions of medieval Europe—notably for the towns and countrysides of northern Italy in the late fourteenth and fifteenth centuries. Within the cities of the late Middle Ages, women seem to have been, in comparison with rural communities, distinctly more numerous than men, and in some cities they outnumbered the males. At Bologna in 1395, there were only 95.6 men for every hundred women; in German towns, the preponderance of women was even more pronounced—83.8 men for every hundred women at Nuremberg, and comparable ratios could be cited for other towns.[11] Even when women were slightly fewer than men, they score higher on another critical index—the average of their ages. At Verona in 1425, the average age of men was 30.4 years, and women 32.2. At Florence in 1427, men averaged 26.0 years of

9 *Speculum naturale* (Graz, 1964), liber xxiv, cap. 67, De vita et morte animalium. "Sed in homine masculini foeminis plus vivunt, quia masculus femina calidior sit."

10 *Alberti Magni ordinis fratrum praedicatorum Opera Omnia,* XII (Monasterium Westfalorum, 1955), liber xv, q. 8, p. 263, Quaestiones super de animalibus. To the question "utrum longioris vitae sit mas aut femina," Albert wrote: "Per accidens tamen longioris vitae est femina, tum quia minus laborant, propter quod non tantum consumuntur, et magis mundificantur per fluxum menstruorum et etiam minus debitantur per coitum ideo magis conservantur. Et istae accidentales sunt."

11 For Bologna, see Paolo Montanari, *Documenti su la popolazione di Bologna alla fine del trecento* (Fonti per la storia di Bolonga, Testi, 1; Bolonga, 1966), p. 8. In the partial census from 1395, there were 2366 men and 2448 women. For Nuremberg and other German cities, see Fritz Rörig, *The Medieval Town* (Berkeley and Los Angeles, 1967), p. 115. At Nuremberg there were 1207 women per 1000 men; at Basel, 1246; and at Rostock, 1295.

age, and women 27.3.[12] Differences of one or two years may not seem impressive, but they are impressive in communities where life expectancy for both sexes never much surpassed 30 years. These are of course cities, which always attracted immigrants, and doubtlessly older women in greater numbers than older men. We are only now pushing our researches into the countrysides, which imposed apparently at all periods of medieval history harsh conditions of life upon women. Even so, in regions with a fairly large urban contingent in its population, women were surviving better than men. We can offer some figures for the population, both urban and rural, of Pistoia in Tuscany—dubious figures, as most must be for the Middle Ages, but not entirely to be disparaged. Women at birth could hope to live to 29.8 years, and men to 28.4.[13] More than the exact values, the advantage held by women is the notable result of these calculations. Albert, in affirming the superior if accidental longevity of women, seems to have been right.

Others believed so too. In a manual on courtly behavior, the *Book of the Courtier* written in 1516, the author Baldesare Castiglione reported a conversation which supposedly occurred in the palace of the duke of Urbino. One participant confidently affirmed that women live longer than men, and that since it is so, they fulfill the intention of nature better than males.[14] The speaker presented this statement as common knowledge, and his hearers accepted it as such. Aristotle had been forgotten. There is, in other words, evidence, both literary and statistical, that women, at least in certain favored quarters of society, had achieved over the course of the Middle Ages that superiority in life expectancy over men which they still possess in Western societies.

Something very basic seems to have shifted in Western civilization between late antiquity and the late Middle Ages—one of the least recognized, but perhaps most fundamental changes to have affected social life in the West. We are still too ignorant to be able to state what factors were conferring upon women an improved chance of survival. Perhaps it was the painfully slow spread of a Christian ethos across and within the fabric of medieval society. Surely, it owed much to the emergence among the aristocracy of a civilized and refined court life, and still more to the growth of cities from the eleventh century. Courts and

12   The figures for Verona represent the average age of 1821 men and 1805 women, taken from unpublished Anagrafi at present in the Archivio di Stato of Verona, concerning which the author hopes soon to publish a more extensive study. The ages from Florence are those contained in a tax survey, called the Catasto, at the Archivio di Strato of that city. They are based on 19690 men and 16550 women for whom ages are stated in the survey.

13   D. Herlihy, *Medieval and Renaissance Pistoia. The Social History of an Italian Town, 1200-1430* (New Haven, 1967), p. 286. Life expectancies calculated on the basis of a single census are distorted by changes in the age structure brought about by variations in births and deaths over time, and through immigration or emigration.

14   *The Book of the Courtier,* transl. Charles S. Singleton (New York: Anchor Books, 1959), p. 219. "And thus, since men dry out more than women in the act of procreation, it frequently happens that they do not keep their vitality as long as women; thus, this further perfection can be ascribed to women that, living longer than men, they carry out the intention of nature better than men."

cities, the courtly and urbane manners they engendered, seem to have brought a milieu relatively favorable to women and to their biological survival.

Survival is of course a prerequisite for the fulfillment of any social role, but the survival of a group in relatively larger numbers does not necessarily convey a social advantage. We turn now to our second indicator of the social importance of women: the wealth they controlled, the power they exercised over property and persons, the eminence they achieved. Here we must look at different sorts of records. From about the middle of the eighth century, there have survived from numerous regions of Europe charters by the thousands, which chiefly record contracts or agreements between private parties, both laymen and churches. Most involve conveyances of land—sales, leases, donations and the like. The charters partially but uniquely reveal the role assumed by women in the management of land, the basic wealth of medieval Europe. In other curious ways, the charters reflect the importance of women. They show, for example, a tendency, quite pronounced at certain times and in certain regions, for the men who appear in the contrasts to identify themselves not by the name of the father, as, for example, John son of Peter, but by the name of the mother, John son of Mary. The assumption would be that the lady who gave her name to her son enjoyed some sort of stature within her community.

Several years ago, I attempted to survey most of the published charters from continental Europe for the period 700 to 1200, in order to assess the importance of women.[15] Specifically, I sought to count the times women appear alone as the first principal mentioned in the charters, the times women alone are described as the owners of contiguous property, and the times men in the charters bear a matronymic rather than a patronymic. The results have already been published, and here we shall offer only some further comment about them. The charters give considerable visibility to women. In one out of ten instances, a woman alone conveyed land in her own right and name. Women appear in about 6 percent of all references to contiguous owners, but many more were doubtlessly included in the numerous but vague references to unnamed heirs as the owners of contiguous lands. About one out of twenty males in the charters identify themselves with their mothers exclusively.

The charters also help show some of the factors which seem to have lent women a particular prominence. Social position was clearly one of these. The higher the social rank, the greater the responsibilities women bore and the stronger the influence they exerted upon society. As far back as the ninth century, in a tract on the administration of the palace under Charlemagne, the queen is allocated a special responsibility for the supervision of the treasury, the

---

15 "Land, Family and Women in Continental Europe, 701-1200," *Tradito,* XVIII (1962), 89–120. In identifying a piece of land, the charters often state not only its location, but the name of the owners of the lands contiguous to it. These references to contiguous owners, random in character and numbering more than 100,000 in the period of our interest, thus offer a means for estimating the distribution of property in the medieval countyside.

distribution of gifts to the court knights, and even the management of estates.[16] She seems to have served her husband as a mayor of the palace, virtually in the office which the founders of the Carolingian dynasty had themselves used as a step towards royalty and empire. Christine de Pisan, in writing of the education needed by noble women, reaffirmed that "ladies and baronesses who live on their lands" needed to know how to read and how to calculate, for the proper administration of their own and their husband's estates.[17] For the husbands of these great ladies would be frequently occupied or absent, and they would bear chief responsibility for the state of the court or palace, and the management of estates. This conferred upon them a limited, but real, power. . . .

Still another corner of medieval society, marked by a high degree of male mobility and a consequent reliance on the managerial skills of women, was the city, and within the city, the class of rich merchants. In Italy, the great center of the medieval commercial revolution, moralists discussed at length whether girls should be taught to read. The discussion in fact was bootless, as a literate wife was an essential asset to a mercantile family. Much more than the medieval Church, the medieval city was thus concerned with the formal education of women. According to the chronicler Giovanni Villani, Florence about 1338 was sending between eight and ten thousand children—both boys and girls—to elementary school, to learn their letters.[18] He does not unfortunately inform us how the number divided between boys and girls, but the city was clearly making provision for female education. The nascent capitalism of the Middle Ages could not neglect the resources which women offered.

In a dynamic, mobile, changing society, women offered a continuity of management over households, castles and estates essential to social progress. But no less remarkable is the prominence achieved by women in quite a different facet of medieval life—rebellious opposition to the social establishment of the medieval world, which similarly grows in strength and vehemence from the eleventh century. Social opposition in a medieval context meant primarily heresy, and "in the history of heresy," a great medievalist has written, "[women] appear . . . as in no other manifestation of [medieval life]."[19] Amid the play of powerful social forces many women could arrive at positions of

---

16   Hincmar of Rheims, "On the Governance of the Palace," in *The History of Feudalism*, ed. D. Herlihy (New York, 1970), p. 219. "The good management of the palace, and especially the royal dignity, as well as the gifts given annually to the officers (excepting, however, the food and water for the horses) pertained especially to the queen, and under her to the chamberlain." See also Charlemagne's capitulary "On Estates," in *Medieval Culture and Society*, ed. D. Herlihy (New York, 1968), p. 45. "We wish that whatever we or the queen should command to any steward, or whatever our servants, the seneschal or the butler, should order the stewards in our name or that of the queen, they should perform as was told them."

17   Cf. Laigle, *Le Livre des trois vertus*, p. 187.

18   *Cronica de Giovanni Villani* (Florence: Magheri, 1823), p. 184.

19   G. Volpe, *Movimenti religiosi e sette ereticali nella società medievale italiana* (Florence, 1922), p. 17. "Nella storia dell' eresia esse appaiono, ora, come in nessun' altra manifestazione della vita."

leadership and influence, but many others manifested a bitter antagonism toward and alienation from the institutions and the values which dominated their lives. . . .

This then was the extraordinary range over which the position of the woman could vary within medieval society. Like Mary and like Eve, she was both hand-maid and rebel, queen and outcast among them. What then can we say about our third indicator, the importance of women in setting the cultural styles of the Middle Ages? The question is rendered the more difficult because today psychologists, to whom we must turn for aid, are not themselves agreed whether there exist specifically feminine tastes or cultural preferences. Do women prefer, for example, tales of romance, and men tales of war? And are such apparent dif-ferences biologically based, or culturally induced by the different educational ex-periences and the different values which our society, over the centuries, has im-posed upon its girls and boys?

Caught amid such uncertainties, the historian can only cite those areas of medieval culture in which contemporaries themselves thought that they dis-cerned a marked feminine influence. These areas are clear and they are large. From the eleventh and twelfth centuries, medieval Europe witnessed the growth among its aristocratic classes of a lively court life. A new culture grew up in close connection with the European courts, first in southern France and then widely across the continent. This "courtly" culture set for men and women proper standards of "courteous" behavior, and especially influenced those two chief human activities, the making of love and the making of war. The new deport-ment in battle was chivalry, but even more remarkable than the polite combat it recommended were its attitudes towards "courtly" love. The love of a man for a woman was divorced from any connection with marriage, and still less with the procreation of children. According to the arbiters of the art, true love could not even exist within the bonds of marriage.[20] Like the heretics, the courtly lovers re-jected marriage as a means of human fulfillment. Love was rather viewed as an analogue to the Christian conception of grace: it was a saving power. If the lover won his lady's favor, so he gained ineffable joy; winter changed into spring, and he came to inhabit a new heaven and a new earth, the promised land of the blessed. Poets and writers wove a rich tradition of romantic literature around the themes of love, chivalrous adventures, sensitive spirits and high emotions.

Did women affect these remarkable cultural departures? A troubadour poet of the thirteenth century celebrates the influence of women in the following lines:

There is no reason enough why
We ought to hold women dear
For we see happen very little
Courtesy, except through women.

---

20 According to a famous decision of a "court of love," recorded in Andreas Capellanus, *The Art of Courtly Love,* trans. John P. Parry (Records of Civilization: Sources and Studies: New York, 1941), p. 171.

Well know I that for love of the ladies
The very peasants become courteous.
Woman is of such a nature
That she makes the coward bold.[21]

A comrade in arms of St. Louis of France is reported to have remarked after a battle, "We shall yet talk of this day in the ladies' chamber."[22] The phrase seems to show that the approval of women had a singular value for this medieval knight. Much later, in Castiglione's *Book of the Courtier*, one of the persons involved in the conversation declares:

> Do you not see that the cause of all gracious exercises that give us pleasure is to be assigned to women alone? Who learns to dance gracefully for any reason except to please women? Who devotes himself to the sweetness of music for any other reason? Who attempts to compose verses, at least in the vernacular, unless to express sentiments inspired by women?[23]

As medieval writers thus viewed their own society, women played a prominent role in softening the art of war, and perhaps in making love an art. In another major field of medieval culture the influence of women seems apparent: religion. The role of women in the medieval Church was, as we have mentioned, fluctuating and ambivalent. They contributed some of its greatest saints, and filled the ranks of its most committed enemies. They seem also partially responsible for certain shifts in the style of medieval piety. An extraordinary veneration for the Virgin Mary marks medieval piety from the eleventh century. The movement introduces new qualities of compassion and of mercy into the religious view of the universe and God's management of it. In hundreds of miracle stories, the sinner is saved from his just desserts by the Virgin's clemency and pity. From the late thirteenth century, the same qualities affect in still another way the character of medieval piety. By statistical count it can be shown that the religious institutions which grew most rapidly in wealth in the late Middle Ages were hospitals, orphanages, and the like.[24] There is apparent a new compassion for one's fellows, and a new social consciousness. Perhaps this unmistakable movement reflects only the disasters of the late Middle Ages—the ravaging plagues and famines. If one could not be moved to mercy amid the carnage of the Black Death, by what could one be moved? But there were those who said that the emphasis on works of mercy as an indispensable obligation of Christian piety reflected a feminine influence. Christine de Pisan, in answering the charge that women were hypocritical in their piety, replied that women primarily comforted the sick, aided the poor, visited hospitals, and buried the dead. "These," she wrote, "are the works of women, which are the sovereign steps that God

---

21   Cited by Thomas Wright, *Womankind in All Ages of Western Europe* (London, 1869), p. 166.

22   Cf. Marc Bloch, *Feudal Society* transl. L. A. Manyon (Chicago, 1961), p. 307. The speaker was the count of Soissons, and the battle was waged at Mansura in Egypt, in 1250.

23   *Book of the Courtier*, transl. Singleton, p. 257-8.

24   See my additional comments in *Medieval and Renaissance Pistoia*, pp. 241-258.

commands us to follow.''[25] If the inclinations of women changed the styles of medieval love and war, so they also in their tendency to mercy and compassion affected the nature of medieval piety. And love, war and religion, which feminine influence touched deeply in the Middle Ages, surely are central parts of any culture.

Of course, in spite of their influence, few women appear among the great authors and thinkers of the medieval world. Christine de Pisan, in her comprehensive defense of her sex, explains this apparent failing too:

> If the custom were to place girls in school, and if they were commonly taught the sciences as are boys, [the girls] would learn just as perfectly and they would understand the subtleties of all the arts and sciences, as do the boys.[26]

Christine's comment points to one great failure of medieval civilization; still, it is notable that such a sentiment could have been expressed and defended in a medieval context, and by a woman.

The experiences of women in medieval society—so varied, so ambivalent, so rich—defy an easy summary. The Middle Ages imposed heavy burdens upon women and formed deep prejudices against them. On the other hand this long chapter in Western history added a few years to their lives and a little to their dignity. The balance of change was in their favor.

25 *Cyte of Ladyes,* transl. Anslay, pt. I, cap. 10, ''Me semethe that these be the werkes of women the whiche ben the soverayne traces that God commandeth us to folowe.''

26 Cited by Laigle, *Le Livre des trois vertus,* p. 120, ''Si la coustume estoit de mettre les petites filles a l'escole, et que communement on les fist apprendre les sciences comme on fait aux filz, qu'elles apprendroient aussi parfaitement et entenderoient les subtilites de toutes les arz et sciences comme ils font.''

—FRIEDRICH HEER—

THE SOCIAL STATUS OF WOMEN

Some illustrations from French history will help to show the extent to which woman's position declined. The Merovingian era had been dominated by forceful, not to say formidable, women; Brünhilde, although the most memorable, was by no means unique. The mother of Charlemagne and

From Friedrich Heer, *The Medieval World: Europe 1100–1350,* trans. Janet Sondheimer (London: George Weidenfeld and Nicolson Ltd., 1961), pp. 261–66, by permission of the publisher.

Hildegard, his third wife, were women of considerable influence, while the Empress Judith, wife to Louis the Pious, his successor, was a stronger and more effective character than her husband, a worthy namesake of the great heroine of the Apocrypha. In the disorders of the succeeding centuries, when monarchy was weak and the baronage powerful, widows of apparently superhuman strength frequently fought to preserve their children's inheritance intact from the depredations of vassals and neighbours. Although a ninth century council held in the diocese of Nantes forbade women to attend political assemblies, there is evidence that in the south of France women took part in elections to the *commune*, the municipal government. From the eleventh century it seems that there was something like equality between the sexes in this region. Still later, in 1308, we hear of certain women in the Touraine who were apparently eligible to assist in the election of deputies to the assembly of estates at Tours. The town charter of Beaumont, which served as model for over five hundred small towns in Champagne and eastern France, has a regulation requiring the assent of the vendor's wife to any sale of goods or property.

There were still great ruling ladies in the France of the twelfth and thirteenth centuries. Eleanor of Aquitaine, the Empress Matilda and Blanche of Castile at once spring to mind. This period opens with the elder Matilda, wife of William the Conqueror, firmly in control of Normandy during her husband's absences in England. Then there was Ermengarde, Countess of Narbonne, who ruled her lands and her troops for fifty years and was the leader of the French royalist party in the south of France in opposition to the English—a nobly-born Joan of Arc. Ermengarde was married several times, but her husbands took no part in the government. She fought numerous wars in defense of her territories, was a patron of troubadours and a protector of the Church, and had great renown as an arbiter and judge in difficult cases of feudal law.

At the time when Philip Augustus was engaged in unifying the country under the crown, large tracts of France were governed by women—Eleanor of Aquitaine, Alix of Vergy in Burgundy, and the Countesses Marie and Blanche in Champagne, where they fostered the growth of the trade fairs and of urban settlement. Flanders, the other great centre of economic acitivity in northwestern Europe and a much fought-over territory, was ruled by women for sixty-five years, first by Joanna and after her by her sister Margaret, who rehabilitated the country after its devastation by war. Margaret regarded herself as the vassal of the French King and of the German Emperor in her own person, and did all in her power to promote urban independence. She was the first ruler to adopt French as the official language of her chancery. This was in 1221; it was not used at Paris until some years later, in the time of Louis IX. The growth of the vernacular languages owed much to feminine influence, as is clear enough from religious and literary sources.

Blanche of Castile impressed her personality on every department of French life in the first half of the thirteenth century. Her political contribution as regent for her son, St Louis, has already been described. She also made a significant social contribution, as protector of the Jews and champion of the poor. St. Louis was persuaded by his Franciscan advisers to adopt a most unhappy policy towards the Jews, and it was during his reign that the first burnings of the Talmud took place. When some Jews came to plead their cause at the royal court in Paris they found the Queen-Mother in charge; she treated them with far more wisdom and understanding than her son in his agony of mind had been able to show. Blanche appears as protector of the poor in an anecdote told by the chronicler of St Denis, who praises her for shielding them from the cruelty of affluent clerks: the cathedral chapter of Paris had imprisoned large numbers of tenants (both dependent and free) from the villages of Orly, Chatenai and other neighbouring places because of their refusal to pay a special tax. The Queen came in person to open the doors of the prison and set free the men, women and children suffocating from the heat inside.

Blanche had a worthy successor in her daughter-in-law, Margaret of Provence, though the two had little liking for each other. A woman of great strength and courage and the mother of eleven children, Margaret made Philip, the heir to the throne, swear to remain subject to her advice until he was thirty years old.

The rise of France in the twelfth and thirteenth centuries thus owed something to the achievements of its great ladies. But then a masculine era set in; in 1317 an assembly of notables meeting in Paris under Philip V declared that women were excluded from succession to the crown. The career of Joan of Arc at the close of the Middle Ages seems to promise a return to women's former political status and prestige. Almost at once, however, she was turned into a figure with largely supernatural associations and made the subject of legend. This was characteristic of the age: what had once been sober reality was now felt to be impracticable and improper.

[A] considerable positive contribution [was] made by noble and other women to Catharism. For the first time women had been admitted to a leading role in a religious society. Women were eligible to become Perfects and were authorized to preach and to dispense the *consolamentum*. A countess of Foix left her husband to become head of a feminine Albigensian community. The women and girls of Toulouse fought alongside their men against the masculine array of crusaders from the North led by Simon de Montfort, the epitome of brutal and ambitious manhood, who met his death under a hail of stones hurled at him by a band of women.

There had been women troubadours as well as women Perfects. Five songs have survived by the Countess Beatrix of Die, an open and unashamed expression of her love for Count Raimbaut of Orange. Other women troubadours included Beatrix's daughter Tiberga, Castellox, Clara of Anduse, Isabella of Malaspina and Marie of Ventadour. The celebrated poetess Marie de France says of herself, with proud and serene assurance, "*Marie ai nom, si sui de France.*" This simple statement, "Marie is my name and I come from France," finds its echo in the equally proud and unaffected avowal of Joan of Domrémy, who withstood the examination of some fifty crabbed theologians only to be broken by imprisonment: "My name is Joan and I came to France from Domrémy."

Around the year 1250 there were some five hundred nunneries in Germany, with a total population of between twenty-five and thirty thousand religious. Even so, it is evident that the Church had not succeeded in giving full scope to the religious energies of women. Hildegard of Bingen, who lived in the twelfth century, had already appreciated the seriousness of the situation. She held that the decadence of Church and society was chiefly caused by masculine weakness: women therefore must act where men had failed; this was the *tempus muliebre,* the era of woman. Since the clergy would not, it was left to women to go and preach against heretics and make missionary journeys up and down the Rhine and the Nahe. The Abbess Hildegard in fact had many masculine traits to her character and for a long time yet the life of the female religious would continue to be ordered along the lines laid down for men. The *Speculum Virginum,* for example, a handbook for nuns composed about 1100 and still extant in versions in Latin, Middle Low German and Swedish, has no section devoted to love, private prayer is not mentioned, nor is there any hint of concern for the soul of the individual nun. The spiritual regime prescribed is harsh and unyielding. No penance could be accepted from the fallen, though all the world knew how easy it was for young nuns to fall from grace, seduced as often as not by clerks.

Heterodox and heretical groups offered women much greater freedom and a wider field of activity. The Waldensians and Cathars, and other sects as well, encouraged women to preach and propagandise and to cultivate their own souls, both actively and passively. When these groups were suppressed—not before many women and girls had gone cheerfully to their deaths, serenely confident, inwardly set free—a number of passionately devout and spiritually awakened women sought refuge in Dominican and Franciscan convents and in Beguinages. But there they often found themselves in little better case, and their position became increasingly difficult during the thirteenth and fourteenth centuries. Men were reluctant to assume responsibility for the spiritual direction of women and evaded it wherever they could; the Church continued to distrust women who were spiritually restless, suspecting them all the time of heresy. For a brief space the omens were more propitious, when Meister Eckhart, Tauler and Suso were bringing their mysticism into the Dominican convents of Germany. They succeeded in absorbing and deflecting much of this restless yearning after personal communion with God, channelling it into forms of expression recognised by the Church; but this was a passing phase.

The increasing gloom and anxiety which spread over Europe in the later Middle Ages, when nations, churches and minorities drew further and further apart, to eye one another with mutual hostility and envy, is closely bound up with the failure to harness to the social and religious needs of the age that feminine spiritual energy which had burst forth so dramatically in the twelfth century. The embers were banked down, but they still smouldered. Cast spiritually and intellectually adrift, women were confronted with the closed ranks of a masculine society, governed by a thoroughly masculine theology and by a morality made by men for men. The other half of humanity came into the picture only when specifically feminine services were needed. Aquinas's ethical system related entirely to men. He speaks blandly of "making use of a necessary object, woman, who is needed to preserve the species or to provide food and drink." "Woman was created to be man's helpmate, but her unique role is in conception . . . since for other purposes men would be better assisted by other men." True, some relaxation of this suspicious fear is evident in a few thirteenth century books of penitence and in some scholastic writers, but the great mass of homilectic literature is still pervaded with hatred and distrust: woman is portrayed as "sin," without qualification. The tradition is an ancient one, going back to Augustine and the early Fathers, above all to St. Jerome, the patron saint of misogynists: "woman is the gate of the devil, the path of wickedness, the sting of the serpent, in a word a perilous object."

The inner schizophrenia of the waning Middle Ages is clearly shown up in the gulf between prevailing theories and social reality. Women, feared by monks and theologians and disdained as the least valuable of all human material, contributed largely by their labours to both urban and rural economic life. Women worked in the fields and sometimes, as among the Germans, were responsible for the entire agricultural routine. Townswomen were active in a wide variety of trades and industries. The women of Paris are known to have been engaged in more than a hundred different occupations. They worked as weavers, embroiderers and retailers; when their husbands died they carried on their businesses with resource and courage, proving themselves master craftsmen in their own right; they were teachers, doctors and merchants, capable of handling the large-scale affairs of foreign trade. In all these fields they acquitted themselves like men. The decline of the German towns in the late Middle Ages is bound up with the suppression of flourishing feminine industries and the replacement of skilled women by men, which created a large female proletariat. This class of distressed women was much augmented by the appalling growth of public prostitution and the moral collapse of Beguinism. We know the extent of the disproportion between men and women in some of the larger towns during the later Middle Ages: for every thousand men Nuremberg had 1,207 women, Basel 1,246 and Rostock 1,295. There was no suitable outlet for their great abilities and no satisfaction for their spiritual and intellectual yearnings.

The women who grew up in the courtly civilisation of the twelfth century had learned to "sing and say," to use their minds and their imaginations, to conduct their lives and loves on a highly-civilised plane. In the later Middle Ages there are a few ecstatic figures, burning with a prophetic flame, who stand out sharply against the undifferentiated mass of oppressed women forced to accept life and men and misery as they found them: these were exceptional women by any standard, women such as Catherine of Siena, who threatened the Popes with dire penalties if they refused to return to Rome from Avignon. The Middle Ages had conspicuously failed to solve the problem of woman's place in society; it was left as a heavy mortgage on the future.

CHAPTER
6

TOWNS AND THEIR DWELLERS

From civic records and other scattered sources scholars have been able to re-create the sights and sounds of medieval town life. Since most urban centers were little more than tiny villages by modern standards, with a population rarely exceeding a thousand souls, the life of the majority of town dwellers usually blended into the surrounding countryside. But some were true cities that by the fifteenth century had grown beyond 100,000 inhabitants. Our selections treat a cross-section of these: London, Paris, Florence, and a few of the more important communities in Germany.

Urban T. Holmes, Jr., recounts the experiences of a twelfth-century youth by the name of Alexander Neckam as he travels from his village to discover the city of London. We are able to share the astonishment and alarm of a country boy at his first sight of densely crowded streets. We observe with him the buildings and houses, the hawkers and artisans, the lame and the blind, the drunks and the toughs, the cries and the smells of a new way of life. We are bound to conclude that medieval society was anything but static and that many urban problems that we regard as modern were well known to medieval people.

Letha Curtis Musgrave focuses on a characteristic creation of medieval town-life: the university. She is less concerned with what students studied than with how they lived, drawing her examples from Bologna, Oxford, and especially Paris. From the beginning, as we can see, town-and-gown relationships were seldom exercises in sweet reason. The institution of student riots, albeit in a distinctly medieval setting, was already well established by the fourteenth century. Students of today are likely to find many of their problems prefigured in the life of their earliest predecessors.

Jean Lucas-Dubreton reconstructs the life of Florentine burghers in the late medieval period. He describes their habits of eating and drinking, and he gives a hilarious rendition of the basic rules of good breeding for the resident of Florence. He also examines the practice of medieval medicine, palmistry, and astrology—all subjects of fad and fashion in the towns of Italy—before closing with a fairly unappetizing account of Florentine funerals.

Fritz Rorig estimates that the German territories still contained few towns of any real consequence before the fifteenth century. Yet the importance of civic tradition, he concludes, should not be neglected. He introduces us to a number of urban types: the merchant, the shopkeeper, the weaver, the worker, the Jew. Finally, he shows the economic and social importance of the medieval trade guilds and thereby locates one important source of future social conflicts.

Social organization in medieval times remained for the most part both personal and local. Apart from the overarching structure of the Church, one finds little evidence in everyday life of large corporations and multi-territorial enterprises. Yet social forms and social concerns do display a remarkable similarity in many areas of Europe, and one might even identify several universal types known to all Europeans: the peasant, the village priest, the artisan, and the small merchant, to name a few. If medieval society was rapidly changing after the twelfth century, many of its characteristic members were steadfast and not soon to disappear from the European scene.

MEDIEVAL LONDON

In 1178 or thereabout, Alexander Neckam, a young clerk teaching in the grammar schools at Dunstable, Bedfords, decided to go to Paris to continue his own studies. The little town of Dunstable was a village in the Chilton Hills, thirty-four miles to the northwest of London, situated at the juncture of two Roman roads. . . .

London, like every other important walled town, teemed with people. The walls were some eighteen feet high. The gates were fitted with double swinging doors of heavy oak, reinforced with iron.[1] Inside the walls, the houses were mostly of wood. Here and there appeared more prosperous ones of stone. These were seldom constructed from regular, hewn blocks of stone. Like the country houses, they were more often made of irregular quartz stones and flints, bonded together by cement. Some of the wooden houses had tile facings; some houses were obviously made with a sort of mud or stucco daubed over a wattle framework or lath. Alexander remarked, at a later date, that foolish people were not content with the practical details of a house. They must have useless ornamental decoration. This comment was highly justified in his day, the Romanesque era. "Gingerbready" is the word that would have come to us if we had beheld what Alexander saw on his visit to London. Stone houses had saw-tooth ornamentations, and elaborate moldings with small lozenges in the intersections, and criss-cross effects. Wooden houses, vastly in the majority, had the same sort of thing executed less skillfully.[2] Exterior decorative paneling such as we are accustomed to associate with Tudor architecture was extremely common. Many of the wooden structures had a little roof lift before the entrance. The beams supporting this could be topped by a heavy ornamental capital, imitating the opening of a flower or the head of a strange bird or animal. Some

From Urban Tignet Holmes, Jr., *Daily Living in the Twelfth Century: Based on the Observations of Alexander Neckam in London and Paris* (Madison, Wis.: Univ. of Wisconsin Press, © 1952 [renewed 1980] by the Board of Regents of the University of Wisconsin System), pp. 18, 25–42, by permission of the publisher.

    1   Naturally we can only imagine the appearance of the wall of London. A city wall and gate are illustrated in a Cambridge MS, Trinity College R. 17.1, dating about 1150. The gate is there flanked by two towers with three upper stories to each tower. The crenelated top of the gate is higher than the walk on the top of the wall. See Dorothy Hartley and Margaret M. Elliot, *Life and Work of the People of England* (New York, 1931), I, Plate 20e.

    2   The description of wooden houses is elaborated from Bayeux Tapestry, No. 48, in Eric MacLagan, *The Bayeux Tapestry* (London, 1945).

wooden piers which extended from the ground to the main roofs had this same type of capital. There were occasional wooden balconies, displaying tile and crossbeam decorations. Around windows and doors the casements were embellished with curlicues, not unlike what we find three centuries later in stone-decorated Gothic. Stone houses often showed the typical Norman chimney stack, that is, a conical cap pierced with smoke holes, rising from a cornice enriched with zig-zag ornaments.[3]

Nearly all the smaller houses were in solid rows, not detached, extending down the street. They housed tradesmen who manufactured their goods on their own front premises. The lower floor of such houses resembled a sort of booth with a low counter extending across the front. An opening in the counter gave passage in and out. This was the type of workshop used by knife-maker, baker, armorer, or other tradesman. To one side there was a small spiral stair which led up to the main dwelling room. The stair well was a little tower which could be placed inside or outside the principal walls of the building. In these rows of houses it was surely inside. Upstairs was the *salle,* or main room, with ornamental windows facing on the street. There the wife of the household reigned supreme—during business hours, anyway. . . . We should notice that the floors of both shop and *salle* were strewn with rushes, green in summer, dry in winter.[4] The houses of wood were smeared with paint—most commonly red, blue, and black—which had a pitch and linseed base and gave constant promise of fires. It was hoped that by providing stone walls, to the height of sixteen feet, between adjacent houses this menace would be reduced.[5]

The street through which Alexander walked after passing the guard at

3   J. P. Bushe-Fox, *Old Sarum. Official Guide* (London, 1934), p. 12.

4   I cannot give my exact references for his impression of the houses of the time. It is a conglomerate of personal impressions acquired over some years from visiting extant houses in England, France, and Italy, combined with a study of illustrations and reading in texts. Some details will be easily traced. Houses at Chartres show the ornamental windows on the principal floor. In *Aucassin et Nicolette,* ed. R. W. Linker (1948), there is mention of the small pillar of stone in the center of such a window: *le noua au piler de la fenestre* (§12).

5   The Assizes of 1189 established certain housing ordinances. The text from which we are quoting is that given in Thomas Stapleton's *De antiquis legibus liber* (Camden Society, No.34, London, 1846), pp. 206–11. The greater part of the city had been built of wood previous to the fire of 1135–1136 which destroyed from the Bridge to St. Clement's Dane (p. 210). To encourage construction in stone the Assizes gave many privileges to the owner of a stone house, over his less affluent neighbor. If anyone should have a stone wall on his own land to the height of sixteen feet, his neighbor must make a drain and receive in it, on his land, the water shed from the stone wall and carry it across his land, unless it can be brought into the King's street, and nothing must be constructed by him on the aforesaid wall when he builds near it. If he does not build he must continue to receive the water shed from the stone wall, without damage to the owner of the wall (p. 208). A common stone wall cannot be altered without the consent of both parties. *Garde-robe* pits, not walled, must be dug five and a half feet away from the neighbor's boundary; if walled, the pit can be only two and a half feet. A window facing upon a neighbor's land can have its view cut off by subsequent building unless a specific agreement forbidding this has once been made. One who is building is forbidden to make a *pavimentum in vico regio ad nocimentum civitatis et vicini sui injuste* (p. 211).

Aldersgate was some ten feet across. It was a main thoroughfare, but not a principal street of the city. It led to Newgate Street and St. Paul's churchyard. Alexander would surely have been aware that the marvelous cathedral of St. Paul's
was still under construction. Its tower was not yet erected. The stone used, like
that of the Temple [the stronghold of the Knights Templar], was being
transported from Normandy. After going around the churchyard by another
street, Alexander and his companion crossed the important thoroughfare that led
to Ludgate and then found themselves in the purlieus of the two keeps, or don-
jons, which hugged the western wall of the city. These were the keep of Mont-
Fichet, and a larger one directly on the river, known as Castle Baynard.[6] These
crenelated towers were badly crowded in by tradesmen's dwellings. Alexander
tells a story—an old folk tale, to be sure—about a monkey which slept on the
wall of such a tower, right above a poor shoemaker's window. The monkey had
a habit of creeping down and imitating the shoemaker, cutting up his leather.
The shoemaker ran the blunt side of his knife across his own throat, thus inspir-
ing the animal to imitate him and commit suicide with the sharp edge.[7] . . .

Alexander's companion may have told him, as they looked over the reaches
of the Thames, perhaps from the wooden bridge, about the water tourney which
was held on the river during Holy Week. A tree was set up in the river, and
young men would stand at the prow of small boats being rowed swiftly down the
stream and aim with a lance at the target on the tree. If a lance was broken on
the target, the boy was hailed as a victor. If he missed, he was tossed into the
water and then picked up by another boat that stood by. For this occasion the
bridge and the balconies of houses facing the Thames were crowded with people.
Perhaps at this point Alexander and his companion may have turned to thoughts
of sliding on wintry ice. On Mooresfield, at the north side of the wall, there was
still a marsh. When this was frozen in winter, young men would strap the shin-
bones of horses to the soles of their feet and slide rapidly along, aided by a pole
shod with iron. Often the more mischievous boys would strike at each other with
the pole as they shot past. There were many accidents. Ordinary sliding on the
ice was also quite common. Still another sport was to seat someone on a cake of
ice and pull him along.[8]

Remembering [an] agreement to call again at Dowgate [where ships from
Normandy liked to tie up], Alexander now turned back toward the western end
of the city.

There is no evidence, one way or the other, that Thames Street was paved,

---

6 "On the west are two castles strongly fortified. . . ." [John Stow, *A Survey of London*,
with Fitzstephen in the Appendix (London, 1908], p. 502. [Hereafter referred to as F. S.]
Marie de France wrote of two such castles, side by side, divided only by a single curtain wall,
in her *Laostic*, vv. 35–44.

7 Thomas Wright (ed.), *Alexandri Neckam De naturis rerum . . . with the poem of the same
author, De laudibus divinae sapiential* (Rollo Series, London, 1863), p. 209. Hereafter referred to
as N.R.

8 F.S., pp. 506, 508–509.

with an old Roman pavement, but it surely was. Otherwise the mud would have been inevitable and the waterfront could not have been approached to any advantage. This was no low quarter of town, despite the crowds of seamen. In summer these sailors wore nothing but *braies,* or wide underdrawers, and possibly a snood cap, tied under the chin. Their hair was often long enough to curl at the back of the neck. Doubtless they had the usual part in the middle, affected by all classes and both sexes. The average man in the twelfth century did not shave more than once a week, and a short, dark stubble was the common thing. Many seaman wore true beards. On cooler days the seaman wore a coarse *gonne,* or frock, which he pulled up at the waist, over a belt, when he was obliged to step into the water.[9]

As we have said, this was not a low part of town. There was much wealth on display. In that time and age, wealth was shown by cloth heavy with gold and silver thread, brocades, and dark and cloudy gems, cut roughly into cabochon shape, which were encrusted on almost anything, from a helmet to the metal covering of a manuscript book. Silks and spices, which were imported at considerable effort and expense from the East, were another indication of *richesse.* When we consider that silks were transported by sea—sometimes by land—from China to India, from there to the Red Sea region by water, and finally down the Nile to the Mediterranean area, where they were picked up by Italian merchants, it is not hard to understand why their price advanced; and yet most well-to-do people had silken garments, and even silken sheets. Thames Street displayed much of this southern wealth, as well as the northern wealth of expensive furs.

There was something in the air of a medieval community such as London which we moderns are apt to forget. This thing was authority. There was unquestionably much mob violence and considerable injustice on all sides practiced everywhere daily. But even an outraged person felt awed by authority, whatever form it took. The *ribauz,* or good-for-nothings, were always on the edge of a crowd. They begged and plundered at the slightest provocation. They hung around outside the door of the banquet hall when a large feast was held. The king of England had three hundred bailiffs whose duty it was—though not all at one time—to keep these people back as food was moved from the kitchens to the hall, and to see that guests were not disturbed.[10] Frequently in twelfth-century romances a beautiful damsel is threatened with the awful fate of being turned over to the *ribauz.*[11] Nothing more horrible can be imagined. These people accompanied armies on their expeditions, helping in menial tasks and plundering what was left by the knights and other fighting men. And yet they were kept under control by authority. I imagine that the news that Walter Fitzrobert, lord

9 Bayeux Tapestry, No. 4.

10 Gaimar, *Estorie des Engleis,* ed. Thomas Wright (London, 1850), vv. 5981-98. Similarly in *Ille et Galeron,* ed. Löseth (Paris 1890), vv. 4100-4102.

11 As in the *Tristan* where Iseult receives such treatment from King Marc.

of Baynard Castle, was coming down Thames Street would have caused such vagrants to scatter out of the way. In similar fashion the *gouverneur* of a seagoing vessel doubtless had a presence of authority as he moved along the quays. A twelfth-century mob could be unruly, but it was seldom completely lacking in discipline. Up the social ladder, the same observations could be made about the men-at-arms. The Count of Baynard, the Lord of MontFichet, the Constable of the Tower, and others of the King's immediate officers allowed their men a liberty which they could control if they wished. These men were bound by feudal oaths, or by villeinage. On the other hand, when the king was weak, as was Stephen, and again John, the serjants and knights of London must have been a plague to every merchant and every visitor. This is what Fitzstephen meant when he said that London was a fine city when it had a good governor.[12] Rebellion in twelfth-century England and France meant attachment to another overlord; it did not mean becoming a law unto oneself, unless the rebel chanced to be placed very high. When a prominent noble came to town, crowds of people of all classes would flock around him on the streets, anxious to see his dress and his equipment.[13]

It was not unsafe for a man such as Alexander Neckam to walk along the quays in the year 1178. He was only a clerk, and the occasional *ribaut* or man-at-arms who was looking for trouble did not make himself objectionable to a stray cleric. These young men dressed in black were under the jurisdiction of the Church, which, in the person of her bishops, was capable of avenging any outrage that might be visited upon her children by a layman, or king's man. Knowing this quite well, the students and other young clergy often took full advantage of their position within a town. They roamed in groups, heading for the ball field without the walls on the afternoon of a holy day, but sometimes just looking for sport at the expense of others. A precept of the time was "Be wise with the wise, but relax and play the fool when you are with fools."[14] The medieval man loved a good laugh. He got this most often in ways that we would consider impolite or cruel. Running off with signs and other objects that were not fastened down, pitching unoffending creatures into the water, baiting an animal, mocking a man who had been the victim of misfortune—these were everyday sources of amusement. The streets of London, or of any other medieval town, showed a high percentage of mutilated and diseased people. The one-armed, the one-legged, the blind, the half-witted, and the just plain drunk were numerous. These unfortunates could furnish much amusement as they moved about awkwardly. The mockery was not often deep, and I dare say the victim sometimes joined in.

---

12 F.S., p. 503.

13 Such was certainly the case in the thirteenth century. Crowds gathered around the Earl of Gloucester in London, and the Earl of Oxford was greeted in the same way in Boulogne. See *Blonde d'Oxford,* vv. 2458ff., 5484ff. Those who have received Ille's charity crowd about him as he passes through the streets—*Ille et Galeron,* vv. 3788–99.

14 Scheludko in *Archivum Romanicum,* XI, 278.

In a town where there was no sewerage, with *garde-robe* pits or privies in the better houses only, it is to be expected that the natural functions were much in evidence. Walls were dirty, and unless there had been a recent rain, the roadway was smelly. The *odeur de merde* was never completely absent from anyone's nostrils. People were used to it; but we must not assume that nobody ever complained. There is a story told by Jacques de Vitry of a man whose job it was to clean out *garde-robe* pits. He did not mind this odor in which he worked all day, but his nostrils were badly offended by the smell of a snuffed candle.[15] The fastidious and very clean persons were rather few in the twelfth century, but they existed. In all ages, except perhaps in prehistoric ones, there have been three kinds of people: the fastidious, the nonfastidious, and those—greatest in number—who are neither one nor the other but conform more or less to circumstances. Today the fastidious are vastly in the majority in those levels of society which most university people frequent. In the twelfth century the proportions were different.

15   *Die Exempla des Jakob von Vitry*, ed. Joseph Greven (SMLT, 1914), No. 97.

—LETHA CURTIS MUSGRAVE—————————

MEDIEVAL UNIVERSITY LIFE

When Oxford draws knife,
England's soon at strife

As the old rhyme indicates, university riots are nothing new. In medieval times internecine disputes often spread far beyond the student community; and frequently the scholars banded together in bloody battles against the townspeople. In fact, "town and gown" riots were an important factor in the gradual development of the early universities. Far from being formally founded, with rights and limitations clearly defined, these institutions grew up haphazard. During the revival of learning known as "the Renaissance of the Twelfth Century," which introduced Arabian arithmetic, texts of Roman law, and the works of ancient

From Letha Curtis Musgrave, "Medieval University Life," *History Today*, 22, no. 2 (February 1972), 120–27, by permission of the author.

philosophers into Western Europe, groups of students gathered, usually at the site of a cathedral school, to hear lectures on the new subjects. For convenience and safety, the students and their teachers soon began to organize into unions, or guilds, called *universitates;* and it was purely by accident that the term came later to mean an accredited seat of higher learning.

At Bologna, the chief center for the study of Roman law, the guilds exercised a degree of power that modern students might consider enviable. The Cismontane University—men from Italy—and the Transmontane University—men from outside Italy—acting together through two groups of deputies headed by a rector, made strict rules for their teachers, even limiting them to one day's absence when they got married. If a master failed to attract more than five listeners to a lecture, he was obliged to pay a fine; and other Southern European universities, such as the great medical schools at Salerno and Naples, used Bologna as a pattern.

At Paris, on the other hand, the model for most universities in Northern Europe, a strong guild of masters governed. As an institution, Paris developed directly from the cathedral school of Notre-Dame, which was renowned for its great teacher and theologian, Peter Abelard. Largely through Abelard's eminence, Paris became the center for the study of theology. It was also an important center for the study of the liberal arts, which were prerequisites for law and medicine, as well as for theology. Thus, although they ranged in age from fifteen to sixty, most of the Paris students were younger than those at Bologna or Salerno. Moreover, the theological interest tended to emphasize authority. Hence, the masters, rather than the students, made the rules. The students, however, had their own organizations. Upon arrival at the school of their choice, they were assigned to a "nation," supposedly on the basis of their homeland, although the divisions were rather artificial, and often led to controversy. At Paris, there were four nations—France, Normandy, Picardy, and England. They chose the rector; and, as each had a key to the fourfold lock of the money-chest, and representatives from all four must be present when the chest was opened, it is scarcely surprising that disputes were numerous.

Quarrels between the two Oxford nations, established in 1252, the Northernmen and Southernmen, were apt to be particularly savage; and, as the couplet quoted above shows, they often spread beyond the confines of the university. One of these fights, which took place in the fourteenth century, and was described by Adam of Usk, ringleader of the southern faction, as "a grave misfortune . . . whence arose broils, quarrels and ofttimes loss of life," lasted two whole years. In the first year, the Northernmen were driven away from the University; but they managed to stage a comeback, and indicted many Southernmen for causing a felonious riot. Although he was finally acquitted, Adam had been much alarmed. "From that day forth," he wrote, "I feared the king . . . and I put hooks into my jaws."

Far more important than brawls of this kind were the "town and gown" riots, in which students, usually supported by the university authorities, united against the townsmen to obtain greater privileges. The theoretical right of the town to exercise control over the university was never denied; the problem in dispute was just how far the town's right extended, and in what manner it should be exercised. Economic problems also played a part—especially the vital question of what constituted reasonable rents; for the earliest university students had to find lodgings in the town.

Thus the aims of the bellicose medieval student bore little resemblance to those of the twentieth-century rioter, who is usually protesting against the policies pursued by the university administration. No less different are medieval and modern tactics. Whereas present-day students often attempt to enforce their demands by occupying and barricading university buildings, at a medieval university they had no such buildings to invade; and the rioters fought their battles in the streets or local taverns. The fact that they had no buildings of their own, however, gave the early universities an important tactical advantage in their struggles with the townspeople—they could threaten to migrate en masse to another city if their demands were not met.

This was a formidable economic weapon; for the university personnel, including the barbers, copyists, bookbinders and others who served the students, and would move away with them, usually exceeded the townsfolk in number. Some universities owed their beginnings to migrations; Cambridge University, for example, was founded after the battle of 1209 (which we shall be describing later), by indignant emigrés from Oxford. A migration to Padua forced the city fathers of Bologna to grant students a number of civil rights, including the all-important right to strike, or migrate, if they could get satisfaction by no other means.

The earliest recorded "town and gown" riot led to the first known charter of privileges, which was granted by Philip Augustus to the University of Paris in 1200. Besides formally recognizing many existing rights, it allowed students to be tried in ecclesiastical courts, rather than in the much more severe lay courts. A more important struggle occurred in 1229, when a few students, out for a walk, decided to stop for some "good, sweet wine." A dispute over the bill passed from words "to the pulling of ears and tearing of hair." The innkeeper called upon his neighbors to help him drive the students out; but they returned next day with reinforcements. Thus the quarrel grew, until the Queen Regent, Blanche of Castile, sent in troops and several students were killed. "Spouting scurrilous poems" about the alleged relations between Blanche and her adviser, the Papal Legate, a large body of masters and students departed for Toulouse, Orleans and elsewhere.

When the remaining masters had threatened to close the university for six years, Pope Gregory IX intervened, and granted the "Magna Carta" of Paris. This document, issued in 1231, recognized the university's right to regulate dress, lectures, funerals and prices of lodgings—above all, its right to migrate if demands were not met; and these privileges were included in grants to new universities for the next two hundred years. But the charter did not satisfy everyone. The Chancellor complained of too much organization and university business, saying that in the old days, when each master taught himself, there was "more zeal for study."

At Oxford, we first hear of a conflict between students and townspeople in the year 1209. Two or three students were then hanged after a pitched battle in which a townsman had been killed, perhaps accidentally, by a rioting scholar. Five years later, the University obtained from the Papal Legate a document that required townsmen who had taken part in the hanging to do penance by marching in procession, barefoot, to the victims' unconsecrated graves, and thence to the cemetery, where the dead were given proper burial. Practical privileges, in the form of rent refunds, a ten-year rent ceiling, and lower food prices, were also obtained by the University. Yet, until as late as 1533, when an attempt was made to force a college election with clubs and swords, Oxford life was often violent; and, according to the nineteenth-century historian, Hastings Rashdall,[1] more blood has been shed in Oxford High Street than upon many a battlefield. Masters often encouraged students to commit crimes, like the professor charged with persuading his students to kill a priest who had offended him, or the proctor who, in 1526, "sate uppon a blocke in the streete afore the shoppe of one Robert Jermyns, a barber, havinge a pole axe in his hand, a black cloake on his backe, and a hatt on his head," and organized a riot in which many townsmen were "stricken downe and sore beaten."

A large percentage of entries on the Oxford coroners' rolls deal with riot-deaths. Indeed, of the twenty-nine coroners' inquests held between 1297 and 1322, twelve were concerned with murders committed by scholars, many of which seem to have been countenanced by the University. Such offences frequently went unpunished. After a riot between Northernmen and Southernmen in 1314, of thirty-nine students known to have committed manslaughter, only seven were apprehended, the others having claimed "privilege of the clergy," fled to sanctuary—thereby incurring banishment—or escaped altogether. Robert of Bridlington, for example, who sat in the window of Gutter Hall and shot an arrow through Henry of Holy Isle, survived for many years, only to lose his life at last in yet another town and gown affray.

Like the Paris riot in 1229, the most famous Oxford town and gown battle, on St Scholastica's Day, February 10th, 1354, grew out of a tavern dispute. In addition to killing and wounding several students, the townsmen scalped their fallen adversaries, removing the skin from some of the university chaplains' heads down to the tonsure. The university sought vengeance through the King, who went so far as to grant it control over the market and a certain amount of jurisdiction over the city itself. The Bishop of Lincoln also placed the townsmen

---

1 1858–1924; author of *Universities of Europe in the Middle Ages,* 1895.

under interdict, which was removed only on condition that the mayor and bailiffs and "three-score of the chiefest Burghers" should "personally appear" in St. Mary's Church every St Scholastica's Day to attend a mass for the souls of the slain. Each of these functionaries was to offer one penny at the altar, of which forty pence would be distributed to forty poor university scholars—a custom that survived until the nineteenth century.

This struggle is typical of the many riots in which the university managed to gain support both from the Church and from the secular government. After a riot, university officials would appeal to the King, who nearly always solved the dispute, as he had done after the St Scholastica's Day battle, by giving the head of the university increased power. If he hesitated, the university could usually rely on support from the Pope, as in the Paris riot of 1229. The limits of town control were largely established both through the riots themselves and through agreements—or, more often, the papal decrees and/or royal grants—that followed them; and thus the universities acquired an independence that helped to make them what they are today.

Yet, oddly enough, the independence they gained had little to do with our modern ideas of freedom. In the Middle Ages, truth was expounded, not sought. It was revealed by authority, not discovered by research, which must be free if it is to be objective. So long as the masters, therefore, stayed within the accepted bounds of dogma, they were allowed to teach pretty much as they pleased. In the climate of their time, they did not feel cramped by the rule of authority, as twentieth-century professors would; and the students they taught willingly accepted the curriculum. Although there were intermittent disputes over the teaching of Aristotle, his works had been reconciled with the Christian faith and become a fixed part of the curriculum by the middle of the thirteenth century. In Paris, during the course of that century only one case is recorded of a teacher being imprisoned for propagating theological errors; and only one other was deprived of the right to teach because of his heretical notions. Thus, in general, the masters taught as they wished. Even if they were accused of heresy, they could usually save themselves by falling back on a convenient doctrine of the time—that what was true in philosophy might be false in theology, and vice versa.

A glance at what was included in the medieval curriculum makes it plain that, apart from questions of theological heresy, there was little chance of controversy over subject-matter. The university course began with the Seven Liberal Arts—the *Trivium* and the *Quadrivium*. The *Trivium* included grammar, usually studied in verse form through Alexander de Villa Dei's *Doctrinale;* rhetoric, the art of letter writing; and dialectic, mainly the study of Aristotle's philosophy and logic. The *Quadrivium* included arithmetic; geometry, which comprised Euclid plus some geography; music, which included notation, singing and the numerical relations of sound; and astronomy, which was little more than astrology. After completing the Liberal Arts, usually at Paris, the student who wished to do graduate work in law would journey to Bologna, to absorb the laws of the Roman Emperor Justinian through an elaborate series of commentaries known as the Glosses. For medicine he might remain at Paris for six more years, to study the works of Hippocrates and Galen, his only laboratory work being the dissection of pigs. If he was more daring, he would go to Italy, where he could learn anatomy by dissecting human cadavers.

For theology, the highest study of all, he would remain at Paris, using as his primary textbook—not the Bible, but Peter Lombard's *Four Books of Sentences,* a series of questions answered by the authority of the Scriptures and the Fathers of the Church. These included such moot points as how many angels could dance at once on the point of a needle, and whether glorified souls spent the next world in the empyrean or in the crystalline heaven—as well as a number of other problems that had a more direct bearing upon human life.

For the privilege of following this rather limited curriculum, most students of the Middle Ages were prepared to go through dreadful hardships. Getting to the chosen school was, in the first place, far from simple. Unless the scholar was a nobleman, he had usually to make the journey on foot, finding free lodging at monasteries. Wearing a coarse tunic, laden only with his wax tablets and a stylus at his girdle, a packet of bread and herbs and salt on his back, he had little to fear from the robbers that infested the roads. But, if he were rich, he might travel by coach with an armed retinue to protect him, his clothing and books, his precious letter of introduction and album in which his professors and fellow students would later sign their names and write mottoes.

When he arrived at his university, he suffered mild persecution from upper classmen. He was called "yellowbeak," "cock of the walk," or "greenie." He might be bullied by being dressed in an oxhide, complete with horns, then sprinkled with earth and made to pass a mock examination, or go through more strenuous antics to rid himself of his beastly nature. The newcomer soon discovered that he had better hasten to brush up his Latin; for all university men were required to converse in that language. Student dictionaries and conversation manuals came to his rescue, providing models of proper discourse for all situations—quarrelling with his roommate; borrowing money; falling in love and recovering; visiting the jugglers in the marketplace; getting into trouble for breaking rules; and even inviting his masters to a banquet, preceded by a free bath, upon the occasion of receiving his degree. To make sure his manners would be acceptable, he might also consult a manual of etiquette, which instructed him to wash his hands in the morning and his face, too, if he had the time; to eat with only three fingers; not to pick his teeth with his knife; and not to gnaw bones but to throw them on the floor.

Once he was settled at the university, his life was not altogether pleasant. Rising at four or five o'clock, he descended a narrow staircase and washed at a common trough in the courtyard. First, he attended mass. Then, usually without breakfast, he made his way through the dark streets to a square, a cloister or sometimes a stable, where he sat on a bundle of straw, listening to lectures until ten or eleven o'clock. After a meagre meal, he returned to school for the "meridian disputations," and spent the afternoon hearing repetitions of lectures. If he were lucky enough to have access to any of the few available manuscripts, he might study the next day's lessons—unless he decided to drink.

For drinking was the chief amusement of most of the students. Everything—the arrival of a new master, the end of examinations, even the funeral of a classmate—might be the excuse for a drinking bout. Among the heaviest drinkers were the wandering students called the Goliards (after Golias, the twelfth-century "Archpoet," who drifted from school to school, sometimes carrying for show only, huge wide-margined, red-bound books). Although they did little studying, they sang songs and wrote poetry, including a large number of ribald or romantic drinking songs. Gambling, too, was so prevalent that, in 1274, the Paris masters had to forbid students to shake dice on an altar in Notre-Dame while mass was being celebrated. Covered baskets of wafers were frequent stakes at dice; the winning students hung their baskets from their windows.

At Oxford and Cambridge colleges, the student had an especially strict routine. Besides "noxious, inordinate, unlawful and unhonest sports"—which included chess—the rules prohibited "light and idle talk," dancing, and musical instruments. The student had only two meals a day, and in his room did without heat and light. At dinner, an upper classman read from the Bible or from a book of martyrology. For one hour after this edifying meal, conversation and walking were permitted. In cold weather, the walk was almost a run, for it was the only means of warming the feet before one went to bed. Yet, despite this Spartan routine and the frequent disturbances to which they were exposed, many students worked hard, and even enjoyed their university career—like Richard Wyck, the thirteenth-century Bishop of Chichester, who felt that "in all his days, he had never after led so pleasant and delectable a life." Though poverty stricken, he even gave up the chance to go home and marry a rich and beautiful girl, saying that a young man "may always get a wife, but science once lost can never be recovered." Wyck must have been as conscientious as the many students who did their best to obey the six rules for study set forth by Robert de Sorbon, the Paris lecturer, active during the later thirteenth century, for whom the Sorbonne was originally named. According to Sorbon, the student should:

1. Consecrate a fixed hour to each study . . .
2. Fix the attention upon what is read, and do not pass over it lightly.
3. Extract from the daily reading . . . some truth, and grave it upon the memory with special care.
4. Write out a résumé, for words which are not confined to writing fly away like dust before the wind.
5. Discuss the matter with fellow students . . .
6. Pray. . . .

If he followed these rules reasonably well, and managed to avoid being killed in a riot—or, like one Bolognese scholar, being attacked with a cutlass in the classroom—the medieval student, at the end of his course, could hope to receive a bachelor's degree. He might go on for a licentiate and a master's degree, which in many places would both entitle him to noble rank and enable him to teach at a university. To obtain it, he had either to bribe his masters or pass a difficult examination, promising not to knife the examiner should he fail. As part of the test, he had to teach a sample lesson to a "shrewd boy," with the aid of a rod and a palmer—for inflicting corporal punishment on the palms. If he wielded these vigorously enough, he qualified as a future teacher and, provided he had the means, could then celebrate with a banquet.

Not many could. A constant need for money is one problem that medieval and modern university students have in common. A six-hundred-year-old version of a familiar letter runs as follows: "I crave your kindness, my respected father, devoutly, so that fatherly reverence may consider it worthy to give me some money with which I can now manage in school until the Feast of St Michael." Often the medieval scholar was able to supplement his father's contribution by copying manuscripts or carrying holy water. But abject poverty was the rule, except among the sons of noblemen; and many students were forced to maintain their existence by begging. We read of a trio of friends who were so poor that they had only two tunics among them. One wore a tunic and their single bonnet to lectures, while the others remained in their miserable room, one wearing the other tunic and the third staying in bed.

To alleviate the students' poverty, as well as to provide better discipline, the collegiate system developed. Bolognese students first organized residential halls as early as the twelfth century; and their plan rapidly spread to Paris and Oxford. During the second half of the thirteenth century, philanthropists, troubled by the plight of poor scholars, founded special hostels for their benefit. The universities gradually assumed control of all these residences, which were called "colleges," and required students to take up residence there. Originally the colleges were only dormitories; later, students were instructed under the college roof by the masters in charge. A few students, however, managed to avoid living in the colleges and continued to lodge in the towns. Known as "chamber deacons," they were responsible for a good percentage of the violence and marauding attributed to the student body. An Oxford statute of 1410 complained that the chamber deacons "sleep all day, and at night roam about taverns and houses of ill fame for opportunity of robbery and homicide;" and, in 1413, King Henry V banished the Irish deacons, hoping to bring greater tranquillity to his realm.

The crimes that chamber deacons committed led to the passing of laws that made it a more serious offence to be abroad after curfew than to shoot an arrow at a proctor with intent to wound him. Yet, although plenty of idlers, like the

Goliards and the chamber deacons, must always have swelled the university ranks, during the Middle Ages, just as today, no doubt the typical university student had a genuine love of learning. Like Chaucer's Oxford scholar, "gladly wolde he lerne, and gladly teche." For, had there not been many such students, the medieval universities could not have exerted so wide an influence both on their own time and on future ages.

—JEAN LUCAS-DUBRETON————————————————

HOME LIFE IN FLORENCE

The Florentine was a home-bird because he was economical. He considered it "harmful, costly, annoying and inconvenient to change houses," and, as far as possible, he tried not to sink to the level of a lodger; but to have his own house in a respectable quarter so that his wife should make only honourable acquaintances. He did not like separating his family because to live under the same roof appeared to him to have solid advantages, if only because it economised lighting and heating.

Like most Italians, he was neither a drunkard nor a glutton; but, though the excesses of the Swiss and the Germans disgusted him, he was not averse to good cheer.

The first family meal was taken between nine and ten in the morning, the second before nightfall. In the days of "modesty and sobriety" these meals had been of the simplest. Husband and wife ate from the same dish and drank from the same cup, the menu being mainly composed of bread, "herbs," jam and fruit. Meat was eaten only on Sundays, and when a pig was slaughtered, one gave black-pudding to one's neighbor, who was angry if one forgot to. The fare became more delicate as the years went by. Boiled kid or peacock might now be served, followed by coloured jellies in the shape of little men or animals. This Florentine invention was made of almond-milk and other ingredients, colored with saffron, or *zafferano* as it was called, and sometimes even scented. Pastry came in only with the sixteenth century.

From Jean Lucas-Dubreton, *Daily Life in Florence in the Time of the Medici* trans. A. Lytton Sells (New York: Macmillan, 1961), pp. 115–23, by permission of Hachette, Paris.

For a burgher or merchant—it was the same thing in Florence—entertaining was an obligation. It meant business-customers as well as friends. Here, according to an expert adviser, were the requisites for a pleasant dinner-party: the guests should not be less than three, or more than nine, because, if more are invited, they will be too many to listen to each other or hold consecutive conversation—which may be profitable—and because asides spoil the pleasure and create confusion. One should therefore invite a reasonable number of people, sociable and on good terms with each other; they should be entertained in a pleasant room, at a convenient hour, and the service should be faultless. The guests should be neither babblers nor of taciturn disposition, but moderate talkers. The topics of conversation should not be subtle, uncertain or hard to understand, but gay, amusing and useful. One must not forget to be practical.

The table is set facing the garden-door which lets in the fresh air. The host has a ewer of water passed round so that the company may wash their hands. They then take their places, ladies alternating with gentlemen. Slices of melon are served, then a *berlingozzo*, which is a cake made of flour, eggs and sugar. This is followed by boiled capon, fat and in perfect condition, prime quality sausages and veal, a good stew, roast chicken,[1] or else thrushes, pigeons or pheasants, and sometimes trout, "to appease the voluptuous and so fit the mind to cope with the things of this world. Something must be allowed to the weakness of the flesh."

This was a rich man's menu for festive occasions. There would be music for merriment: the kettle-drum, played with two sticks, or the jew's harp, an iron band bent double and fitted with a steel tongue to serve as a spring. It was held between the teeth, and the tongue vibrated as you pushed it with your finger. While this was going on, the servant would be running backwards and forwards from the kitchen and grumbling about her mistress: "She works hard talking, and I walking, and I have only two legs and down-at-heel shoes."

These Florentine banquets were, by the way, matched by the meals usually eaten in France, at least in the sixteenth century, if we are to believe the economist Jean Bodin, whose strictures are violent: "People are not satisfied, at an ordinary dinner, to have three dishes; boiled meat, roast meat and fruit. They must have meats prepared in five or six different ways, with so many sauces, mincemeats, pastries and every kind of hotch-potch and other fancy dish, that there is great intemperance."

But Florence was ahead of France in the use of that instrument which the Latinists designated as a *fuscina* and we call a fork. It was considered vulgar to dip one's fingers in the gravy; one should pick up the food one wants either with a knife or a fork.[2]

---

1 Did all the guests take all these courses? Probably not, but we do not know. If however (another query) the Florentines were still on the two-meal-a-day régime, this would make a great difference to their capacity. (Translator)

2 The fork, like so many of the amenities of civilisation, was invented in Italy. It does not appear to have been much in vogue in England before the end of the seventeenth century. (Translator)

The average Florentine, of course, dined less expensively than the rich merchant. He would begin with a salad, followed perhaps by a small pigeon, goat's milk cheese and fruit. He was very fond of *fegatelli,* a sort of liver sausage. But his basic diet was already *pasta,* which he prepared in various ways, while the preachers railed at his self-indulgence. "You are great gourmands," cried one of them. "It's not enough for you to eat fried *pasta,* but you must flavor it with garlic. When you eat *ravioli,* it's not enough for you to boil them in the pan and eat them with the broth, but you must then fry them in another pan, together with cheese."

Wine, too, had its votaries, and everyone sang the praises of Vernaccia, Trebbiàno, etc. "Drunk in moderation, it nourishes the body, improves the blood, hastens digestion, calms the intellect, makes the heart joyful, enlivens the spirits, expells wind, increases the warmth of the body, fattens convalescents, rouses the appetite, purifies the blood, removes obstructions, distributes nourishment in the right places, gives color and health to the cheeks," and so on. It was the object of a cult. Luigi Pulci writes in the *Morgante Maggiore:* "I believe no more in black than in white, but I believe in boiled or roasted capon, and I also believe in butter and beer. . . .[3] But above all I have faith in good wine and deem that he who believes in it is saved."

Drunkards and gluttons were not however in favour. To have a good time but without swilling and gormandizing—that was the rule for most people, and they practised a delicate epicureanism. An English protonotary apostolic, who was staying in Florence and had been accustomed like his fellow-countrymen to spending four hours at table, was amazed by Florentine sobriety and ended by conforming to it.

There was no lack of inns and taverns in the city, and one of them, the Tavern of the Snail, near the Mercato Vecchio, was famous. Better-class citizens did not usually frequent them; but if a merchant's wife and children had left for the country, he would take his meals there—unless friends had invited him out—and return home only at bedtime.

The rules of courtesy and good manners are set out by a talented writer, Giovanni della Casa,[4] in the *Galateo,* a sort of manual which shows how Florentines behaved—or should behave.

When you are eating, do not masticate noisily[5] "or crouch gluttonously over

---

3   "Cervisia," to be exact. It was the kind of beer the Romans made.

4   Della Casa was born in the Mugello; he published the *Galateo* in 1558. He is famous also for his sonnets, of which the form influenced Milton. (Translator)

5   A Frenchman observed in this connexion: "The Germans keep their mouths shut when masticating, and consider any other way unsightly. The French on the contrary half open their mouths and consider the German way unsightly. The Italians go about it very gently, the French rather more briskly, and they consider the Italian way too refined" (cf. A. Lefranc, *La Vie quotidienne au temps de la Renaissance,* p. 150).

the food without raising your face, as if you were blowing a trumpet. Don't hic-cup. That is not eating but devouring; and then too you soil your hands and even your elbows, and dirty the cloth.''

Avoid rubbing your teeth with your napkin, or, worse still, with your fingers. Do not scratch yourself, or spit, or at least only do it ''reservedly.'' ''I have heard,'' remarks Della Casa, ''that there are nations so polite that they never spit; and we might well refrain from spitting. . . . Inviting people to drink repeatedly is not one of our habits and we describe it by means of a foreign word: *'fare brindisi,'* a reprehensible custom which one should not adopt. I thank Heaven that, among the scourges that have come from beyond the Alps (a reference to Germany and France), this one, which is the worst, has not gained a footing here; I mean, to consider it amusing and even estimable to get drunk.''

In no circumstances should you bend over the glass of wine or the plate, where someone else is going to drink or eat, in order to take a sniff. And do not offer your neighbour a pear or other fruit which you have already bitten.

On rising from table, do not stick your toothpick in the back of your mouth, which makes you look like a bird carrying a twig to its nest; and do not wear your toothpick in your collar—a strange accoutrement for a gentleman. After blowing your nose, do not look into your handkerchief as if pearls or rubies had been deposited in it; and do not drum with your fingers on the table or wave your legs about. This shows little consideration for other people.

If you wish to speak with someone, do not go so close to him as to be breathing in his face. One does not always like to smell other people's breath. And do not nudge people with your elbow, and repeat: ''Isn't that true? And what do *you* think? And Messer So-and-So?''

Avoid expressing yourself affectedly, ''with the point of the fork''—*favellar in punto della forchetta.* Do not for ever be talking about your wife, or the children, or the nurse; and refrain from long descriptions of your dreams, as though they were wonderful or important.

To lavish advice on those who have not asked for it is equivalent to saying that you are wiser than they, and that they are incompetent. This can only be done between close friends. And the same applies to counsels of health. To say with the gravity of a physician: ''You ought to take *this* electuary, or *that* kind of pill,'' is like trying to clean another man's field when one's own is full of thorns and nettles.

In conversation, generally, do not be so anxious to hold the ball that you snatch it from your neighbour, ''as one often sees a hen in a farmyard snatching a straw out of the beak of another.'' And if you want to make the company laugh, refrain from twisting your mouth, rolling your eyes, puffing out your cheeks or making other grimaces. ''The goddess Pallas amused herself for a time by playing on the bagpipes. She became an expert player. But one day, being thus occupied at the edge of a pool, she happened to see her image in the water and was so much ashamed that she threw away the instrument.'' Imitate Pallas, and shun ridicule. . . . And stop making noises with your mouth to express surprise or contempt.

A few instructions now as to how one should appear in public. Do not be seen wearing your nightcap, or put on your garters in front of other people. Do not leave your office with your pen above your ear, or holding a handkerchief between your teeth. Do not put a leg on the table; avoid spitting on your fingers.

Your dress should be neither so pretty nor so elaborate as to make people remark that you are wearing Ganymede's hose and Cupid's doublet. If your legs are too fat or too lean, or slightly twisted, do not order from your tailor hose in gaudy colours or of a conspicuous cut, which would simply invite attention to your defects.

Observe the code of the *Galateo* and you will be an accomplished man of the world.

Well-informed though he was, the Florentine did not refrain from consulting palmists and having his hand read. It has in fact been established that the hand is the organ of every part of the body and that the natural disposition of the individual is revealed in its lines and contours. Why are there four lines in the hand? Because we have four principal organs: the heart, the liver and the brain, which counts for two. The palmist Bartolomeo Cocles says so. A short hand is the sign of a person subject to "cold humors"; a long hand with short, stiff fingers denotes a phlegmatic individual, without much courage; a long hand with a broad palm warns us that the person will be mischievous, even a knave and a thief. As to a woman, if her hand is short but her fingers excessively long, she will be "in peril of child-birth."

Palmistry was of course no antidote for sickness. What then of the physician? He belonged to the fifth of the major "arts," the art of drugs and groceries, which included the *speziale,* or apothecary, with whom the physician sometimes lodged. He had formerly been a man of modest appearance, in spite of his tall hat trimmed with fillets. He had worn a long fur gown, so shabby and threadbare that "a furrier could not have guessed what animal had provided the skin." In these days, however, he dressed with studied elegance, wearing a long and capacious robe, trimmed with squirrel-fur and bands of scarlet, heavily begemmed rings, and gilded spurs, like a knight's. Following the example of Pier Leoni, Lorenzo's doctor, he had abandoned Arabic medicine in favor of Greek. Educated until recently in the medical school of Salerno, he practised astrology as much as medicine, and was now acquiring a reputation abroad, especially in France.

In 1479 sixty-six doctors are recorded as practising in Florence. They mainly prescribed simples, cabbage for example, which they regarded as a panacea. But in spite of his noble appearance, the physician was not taken very seriously, hardly more than the pedant. Years before this, Petrarch had described doctors as ignorant "spectators of maladies and sick persons." The facetious Poggio addressed them as follows:

> You visit the patient, inspect his water and excrement with attentive eye and puckered brow as if his malady required the most important attention. Then you feel his pulse, where you recognise the forces of nature. Next you consult your colleagues and after much discussion agree as to the remedies, as you call them. If by chance the beverage you prescribe has been effective, you never cease from extolling the cure; if it has done harm, you blame the patient.

Machiavelli is said to have died from taking too many pills containing aloes and cardamom, which a doctor had prescribed for him.

In cases where the patient entered one of the city's numerous hospitals, he found a high degree of comfort: abundant food, choice wine, competent nurses, and great cleanliness in his room and bed.

When a Florentine died—or "entered the great sea," as dying was called—the Signoria regulated the procedure. The body was to be simply dressed in white muslin lined with taffeta, with a plain cap on the head. In burying a woman, no ring was to be left on her fingers, unless it had little value. With a man, no armour was to be buried, no doublet, penon, flag or shield. The body rested on a common palliasse.

At the interment, two candles were permitted, or two torches containing at most thirty pounds of wax between them, or else four small torches. Candles or torches were to be extinguished immediately after the ceremony and returned to the dealer, the *speziale* in this instance, who was not allowed to sell candles weighing more than fifteen pounds, including the paper and candle-end. It was unreasonable to provide lighting for the dead, a useless display; and those who infringed the law were liable to a fine. This went into the *opera,* the fund for church-building and repairs.

The body was followed to the grave by mourners garbed in black; but this funeral attire was only loosely stitched "so as not to spoil the material which would later serve to make clothes." The wages of those who "announced" deaths and of the undertaker's men—the *beccamorti*—were fixed at a maximum of eight soldi. The widow was not to receive from the heirs either a gown, or petticoat, or girdle, or headdress, but simply a skirt and a cloak lined with taffeta. Two courses only might be served at the funeral dinner.

The interment took place at the charnel-house, or in the case of important persons, in the church. In Paris it was not until the middle of the sixteenth century that, on the occasion of an epidemic, the famous Dr. Fernel and a colleague, having heard of the fetid smell that hung over the Cemetery of the Innocents, recorded the fact that "in dangerous times the houses near the said cemetery have always been the first to catch the contagion and have remained infected longer than other houses in the city." But this warning remained a dead letter.

In Florence, however, as early as the fifteenth century, Bishop Narcissus, who was of Catalan origin and who had observed how crowded the Florentine churches were with sepulchres, gave the following warning: "The House of God, being clean and pure, should not be sullied with the presence of corpses. It is the monks who have introduced this custom. The primitive Church not only did not permit the burial in church of those who are now buried there, but even raised objections to the interment of holy men." And Narcissus cited the reply which a Pope had made when asked by some prelate for permission to inter the bodies of two martyrs in his church: "Place them at the entrance, but not elsewhere."

The Florentines unfortunately remained deaf to the words of this foreigner who was so concerned for the purity of a holy place and, perhaps without realising it, for public health.

—FRITZ RORIG————————————————————————

URBAN TYPES IN GERMANY

. . . The difference in population of medieval towns indicates the various degrees of activity and the various functions of individual towns. Not all so-called towns, not even those which may, legally, have been a town in the sense that this or that little place may have had "urban rights" bestowed upon it by some lord, can be included in an exposition whose aim is to elucidate the essential elements that made the medieval town into one of the most important impulses in world history. Nowadays we have freed ourselves from the notion that the medieval map of Germany was dotted with about 3,000 towns, each of which had the same aim—namely, as the central point of a minute territorial economic area, to lead as self-contained a life as the old manor farm of the local seigneur

From Fritz Rorig, *The Medieval Town* (Berkeley and Los Angeles: The University of California Press, 1967), pp. 111–114, 119–121, 146–150, 154–156, by permission of B. T. Batsford Ltd., London.

had once led. By far the greater part of these 3,000 "towns"—about 2,800—had populations of less than 1,000; in other words, there is no question of their being considered as truly urban economies, least of all as self-contained ones, because there was really no possibility that within these tiny little populations there would be room enough for all the trades necessary to the self-sufficiency of a town, however modest. A further 150 "towns," roughly speaking, also very modest even by medieval standards, had populations of between 1,000 and 2,000. Only the remaining ones, about fifty of them, were towns of any real importance within the German economy, over half of which, with populations of less than 10,000, formed the German medium-sized towns. Finally there was a group of about fifteen large German towns whose populations were in excess of 10,000. Cologne was the largest with more than 30,000 inhabitants; the second largest was Lübeck with no more than 25,000 around 1400. Apart from these only Strasbourg, Nuremberg, Gdansk and perhaps Ulm would have reached and exceeded 20,000 in the fifteenth century. Towns of the rank of Frankfurt am Main, Wroclaw, Zürich and Augsburg grew from 10,000 to 18,000 in the course of the fifteenth century; in 1493 the population of Erfurt amounted to about 18,500. If the population of Leipzig is calculated at around 4,000 in 1474, then this is the clearest possible indication of the huge increase which this town experienced since then, mainly as an ancillary member of the Nuremberg trading system.

Similar conditions obtained in the northern European towns outside Germany. Of English towns only London had more than 10,000 inhabitants, and this certainly by a considerable amount; it already had 30–40,000 in the fourteenth century. An even higher incidence of population in a capital is certainly known to have obtained in Paris. This town, as the royal residence, as an episcopal see and as the seat of the famous university, exercised at the height of the Middle Ages a power of attraction such as did no other town north of the Alps. Among the Flemish towns Bruges appears, at least at the time of its greatest prosperity, to have had the largest population within its walls. It is somewhat surprising that Ypres had only a little more than 10,000 inhabitants; admittedly this was in 1412, when the Flemish weaving towns were already in decline and the weavers' suburbs depopulated. Ypres, but also particularly Ghent, would have had far greater numbers in the fourteenth century. Figures far in excess of the German towns were to be found particularly in Italy. Florence is supposed to have had 100,000 inhabitants around 1340; its decline from that time on is well known. Milan is said to have had 85,000 inhabitants towards the end of the fifteenth century. In the sixteenth century the respective populations of Venice, Naples and Palermo are all believed to have exceeded 100,000.

But nothing would be more mistaken than to underestimate a medieval German town of 20,000 people in terms of the function that it fulfilled in the Middle Ages simply because in modern times a town of this size is not usually very important. Within the framework of the whole, a German town of around that number of inhabitants in 1400 fulfilled a political, economic and cultural function of which many a present-day town of several hundred thousands would be envious. Even if one evaluates Aeneas Sylvius Piccolomini's account of German towns, particularly Cologne, Strasbourg and Nuremberg, in the middle of the fifteenth century as conscious exaggeration—nevertheless he was not the only foreigner to emphasise the outstanding importance of German towns; Cologne, particularly, was a match for any other town of Europe. Machiavelli even saw in the German town the heart of Germany's strength.

Certainly this urban population was subject to a terrible danger which could reduce its numbers very considerably. This was the scourge of the plague—the Black Death—which particularly in the middle of the fourteenth century held its slow but ineluctable victory procession throughout the countries of Europe, of which the best propagators were the flagellants, driving the terrible disease before them. The towns, with their populations squeezed within their walls, had the largest sacrifices to make. It is assumed that the population of Florence was reduced by a third in the terrible mass death of 1348. It was the lowest classes, the weavers, who were the most thoroughly depleted; a renewed outbreak of the plague hit the town in 1374. Western Europe was no less badly hit; England is thought to have lost up to half her population. Germany, too, hit by the first wave of the plague in 1349–50, suffered greatly. According to an entry in the citizens' book of Bremen, 6,966 known and named persons were carried off by it in the town. . . .

The Jews, who led a special existence by religion and by law deserve a special note. It was not as though there were Jews in every town; the chronicler remarks of Lübeck—a town which was highly self-conscious as a place of commerce: "There are no Jews in Lübeck; there is no need for them either." He was right; for even without Jews such things as money-lending and usury, mortgages and foreclosures were everyday things in Lübeck; in the same way Florentine banks were created by Italian entrepreneurs, and Italian, Hanseatic and English merchants of the fourteenth century carried on money businesses of considerable size for the English crown. The good and bad results of a commercial enterprise directed towards personal gain also affected towns which had nothing whatever to do with Jews. All this in spite of ecclesiastical prohibition of usury—a prohibition which, like so many, is to be taken rather as evidence that in fact things happened quite differently from the way in which the prohibitors, in this case the ecclesiastical moral theorists, supposed and demanded. Quite unabashed, the council of Constance forbade its townsmen to take more than eleven percent on the money they lent. Moreover, the behavior of the church itself was most strangely at variance with the demands of its moral theoreticians. On the other hand it is wrong to imagine that the Jews were restricted to money-lending. Like the Christians, they, too, combined trade in goods with money-lending—in the early centuries they were pioneers in foreign trade. Certainly in the later Middle Ages they concentrated on money-changing and banking, and particularly pawnbroking. Lords of the manor, knights and towns found themselves among the debtors of Jewish money-lenders; but also did a whole lot of small people—cobblers, tailors and saddlers. If the hatred of Jews in many towns reached special intensity in the fourteenth century, then this is connected with the fact that the small people, too, saw in them the burdensome, and certainly also frequently usurious creditor. To this, moreover, was added the religious contrast which divided Jews from Christians far more sharply than did the economic contrast, which in any case was to some extent artificially engendered by the church.

The first wave of persecution of the Jews in Western Europe was bound up with the crusading atmosphere, the second with the advance of the Black Death in the fourteenth century. It was at the beginning of 1348, when the plague was raging in a town of Provence, that in May of that year the first Jews were burnt. From there the rumour that the Jews had poisoned the wells of the town buzzed through the land, even throughout South, West and Central Germany. In most cases the Jews had already met their fate before the plague even hit the town, as in Strasbourg, where the chronicler confesses that money was the sole reason for the killing of the Jews. If they had been poor and the lords had not been indebted to them, they would not have been burnt. If the picture given of the burning of the Jews in Strasbourg is correct—apart from the certainly exaggerated total given of Jews burnt (two thousand)—then it becomes clear that religious hate was stronger than racial antipathy. If a Strasbourg Jew consented to be baptised he stayed alive; many small children are said to have been taken from the burning pyre and baptised against their parents' wishes. Frederick I's Jews' Charter of 1157 had already forbidden the baptism of secretly stolen Jewish children. Subsequent rulers were not able to withstand the temptation to exploit their rights of protection of the Jews ruthlessly for their own enrichment. However it would be wrong to assume that persecution of the Jews was the rule; decades of peace and lawfulness were suddenly interrupted by catastrophes. In the large towns it was in fact the circles of council and merchant families which energetically protected the Jews at least from arrest without trial, mob law and the like in the interests of law and order within the town until far into the fourteenth century. The worsening of the Jews' position in the towns is reflected also in the circumstances of their living quarters and the property they owned. The real obligation to live in a spatially enclosed Jewish settlement within the town, which was locked up at night—the ghetto—only set in towards the end of the thirteenth century. After the persecution of the Jews in the fourteenth century, remote streets and corners were set apart for them. . . .

The merchant, following a tradition which went back to earliest times, was an itinerant foreign trader; he was not a local middleman who only supplied what was absolutely necessary in raw materials and goods that could not be manufactured in the town, in order to keep the town's own economy going. It was quite a different story with the worker. His field was not the world, but primarily the market of his own town. The goods the merchant procured from foreign parts aroused the suspicion and ill-will of the manual worker. In his view he could have satisfied local needs just as well with his own goods; but that was his view, not that of the buying public. This is the reason why quality goods which came from outside, and of which the local shopkeeper and worker had no specialised knowledge, were generally retailed by the same wholesale traders who procured the goods. We may remember the "cutting rights" of the valuable Flemish materials held by the leading men of the wholesale and foreign trade in the German towns which lasted until a circle of local retailers having specialised knowledge, and devoting itself to the retailing of Flemish cloths, was formed, which allowed the wholesale traders progressively to renounce their "cutting rights." This happened in Lübeck in the fourteenth century. We may also remember such a large-scale business as that of Antonius Koberger the publisher, with his agents in Paris and Lyons, who at the same time systematically sent out men who had been specially schooled in the job of retailing the published works. Finally there were those Nuremberg merchants in the Hansa who also retailed their richly varied collection of Italian silks, their valuable silver and golden ornaments decorated with jewels, and found a receptive market for them. But one can also understand the troubled complaint of the Lübeck shopkeepers to their council about 1400 that a Nuremberg merchant in Lübeck sold twenty times as much as any other, and as much in one day as a Lübecker did in a year!

If the shopkeeper was the sworn enemy of free trade for foreign merchants in his own town, and would have liked to see their wholesale selling limited, things were different for the workers—or at least more complicated. For it was not only the local market which determined the selling conditions for medieval urban trades. Certainly the provision trades—bakers and butchers—had their circle of customers in the town itself. But even the shoemakers also worked for export, as for instance those of Lübeck worked for the Norwegian market. This was even more true of the metal-working trades of towns like Nuremberg whose products in this field had a good and widespread reputation. The textile trade was least concerned with the home market—particularly in those places whose products had a world-wide reputation, such as the Flemish towns or Florence. The linen and fustian weavers in the small South German towns near Lake Constance, and the linen weavers in Saxon and Lusatian towns also worked for consumers they did not know, who might be hundreds of miles away. However, it was not the worker's job actually to supply the goods to the consumers, but that of commerce. The framework of the relation between worker and merchant was a system of credit which could often bring about the complete dependence of the worker on the merchant, as was the case in Flemish towns and in Florence. It was as no more than a reaction against such grave abuses—in cases where the weavers' enmity towards the merchant upper class in the large weaving towns was especially strong—that the most bloody conflicts ensued, even though the economic interests of these same groups of workers were related not to the urban but to the world market. Relationships were better where the merchant with capital did not make contracts with individual workers but with a whole union, where it was thus a question of collective contracts. The first instance known of such a contract was in 1424—between the Lübeck amber-turners and a group of merchants for the selling of the greatest part of their production; Venice, Nuremberg, Frankfurt am Main and Cologne were the projected selling areas. The manual worker was really best off if he was himself in a position to carry on outside sales. But this was only possible for a few workers who produced quite valuable wares. Goldsmiths from Cologne, Augsburg and Nuremberg went in great numbers to the Frankfurt fair, where they found their best buyers in the international wholesale trade which was there to buy in bulk. But the trade of goldsmith counted as the most elevated trade in any case; it was no coincidence that many members of this trade transferred to the merchant upper class. Nor that the only surviving business book of a medieval manual worker belonged to a goldsmith. This was Stefan Maignow, who died in 1500, a man who failed to attain the degree of importance and artistic skill possessed by his colleagues in Nuremberg, Augsburg and Cologne, but who had numerous customers among the noble families in the region of Constance who bought eagerly from him, even if they were not quite so keen on paying up.

Shopkeepers and those workers who, unlike the weavers, were economically independent and mainly interested in the local market were, with their xenophobic tendencies, the real eulogists of the urban economy. Their aim was to assure all the advantages of the local market for local people and to organise foreigners' selling in such a way that local trade should not be at any disadvantage on account of it—the foreign merchant, if they had their way, would only have been permitted to sell wholesale. In this way he was robbed of a large number of potential customers in the town; moreover, on account of the prohibition on business with foreigners, he was eventually dependent on unions and shopkeepers as his only customers. They were, therefore, exceptionally favoured. Yet the simple fact that trade dominated the economic, social and even political aspects of the more important medieval towns meant that such aims remained unrealised, or were only tolerated and partially achieved later on. Even the economically independent worker was himself in all ways dependent on the merchants, and on the merchant-dominated council. A Lübeck master-baker baked his bread in a bakery belonging to one or other of the old families, sold it in the booths by St Mary's church, which were at the disposal of the council, and lived in a house for which, as a rule, he paid a percentage to a distinguished merchant, or for which, as in Cologne, he only paid rent. Although the individual worker was of no consequence by comparison with the ruling families, the organised association of the workers of any particular trade was.

For this reason alone the development of the guild is one of the most important problems in the history of the German town; it is highly improbable in view of the element of necessary compromise and the variety of individual development that in Germany, or in Europe, it was solved by equal bargaining by the three parties involved—the lord of the town, its council and the workers themselves. In the towns of Flanders and Brabant, where a thorough-going sovereign power soon gained influence on working conditions alongside the patrician council, several attempts at a solution were made within a small area. Nevertheless, for Germany, the following characteristics of the development may claim a certain validity. To begin with it was the lord of the town who, aided by his supporters within the town, exercised what was frequently a very effective ruling power over the trades; the best examples of this are the regulations of the older town laws of the lord of Strasbourg. Very soon, as early as the twelfth century, the developing merchant councils exercised similar functions, above all the control of the provision trades and the market. Limitations as to the number of members in a particular trade resulted less from the efforts of the workers themselves than from the official power of the authorities. This was due either to the fact that a fixed number of trading concessions were officially granted to the members of a trade when the town was founded—as happened in Strehlen, Silesia, in 1292, where thirty-four butchers' stalls, thirty-two bread stalls and thirty cobblers' stalls were set up with the express condition that this number was not to be exceeded—or to the fact that the town council wished to limit the numbers in a particular trade for other reasons such as control, or even punishment. In Lübeck in the fourteenth century the council reduced the number of needle-makers to fourteen and the butchers from one hundred to fifty because of their part in disturbances. In the earliest documents which determine the relations between the government and traders, it was an important fact that the authorities disposed of and supervised everything concerning the trades. Nevertheless as soon as the members of a trade claimed and received the right to belong to a group recognised by the authorities, wide opportunities were opened up for their initiative and effort by means of which they could build up their groups in a way both useful and advantageous to the members. The occasional limits on the number of members of a trade by the authorities at the same time gave very valuable economic privileges to the lucky ones who were left in; only those authorised could practise a trade. This also meant compulsory membership of a guild—and without membership no-one could ply his trade. Only the authorities could grant this right; they also decided whether and how far the guild might exercise its own jurisdiction over offenses against the constitution of the guild or its regulations. . . .

In economic matters, the supposed harmony of the medieval town was broken by sharp differences between the commercial and the working classes. Obviously this contrast was reflected in the political field; the guildsmen could only achieve practical realisation of their economic ideal if they shared in membership of the council, or occupied all of it themselves. The conflicts between guilds and patriciate often began in political terms—the guilds formed the core of the resistance to the actual or alleged financial mismanagement of the council. The story of the Flemish towns has shown with what bitterness these conflicts were fought out; here, too, the inseparability of political, economic and social aims within the opposing classes is clear. The conflicts also took a particularly acute form in German towns which had a large number of weavers— Cologne and Brunswick for example. Almost everywhere in the southwestern towns in the thirteenth and fourteenth centuries the guilds gained some degree of a share in the government of the town. Sometimes they were directly represented by councillors on a council which had previously been the exclusive preserve of the leading families; at other times there were two councils in existence at the same time, the old and the new; in which case the constitution provided that the new council should be consulted on certain questions concerning the town. It also happened that the previous council was completely abolished so that the guilds formed the group from which the new council was to be elected. This occurred in Cologne in 1396, when twenty-two political guilds or *Gaffeln* were formed for election to the council. In each of these one of the commercial guilds was the main guild with which the others were associated. The first group was known as the weavers guild, along with related trades; it had the largest number of councillors to elect—four. The remaining twenty-one groups elected thirty-two between them. A further forty-four representatives of the groups were to be called in on the more important matters. All the inhabitants of the town who were not members of a guild—which included also the merchants and leading families—had to associate themselves with one of the groups. Radical as this change of constitution appears, it turned out in practise to be less so. Actually it was still the merchants and not the workers who ruled in Cologne after 1396—although they were prepared to make all kinds of concessions to the lower classes.

This was true of most of the larger trading towns in the fifteenth century. In a town like Lübeck, where the constitutional demands of the workers and those merchants who did not belong to the select families were not met, and where it became clear, at the beginning of the fifteenth century, that the workers simply could not do without the leading families' centuries-long experience in foreign politics, the leading class went an extraordinarily long way towards meeting the economic wishes of the workers and shopkeepers. In German towns the weaver proletariat did not have anything like the importance it did in Flanders, and independent master-craftsmen, often of sound economic standing, stood alongside the patriciate; even so a *rapprochement* was all the more possible because towards the end of the fifteenth century the upper section of guild-masters, which also had a share in the municipal offices, was terrified by the growing ill-will amongst the depressed population. Journeymen who could not manage to become masters, day-labourers and people who had to earn their bread without the protection of a guild played a dangerous role in this. Their fury was directed both against the patriciate and the guild-masters who ruled alongside them. Resentment over increasing burdens imposed on the small man by the monied classes through indirect taxation already mingled with the simple hate borne by the have-nots towards the haves. The council of Erfurt fled before this hate in 1509; in 1513 seven Cologne councillors ended up on the scaffold. Strasbourg, after dramatic struggles and endless compromises between the upper class and the guilds, had arrived in 1482 at a permanent constitutional reform of finely calculated equilibrium, and with its cautious financial politics and the goodwill of all groups participating in its apparently democratic, but in fact oligarchic constitution, appeared to the leading spirits of around 1500 like an oasis in the desert. In the famous words of Erasmus, he believed he could see here a monarchy without a tyrant, an aristocracy without factions, a democracy without uproar, wealth without luxury and happiness without presumption.

INERTIA
AND MOTION
IN EARLY
MODERN TIMES

Few periods in history can rival the age of religious conflicts in Europe after 1500 for sheer complexity. Everywhere, it seemed, traditional modes of thought and accepted means of action came under challenge. In the sixteenth century the Reformation was not simply a huge abstraction but a dynamic series of events that troubled and confounded an entire civilization. Old assumptions and pieties were swept aside and, both politically and theologically, Europe became the scene of a sprawling free-for-all.

This was also the epoch of a remarkable European expansion into the New World, Africa, and Asia. But that vast effort of exploration and colonization by the Europeans is not our central interest here. We are primarily concerned with the many ordinary people who stayed at home, not the relatively few adventurous souls who decided to try their luck elsewhere. The spotlight falls onto the seventeenth and early eighteenth centuries, when increased commercial activity and nascent capitalism were beginning to be felt, but when the industrializing process had not yet begun to transform the bases of European society.

As the title of this part of the book is intended to indicate, this was for Europe a phase of deepening contradictions. There was much visible evidence of movement but also, in reaction, an abiding conservatism and a stiffening resistance to innovation. If a major redistribution of resources did not occur, the chasm between rich and poor was meanwhile becoming all the more conspicuous because of increased opportunities for the happy few to deploy and display their wealth.

Thus, at an exalted level the circumstances were favorable for the growth of European states, with all the elaborate splendor of absolute monarchies and aristocratic courts. History textbooks are ordinarily filled with the military and cultural exploits of these upper classes. Less often are we invited, as in the pages that follow, to enter a more modest world of cottages, farms, villages, and commonplace homes. It is no doubt of great value to study the theoretical advances dating from the seventeenth century and to learn of Copernicus, Kepler, Galileo, Descartes, and Newton. But we should keep in mind that this "scientific revolution" left the daily lives of most people totally untouched. Even printing still remained of limited importance for a society in which only a tiny minority was truly, and sometimes magnificently, literate.

This volume brings us to the edge of that time in European history that we, perhaps egocentrically, call modern. Just ahead lie the Enlightenment, the industrial and political revolutions of the late eighteenth century, and the onset of a new era for Everyman in Europe. We can observe how, quite unconsciously in most instances, the ground was being prepared for what was to come. Yet we should realize, too, that few people in any time or place conduct their affairs in anticipation of dramatic future events. For the most part they are simply attempting to enjoy or to survive the routine of every day.

CHAPTER
7

THE PEASANT
GRINDS ON

As we advance in time it is crucial to retain some perspective and recall that Europe remained an overwhelmingly rural society right through the eighteenth century. Agriculture was still the principal occupation of most people, and even those who might be classified as nonpeasants found that the quality of their lives depended in large measure on the success or failure of seasonal crops. One important fact began to emerge, however, that suggests a long-range theme in European social history. In England and the western portions of the mainland methods of cultivation and patterns of landholding were changing to the extent that the entire notion of feudalism became of dubious applicability to the lands west of the Elbe River. In central and eastern Europe, on the other hand, the serf status of the peasantry was if anything retrenched. By the time of the French Revolution, therefore, it had already become more appropriate to conceive of an evolving social and economic dichotomy between West and East than to dwell on the longstanding ideological division between a Catholic South and a Protestant North. Thus, it is not surprising that the political and industrial revolutions that began in the late eighteenth century were to have a more immediate impact in western Europe, where the process of social transformation was less hindered.

C. B. A. Behrens examines western Europe, particularly France, from the age of Louis XIV to the French Revolution. She portrays a society in which there still existed no industrial cushion against the calamity of poor harvests. The European population was periodically stalked by the twin monsters of war and poor harvest, and plagued by their greedy offspring: conscription, taxation and starvation. This is hardly an idyllic picture of country life, nor is it intended to be. Poverty was the primary fact of life. The volatility of the peasants, or at least their latent hostility toward the privileged, is consequently not difficult to grasp.

Walter H. Bruford looks to the German lands where the first intimations of change were to be detected in the western sections of Europe. Although Prussia and Austria were not without their enlightened administrators in the eighteenth century, the practical results for the rural laborer were seldom commensurate with the visions of reform. In large areas serfdom remained very much intact, whatever the variations of nomenclature, and farming was often as primitive as ever. For peasants under these circumstances, life remained a struggle for survival.

Jerome Blum considers the deteriorating condition of the Russian peasantry. Millions of people were constantly being pressed down into a serfdom barely distinguishable from the most wretched slavery. When freed from legal or moral restraints, masters were left to buy and sell their human property at will—in a manner much like the American slave market of the same era. At the complete mercy of their lord, the serfs were thus subject to the extremes of kindness and cruelty, their individual fate being entirely dependent on the whims of their social superior.

These readings confirm the impression that change, not stagnation, produces the stinging indignities and frustrations that may lead to revolt. In this case the implications are clear. European society was unconsciously preparing itself for a long season of turmoil that would begin in the West and, taking different forms, would eventually spread eastward.

RURAL LABOR IN THE WEST

THE PEASANT PROBLEM

In every country in Europe in the eighteenth century, the vast majority of people earned their living from the land. In France the category commonly described as peasants—that is, everyone who was not a nobleman, a cleric, or engaged full-time in some occupation other than agriculture—must have included by 1789 some twenty-two or more million souls out of a total population reckoned at twenty-six million.

The civilization on which the eighteenth century prided itself was the prerogative of only a very small minority, even in France, where the educated were more numerous than in most other countries. For the vast majority, life was a continual, and often a losing, battle to wring a bare livelihood from the soil. The calculations of governments and of private individuals revolved round the harvest. In France in the eighteenth century, the Contrôle Général (the department responsible for financial and economic affairs) issued every year to each of four hundred local officials a form divided into columns—one for wheat, one for rye, one for oats, etc.—with instructions to note the amounts that were harvested in the current year and that remained over from the previous harvest. In the words of Professor Labrousse: "the problem of grain dominated all the other problems."[1]

Bad harvests, though the substantial landowners and merchants benefited from the rising prices, meant shortage if not starvation for most people, in town and country alike; for most people, in France as in the greater part of the rest of Europe, either owned no land, or owned an amount insufficient to support a family, or worked land belonging to other people on terms that, for the most part, barely sufficed to meet their needs even when times were good.

The price of bread (and of wine in the wine-growing areas) was always the determining factor in the economy. As it rose in times of scarcity it diminished the amount that the poor could spend on other things. Consequently, agricultural calamities had repercussions on the urban and rural industries, which gave employment in the towns and supplemented that in the countryside, and whose

From C. B. A. Behrens, *The Ancien Régime* (New York: Harcourt, Brace, and World, Inc., 1967), pp. 25–42, by permission of Thames and Hudson.

1 C. E. Labrousse, *La Crise de l'Economie Française* (Paris 1943), vol. I, p. 15.

products the majority in town and country could only afford when the price of bread was low or moderate.

Bad harvests also had repercussions on the government's revenues, since the yield of the taxes fell, and on its projects for moving about and provisioning its armies. In addition, they created administrative difficulties, since people who are starving have various ways of making themselves a nuisance to the authorities. Throughout the greater part of Europe in the eighteenth century peasant revolts were endemic. In some of the countries of central and eastern Europe—in Bohemia in 1772, in Russia during the Pugachev revolt of the following year—there were times when they reached the proportions of civil war. They had done so in France in the reign of Louis XIV, but this did not happen again until the spring of 1789, partly, no doubt, because there was no general famine, but partly also, it has been suggested, because the royal administration became more efficient. Scarcity nevertheless remained common, and hunger the fear and experience of most people. In bad times in France the unemployed and starving would band together and roam the countryside in search of food. They would attack the wagons carrying the grain to market and break into the barns where it was stored. Illiterate and brutalized by misery, the victims of irrational fears and superstitions which, if the strong hand of authority were removed, could set whole districts on the march against the scapegoats of the moment, they were always a potential menace to law, order and property, even in France where, if Ségur may be believed (and the facts seem to support him), they were normally more docile, and less hostile to the landlords, than in the serf-owning countries of Prussia, Russia and Habsburg dominions.

In these circumstances, no government could be indifferent to the fate of the peasants, and none, the French government included, in principle ever was. Self-interest and Christian morality alike preached the same lesson: that the peasant had to be helped as far as possible in times of natural calamity; that he had to be protected against exploitation by the landlords; that he should not be subjected to unduly heavy taxation; above all, that the government should rigidly control the grain trade and maintain buffer stocks, in order to mitigate the effects of bad harvests and their attendant troubles.

Between the ideals of the paternalistic monarchies and the treatment the peasant received in practice, however, there was always a large gap, since the monarchs continually found themselves forced or tempted into pursuing policies contrary to the peasants' interests, and were unable or unwilling to prevent their officials and other classes of the population from doing the same. Until the days of the Enlightenment, and indeed often afterwards, the absolute monarchs were given to the pursuit of glory by means of war and conspicuous consumption. Louis XIV built great palaces, kept a splendid court, and—at vastly greater expense—maintained an army that, at its peak, is said to have numbered a million men, of whom one-third were mercenaries but who still had to be paid and fed. This was a larger army than the French ever raised again before the present century, and in Louis' long period of personal rule, which lasted for fifty-five years, war, after the first seven, was almost continuous. The enormous cost of his military operations inevitably fell, for the greater part, on the bulk of the population which consisted of peasants.

In the reign of Louis XIV, the peasant thus paid heavily for the glory of his king and country, and he continued to do so throughout the eighteenth century. Apart, however, from the prestige of belonging to a great nation (which there is no reason to suppose he appreciated), the sums of which he was mulcted brought him in no return, even in the long run, since they contributed nothing to the productivity of the land from which he lived and did much to diminish his own incentive to increase it. . . .

When Arthur Young, in his travels, once met a peasant woman, whom he discovered to be twenty-eight years old though she had the appearance of sixty or seventy, she exclaimed to him: "Les tailles et les droits nous écrasent."[2] This cry has echoed down the centuries, repeated by one generation of historians after another, who have usually assumed, as the peasant woman doubtless did herself, that the state of affairs which provoked it was due to some peculiar degree of wickedness in the nobility and the high officials of the church. Tocqueville, a repentant aristocrat, whose indictment of the Ancien Régime has formed the basis of most later attacks on it, nevertheless knew better. Selfishness, he said, was a vice as old as the world and no more characteristic of one form of society than another, though it manifested itself in different societies in different ways. Comparing the society of pre-Revolutionary France with that of America at the beginning of the nineteenth century, he noted how strong had been the sense of family and kinship in France, and the ties of personal loyalty. These, he believed, could elicit a degree of individual self-sacrifice rarely found in the new societies. On the other hand, he noted how weak in the old societies had been the sense of duty to the community and of obligation to one's neighbor.

The peasants had occasion to know this, notwithstanding the communal organization of agriculture, which was naturally, in a society so organized, used by the strong to oppress the weak. At every level of social life, the people with the greatest wealth and influence framed, twisted or evaded the law to their own advantage. The mass of the peasantry was far from being the only victim of these circumstances, though it suffered most; nor, apart from the state, were the church and the nobility its only oppressors. The record of the bourgeois, who owned many *seigneuries* and farmed the dues in many others, was no better and is often said to have been worse. That of the small class of rich peasants was in some ways worst of all.

The village, like every other group, had its hierarchy. In the more prosperous districts there grew up a class of substantial tenant-farmers, comparable to those in England; but even over the greater part of the country, where the

---

2 Arthur Young, *Travels in France,* ed. Maxwell (Cambridge: 1929), p. 173.

system of share-cropping prevailed, the villages had their *coqs de village*. These were well-to-do peasants, possessing carts and oxen, and enough land to feed their families. They could sometimes even save enough to buy themselves an office in the neighboring town, which served their children as a stepping stone for the ascent of the social ladder. In his analysis of the members of the Paris Parlement in the eighteenth century, Professor Bluche tells us that it was not uncommon for peasant families to climb into the nobility in three generations. No class, however, drove harsher bargains than these successful peasants, or showed more skill and effrontery in cheating and intimidating the tax-collectors; and the burdens they evaded, unlike those of the nobility which was separately assessed, fell directly and immediately on their neighbors because of the collective responsibility for the *Taille*.

In the poverty-stricken societies of eighteenth-century Europe, it seemed a law of nature, as Quesnay, the founder of the school of Physiocrats, said, that "A man can only acquire wealth by means of the wealth he already possesses."[3] Those who started destitute were more than likely to remain so. Money and education conferred advantages that grew in a geometrical progression, while the poor and ignorant were pushed to the wall. Tocqueville said of the mass of the peasantry that civilization seemed to turn against them alone. They were the predestined victims of a royal policy directed to the pursuit of objects other than agriculture; of a conservatism, of which admittedly they were themselves the principal exponents, that blocked the road to change; and of an administration in which, notwithstanding the paternalistic ideals, educated officials of goodwill were too few, and other officials too ignorant, poorly paid and open to bribery and intimidation, to protect the weak against the strong.

---

3   *François Quesnay et la Physiocratie* (Institut National d'Études Démographiques, Paris, 1958), vol. II, p. 537.

COUNTRY LIFE IN GERMANY

. . . The peasant, it will be seen, besides being dependent on the vagaries of the weather and exposed more than any other class to the ravages of war, was less of a free agent than the average townsman, being more closely bound by the routine of the little society into which he was born. On the other hand he was seldom in danger of actual starvation, as a "free" townsman might be, and although he had to work hard, he never experienced the still more unhappy situation of being out of work. Naturally his personal dependence was looked upon as a great evil by the liberals of the Aufklärung, while agricultural reformers criticized the inefficiency of forced and therefore scamped labor. We meet with many reflections in literature of the movement for the freeing of the serfs. In the strict legal sense there were no actual "serfs" (Leibeigene) in Germany like those of the early Middle Ages and of classical antiquity. The feudal dues and services still exacted were a burden on the *land,* not on the *person* of the peasant, and had mostly been commuted for money. Most of the restrictions on their freedom had had their origin not in medieval serfdom but in later developments, particularly in the "Gutsherrschaft," of the lands east of the Elbe. But even if the peasants were at worst only what Knapp has called "erbuntertänig" (hereditarily subject) it was natural that the reformers should use the familiar word serfdom for a relationship which in practice was very little better than slavery. The movement for the freeing of the serfs made little progress in Germany until the nineteenth century.

It was only from the prince of the territory that the peasant could hope for relief. He did not always look to him in vain, for in Prussia and Austria the state needed a flourishing peasantry, to provide healthy recruits for the growing armies, and billets in their houses and barns for the soldiers. Actuated in the main by these motives the Prussian and Austrian rulers endeavored by a number of ordinances to prevent the confiscation of peasants' land (Bauernlegung), but they were not so successful, or perhaps so desirous of success, when they joined in the attempts at the abolition of serfdom that began to be made in Germany in this century. The demesne peasants were freed in Prussia in 1798 and the following years, but the rest did not obtain their freedom until between 1808 and 1816, and then only at the cost of concessions that made the landowners' position even

From W. H. Bruford, *Germany in the Eighteenth Century: The Social Background of the Literary Revival* (New York: Cambridge University Press, 1935), pp. 111-12, 118-24, by permission of the publisher.

better than before. In Austria, in spite of Joseph II's humane attempts, the peasants were not freed till 1848, but other German-speaking territories were not so backward. In the north and west, where conditions were better to begin with, it was only a small step to release the peasant from feudal dues and give him an independent holding, yet here too it needed the impetus of the French Revolution to induce the peasants to assert their claims. . . .

The everyday life and thought of the country dwellers were such as one might expect, given the fundamental conditions of their life. . . . There were naturally great differences between family and family, both amongst the nobility and the peasantry, according to the economic position and inherited privileges of each. As in France, there were some families of noble extraction whose standard of life was no higher than a peasant's, and there were free peasants here and there, particularly in the south, who were little lords in everything but name.

The average peasant and his family, as we have seen, had never much more than was necessary to keep body and soul together. There could be no question of luxuries in their life. It was necessary for them to buy from the towns only what could not possibly be dispensed with, a few spices perhaps and metal ware. For the rest they depended on what they themselves or their neighbors could grow in their fields and gardens and make with their own hands. Houses and furniture and the clothing of both men and women were the work of members of the household, assisted occasionally perhaps by a neighbor, or more rarely by a traveling craftsman. The following description of English rural life at this period could be applied in almost every detail to German conditions:

> The inhabitants had little need of communication with their immediate neighbours, still less with the outside world. The fields and the livestock provided the necessary food and clothing. Whatever wood might be required for building, fences or fuel, was provided on the wastes. Each village had its mill, generally the property of the lord of the manor; almost every house had its oven and brewing kettle. Women spun wool into coarse cloth; men tanned their own leather. Wealth only existed in its simplest forms, and natural divisions of employment were not made, because only the rudest implements of production were now used. The rough tools required for the cultivation of the soil, and the rude household utensils needed for the comfort of daily life, were made at home. In the long winter evenings farmers, their sons, and their servants carved the wooden spoons, the platters, and the beechen bowls; fitted and rivetted the bottoms into the horn mugs, or closed, in coarse fashion, the holes in the leather jugs. They plaited the wicker baskets; fitted handles to the scythes, rakes and other tools; cut the staves, and fixed the thongs for the flails; made the willow or ashen teeth for rakes and harrows, and hardened them in the fire; fashioned ox yokes and forks, racks and rack-staves; twisted willows into scythe cradles, or into the traces and other harness gear. Travelling carpenters, smiths and tinkers visited farmhouses and remoter villages at rare intervals to perform those parts of the work which needed their professional skill. But every village of any size found employment for such trades as those of the smith and the carpenter. Meanwhile the women plaited the straw for the neck-collars, stitched and stuffed sheepskin bags for the cart saddle, wove the stirrups and halters from hemp or straw, peeled the rushes for and made the

candles. Spinning wheels, distaffs, needles were never idle. Coarse, home-made cloth and linen supplied all wants. The very names of spinster, webster, shepster, litster, brewster, and baxter, show that women span, wove, cut out and dyed cloth, as well as brewed and baked for the household.[1]

In the matter of clothing the villagers were almost beyond the reach of fashion. They used their clothes until they were worn out. Styles of dress did, of course, change over long periods. The great variety of peasant costumes worn as best clothes on special occasions all embodied features of the town dress of much earlier periods, perhaps of the sixteenth century or earlier.[2] The peasantry had at some time or other adopted modified versions of town fashions, but these had become stereotyped, because the conditions necessary for quick changes of fashion, above all a surplus of means and variety of stimulus, were not present in the country. It was the same with many other features of their material civilization and even of what higher culture they possessed, as has been pointed out by Hans Naumann and those who like him believe in the "Sinken des Kulturguts."[3] But the opponents of this theory are no doubt right in claiming a considerable degree of creativeness for the peasant. It was by no means all the features of his culture that had been passively received by him from "higher" social classes. Many of the most important went back to a time when there were no other classes—the form of the peasant house and of the chief agricultural implements, as well as innumerable customs and beliefs owed little or nothing to either knighthood or bourgeoisie, for they were older than both. And though admittedly strongly attached to tradition, the peasant was no more incapable than any other man of modifying what he borrowed to serve his own purposes, and of having occasionally good ideas of his own.

What prevented rapid change was the strength of community feeling in the village, and institutions like the three-field system, with its rules of common cropping, which both expressed and fostered this feeling. It is now fashionable in Germany to praise the traditionalism of the peasant, by a reaction against the views expressed when the individualistic middle class led public opinion. For the townsman from the Renaissance age onwards, however, the countryman was "der dumme Bauer." He was held to be coarse, stupid, dishonest, drunken and quarrelsome, and it was not until the time of the Romantics, after hints from Rousseau and the "Sturm und Drang," that it was discovered that the countryman was in his own way a completely civilized person who was even superior to the townsman in much that was now held to be important in life.

In reading eighteenth-century descriptions of peasant life the change of attitude, by which our present-day views have been affected, must be kept in

---

1   *Social England,* ed. Traill, V, 101 (article by R. E. Prothero).
2   See K. Spiess, *Die Deutschen Volkstrachten,* Leipzig, 1911.
3   See H. Naumann, *Grundzüge der deutschen Volkskunde,* Leipzig, 1922.

mind. It was not the townsman's feeling of superiority, however, that inspired the following description of the peasant's life by a man revered by Goethe in his youth, J. M. von Loen:

> The peasant is brought up in complete ignorance like a mere animal. He is plagued continually with feudal services, running messages, beating up game, digging trenches and the like. From morning till night he must be digging the fields, whether scorched by the sun or numbed by the cold. At night he lies in the field and becomes little better than a beast of the fields, to keep the beasts from stealing his seed, and what he saves from their jaws is taken soon afterwards by a harsh official for arrears of rent and taxes. The countryman today is the most wretched of all creatures. The peasants are slaves and their men are hardly to be distinguished from the cattle they tend. The traveler comes to villages where children run about half-naked and call to every passer by for alms. Their parents have scarcely a rag on their backs. A few lean cows have to till their fields and give milk as well. Their barns are empty and their cottages threaten to collapse in a heap any moment. They themselves look neglected and wretched; one would have more pity for them, if their wild and brutish appearance did not seem to justify their hard lot.[4]

These general impressions are confirmed by such different writers as Laukhard, *Der reisende Franzose,* Nicolai, Knigge and Crabb Robinson. The references to the peasantry by Crabb Robinson in his *Letters* are particularly interesting because he is able to compare German with English conditions. The condition of the peasantry varied greatly in the provinces he visited. He was never in the eastern and northern states, where the lot of the peasantry was hardest. Of those he saw, the peasantry of the Catholic ecclesiastical states like Bamberg and Würzburg seemed the best placed. Even where the material prosperity of the peasant was equal to that of the English villager, he seemed to Crabb Robinson to be more subservient, owing to the feudal burdens he still bore, and it seemed wrong to him that so much field work should be left to women. Howitt, writing forty years later, but before the Industrial Revolution had seriously affected Germany, was inclined to minimize the hardness of the German peasants' lot because he was so pleased to find that the majority of them owned the land they cultivated, whereas the average villager in England was a laborer dependent on a master. Howitt too was only familiar with the south and the Rhineland, where it is true that the peasant proprietor preponderated, and where he had, by this time, commuted his services for money payments. His picture would not have been so favorable if based on conditions in Mecklenburg or Prussia. He was struck by the patient laboriousness of the German peasants, men and women, and by the economy they practiced, collecting as they did every scrap that could be used for fodder, manure or firewood. These habits he explained as the result of their working for themselves and not for a master. Aesthetically, however, he preferred the English countryside, with its variety of large and small estates, manor-houses and cottages, and the neatness and

---

4 J. M. v. Loen, *Freye Gedanken vom Hof,* 3rd ed. Frankfort and Leipzig, 1768, p. 28.

cleanliness of even the smallest homesteads. The rarity of gentlemen's seats in the country was a point noted by all English travelers—it was due to the attraction of the nobility to the courts. The cottages were less spick and span than in England because the women worked so much more in the fields, and perhaps also because there was no Hall near by to set a higher standard in these matters.

The chief civilizing influences in the village were the minister and the schoolmaster. The power of the minister was so largely a matter of personality, whatever the sect he represented might be, that no brief general statements can be made about it. . . . The power of the village schoolmaster can be more usefully discussed at this point. Generally speaking, it was very slight indeed, for though, in an age that believed so passionately in education, country people were not neglected by the reformers, most of their proposals remained on paper. In Prussia, for instance, the most advanced of the German states in this respect, the village schools seem to have remained wretched in most cases until after the end of the century. From official reports of an inspection made in 1802 and 1803 in Cleve, a Prussian province where conditions were favorable, it appears that Frederick the Great's admirable General-Landschul-Reglement of 1763 had remained a dead letter. Theoretically, attendance at school for six hours a day was compulsory for all children between the ages of five or six and thirteen. For the poor no fee was charged. The qualifications necessary for a teacher were defined, classes were to be duly graded and uniform textbooks to be used. But at their inspection it was found that forty-three teachers out of sixty-seven were incompetent. Hardly any had attended the training school set up for Cleve in 1784, they had usually been appointed without being examined and once in office they had neither the leisure nor the books they required to improve themselves. They were so wretchedly paid that all had some other occupation. Many were organists or vergers or both, some were tailors or exercised some other craft, some sold brandy or collected tolls. The school buildings, where regular buildings existed, were almost always in bad repair. Often a room had to be hired for the purpose in a house, and sometimes the teacher slept in the school room. There were often no separate classes. Each child came up book in hand and said its lesson. The curriculum was extremely narrow, reading, writing and perhaps a little arithmetic, and a good deal of religion. Little was read beyond the Bible and catechism. Attendance was extremely irregular. In summer the schools were empty.[5] If these were the conditions in an enlightened state, it can be imagined what they were like in the average small state. But in the second half of the century a considerable number of peasants could at least read and write, as is indicated by the large sales of the calendars and so forth that were written for them.

5   W. Meiners, "Landschulen und Landschullehrer im Herzogtum Cleve vor hundert Jahren," in *Archiv für Kulturgeschichte*, III, 1905.

SERFDOM IN RUSSIA

. . . During the years in which millions of free peasants were forced to become serfs the nature of serfdom grew ever more oppressive. By the last part of the eighteenth century the Russian serf was scarcely distinguishable from a chattel slave. That was able to happen because the state withdrew almost entirely from supervision and interference in the relationship between lord and peasant, and thereby allowed the serfowners to gain nearly unlimited powers over the people they owned.

The deterioration in the status of the seignorial peasantry had been going on since the fifteenth century. But the concessions to the dvorianstvo made by Peter I and his successors up to the accession of Paul in 1796, gave a great new impetus to the decline in the position of the peasants. Peter, who needed a large and steady supply of men and money to carry out his grandiose schemes, introduced more efficient systems of taxation and conscription, and made the serfowners responsible for their successful operation. To make it easier for them to perform these duties he allowed them to have new rights over their serfs, and gave legal sanction to powers they had preempted. The rulers after Peter followed his precedent, so that seignorial authority continued to grow. In the last part of the century the increase in prices and the rise in the standard of living of the nobles, made it harder for them to make ends meet. Inevitably, they took advantage of their favored position in the state to demand still greater controls over their peasants, in order to be able to extract greater quantities of goods and services from them. . . .

In a ukase of 15 April 1721 Peter stated that it had been, and still was, customary in Russia for peasants and domestics to be sold "like cattle," and for families to be split up in these transactions. With obvious censure (but complete inaccuracy) Peter stated that there was nothing like this in the whole world, and commanded the practice to cease.[1] Yet in earlier decrees he had not only given recognition to the sale of human beings, but had encouraged it by allowing persons subject to military draft to buy substitutes.[2] In fact, in the very ukase in which he condemned the trade in serfs, he went on to say that if it was impossible

Excerpts from "Masters and Serfs," in Jerome Blum, *Lord and Peasant in Russia: From the Ninth to the Nineteenth Century* (copyright © 1961 by Princeton University Press; Princeton Paperback, 1971), pp. 422–440. Reprinted by permission of Princeton University Press.

1   *PSZ,* VI, no. 3770, p. 377.

2   Engelmann, *Die Leibeigenschaft,* p. 104.

to stop it the serfs should be sold only in cases of need, and then by family rather than by individual. He repeated these pious sentiments three years later in another decree. But the sales went on, and families continued to be broken up, without reproof from the government.

The trade in peasants reached its peak—as did so many of the cruelest aspects of Russian serfdom—during the reign of Catherine II. To give that self-proclaimed disciple of Voltaire her due, she did try to do something about this. In 1771 she decided that the spectacle of human beings on the block should be banned, and ordered that the serfs of bankrupt seigniors could not be sold at public auction. Her prohibition was disregarded, and so in 1792 she amended the law to allow these sales—but forbad the use of the hammer by the auctioneer! She also took measures to cut down on the commerce in recruit substitutes. This traffic always boomed whenever the army issued its draft calls. In 1766 Catherine decreed that men suitable for military service could not be sold during the recruiting period, or for the three months that preceded it. This law, too, was generally evaded.[3]

The sale of peasants without land had been illegal in the White Russian provinces when they had been part of Poland. After their annexation by Russia the landlords there began to follow the example of their peers in the rest of the empire, and a lively business in humans grew up. The terms of the annexation, however, had guaranteed the maintenance of the existing laws, so the legality of the trade was brought into question. The Senate, after deliberating on the problem, solemnly informed Catherine in 1775 that "the proprietors of White Russia as subjects of Your Majesty must enjoy the same rights that the Russian nobility enjoy, and therefore they cannot be deprived of the right to sell their peasants without land."[4] In Lifland the provincial diet in 1765 ordered the imposition of heavy fines on serfowners who sold peasants without land. This measure, inspired apparently not by humanitarianism but by the desire to keep peasants within Lifland, proved unsuccessful, and in 1804 new legislation was adopted to end the practice.[5] In 1798 Paul, overruling a recommendation of the Senate, declared the sale of serfs without land in Little Russia illegal and ordered it to cease. Yet fifty years later the seigniors there were reported to be evading the law, and selling recruit substitutes to buyers in the Central Industrial region.[6] . . .

The increase in the judicial and police powers of the serfowners had as its corollary an increase in their control over the private lives of their peasants. The marriages of their serfs were a matter of especial concern to the seigniors. They preferred to have their peasants wed one another and produce more serfs for the master, rather than have their female serfs marry a man who did not belong to

3   Semevskii, *Krest'iane,* I, 148–49, 151.
4   Engelmann, *Die Leibeigenschaft,* pp. 143–44.
5   Semevskii, *Krest'iane,* I, 158.
6   *PSZ,* XXV, no. 18706, 16 October 1798, pp. 419–20; Samarin, *Sochineniia,* II, 409.

them. If one of their women did want to marry someone outside her master's property, the law required her to get his consent. He could refuse to give it except in the event the girl wanted to marry a soldier (Peter I had ordered this exception). Some proprietors demanded a fee for their permission. Often the amount they asked varied with the wealth of the applicant, and on occasion it amounted to hundreds and even thousands of rubles. Thus, two rich serfs of Ivanovo had to pay Count Sheremetev seven thousand and nine thousand rubles each for his consent.[7]

The law did not require serfs of the same master to get his permission if they wanted to marry. But this was a universal custom, and some lords charged a small fee for their consent. Often, too, serfowners who felt that their peasants' obligations to them included producing children and thereby adding to their master's assets, ordered two of his serfs to wed one another without regard to the couple's own wishes. Peter I had forbidden this practice in 1724, but serfowners paid no heed to the ban. Serfs tried to defend themselves against these unwelcome matches by standing together as sponsors at a christening, for church law prohibited a marriage between godparents. This stratagem had its obvious limitation; infants in need of baptism were not always available to a man and woman who had just been told to get married. But farsighted peasants who had always felt distaste for one another could use it, and so foil their master's wish if he should later decide to pair them off.

Another matter that interested seigniors was the real and personal property held by their peasants. This had long been considered as belonging ultimately to the master. Usually serfowners allowed their peasants to keep their property, and to take it with them when they were sold to another master. The law did not allow serfs to buy real property until a few years before the emancipation, but . . . many lords permitted their peasants to buy land and even serfs in the lord's name. But the lord always had the right to take anything he wanted from his serf's property without paying for it. Sometimes that happened. A group of serfs who belonged to Count Panin pooled their savings and bought a piece of land near Riga to raise vegetables. They made the purchase, of course, in Panin's name. A little while later Panin, inspired no doubt by patriotic ardor, gave the land to the state for a new railroad line. The serfs who had paid for the land received nothing. A wealthy serf owned by Count Sheremetev left 150,000 rubles in bank deposits when he died. His children, who had bought their freedom from the Count, tried to get the money as the heirs of their father, but the court awarded it to Sheremetev on the ground that he had owned the dead man and therefore owned his property.[8]

In return for its grant to the serfowners of nearly complete powers, the government did charge them with certain responsibilities for the well-being of

---

7   Schepetov, *Krepostnoe pravo*, p. 78; Berlin, *Russkaia burzhuaziia*, p. 87.

8   Kulischer, "Die kapitalistischen Unternehmer," p. 352n; Turgenev, *La Russie*, II, 129.

their serfs. But the nature and extent of these obligations were far from commensurate with the privileges allowed the seigniors, while the ease with which they were avoided gives testimony to the government's lack of interest in the lot of the common people.

The only provisions in the Code of 1649 concerned with welfare dealt with slaves and not serfs. The slaveowner was ordered to feed his thralls in time of famine. If he failed to do this, and his slaves had to seek alms, they were to be taken from him. When a captured runaway slave was returned, his owner had to pledge that he would not punish the fugitive by maiming or killing him, or starving him to death.[9] These pitifully inadequate ordinances provided the foundation for the legislation of the next two hundred years on the duties the proprietor owed his serfs.

In 1719 Peter ordered that if a serfowner's conduct worked undue hardships upon his peasants his land and serfs were to be placed under the guardianship of his kinsmen until he mended his ways. If he failed to reform he was to be sent to a monastery and put under ecclesiastical censure. Peter justified this law not by any reference to the need to protect peasants from cruelties and injustices they might suffer from their masters. Instead he pointed out that mistreated serfs were likely to run away, thereby depopulating properties and so reducing the government's tax revenues.[10] Empress Anna in 1734 enjoined private proprietors, and also the managers of lands owned by the crown, to care for their peasants during famines and see to it that they did not become beggars. This command was repeated a number of times in succeeding years, and seigniors were threatened with punishment for noncompliance. In 1775 Catherine II instructed provincial officials to be on the watch for lords who cruelly mistreated their serfs, or who lived so lavishly that they brought ruin to themselves and their peasants. She also tried to make it more difficult for nobles to free serfs when they became too old to work. These unfortunates were turned out of their holdings to fend for themselves. Catherine did not abolish nor even question the right of the seignior to do this, but she ordered that the serfs had to give their consent to be emancipated, and she made the lord responsible for the taxes of the freed peasants until the next revision was made. Her successor, Paul, issued a series of decrees ordering the construction of bins in every village to store food for emergencies, and instructed the serfowners to see to it that their peasants kept these granaries stocked.[11] . . .

The inadequacies of the legislation and the government's lack of interest in protecting the serfs did not mean, of course, that every serfowner mistreated his peasants. Many, and probably most of them, moved by economic considerations and by fellow-feeling, looked after their people. They did not need the goad of

9 *Ulozhenie,* Chapter XX, sec. 41, 42, 92.

10 Semevskii, *Krest'iane,* I, 316; Miller, *Essai,* pp. 268n.

11 Engelmann, *Die Leibeigenschaft,* p. 141; Dodge, *Abolitionist sentiment,* p. 127.

law and the threat of punishment to feed their serfs when crops failed, or to take care of their aged and incapacitated serfs at their own expense.[12] Nonetheless, the nearly unlimited control the seignior had over his people, the fact that the serfs had no legal way to protect themselves against his excesses, and perhaps most important, the absence of social disapproval among the serfowner's peers if he did mistreat his peasants, opened the door to callousness, and often to brutality. Foreigners were shocked when they listened to people of fashion and prominence chat about whippings they had meted out to their serfs, or heard a noble at his club preen himself before an appreciative audience because he had sentenced three of his serfs to nearly triple the legally allowed number of strokes with the cane.[13]

The serf lived always at the mercy of the whims, appetites, and temper of his owner. Women, and especially those who served in the master's house, could not defend themselves against a lustful seignior. Some proprietors kept harems of slave girls, and there were even seigniors (and in some cases stewards) who practiced *ius primae noctis,* though this had never been an established principle of Russian seignorial law. Captious or finical seigniors had a serf whipped because he upset a saltcellar—a serious offense because it was believed to foretell the coming of some misfortune—or because he made the soup too salty, or had not roasted the chicken to his master's taste. General Kropotkin lost his temper because he thought his serfs were stealing from him, became still angrier when he discovered he was mistaken, and vented his rage by having a serf beaten with one hundred blows of a birch rod. Ivan Turgenev's mother sent two of her serfs to Siberia because they neglected to bow to her when she passed by while they were working.[14]

The helplessness of the serfs proved too great a temptation for those proprietors in whose natures sadism lay close to the surface. These people inflicted frightful cruelties upon their peasants.[15] One of the most infamous cases was that of Dařia Saltykov who in 1756 inherited six hundred serfs from her husband. In seven years she tortured scores of them to death for petty or imagined offenses. Her conduct became so notorious that the authorities decided they had to do something. So in 1762 they began an investigation. It lasted for six years. Finally, she was stripped of her noble rank, pilloried for one hour in Moscow, and then sentenced to spend the rest of her life in confinement in a convent. In contrast to her mild punishment, the serfs who at her command had aided in the torturing of her victims were beaten with the knout and then condemned for life to hard labor in Siberia.

---

12   Cf. Le Play, *Les ouvriers,* II, 58; Haxthausen, *Die ländliche Verfassung,* pp. 121-22; Semevskii, *Krest'iane,* I, 238-40; Grekov, "Tambovskoe imenie," pp. 513-14.

13   Passenans, *La Russie,* II, 124-30; Bernhardi, *Aus dem Leben,* II, 69.

14   Kulischer, "Die Leibeigenschaft," p. 9; Passenans, *La Russie,* II, 120-23; Kropotkin, *Memoirs,* pp. 49-51; Yarmolinsky, *Turgenev,* p. 13.

15   Cf. Semevskii, *Krest'iane,* I, ch. VII.

Daria Saltykov and the people like her were psychopaths. But thoughtless and unconscious cruelty was omnipresent. A story told by Peter Kropotkin about his father is a revealing, and at the same time wryly amusing, illustration of the inhumanity inherent in a society where men owned their fellow humans. The elder Kropotkin, as he emerges from his son's memoirs, is a familiar figure to readers of the great nineteenth century Russian novels—the bumbling, pompous, bigoted, self-indulgent landlord. He had been decorated for gallantry in 1828 during the war with the Turks and was inordinately proud of this honor. When his children asked him to tell them about it, he explained that he had been billeted in a Turkish village when fire broke out. His bodyserf, Frol, rushed into the flames to save a child trapped in a burning house. Kropotkin's commanding officer saw this and was so impressed that he awarded the Cross of St. Anne for bravery on the spot—to Kropotkin. The children, of course, pointed out that Frol had saved the child and so deserved the decoration, whereupon their father, nettled by their obtuseness, exclaimed, "What of that? Was he not my man? It is all the same."[16] . . .

The peasants themselves had no legal way of calling official attention to injustices inflicted upon them by their masters. The code of 1649 had not outlawed the right of serfs to present petitions of complaint against their lords, but had declared that no credence was to be placed in them unless they contained proof of treason by the person against whom the complaint was lodged.[17] Despite this rule it had been customary for serfs to send petitions to their sovereigns, and especially to tsaritsas, presumably because women were thought to be more tenderhearted (a serious error in judgment so far as Russian empresses were concerned). Then Catherine II, after a tour in which she had been besieged with petitions, decided that this nuisance must cease. In a ukase of 22 August 1767 she decreed that henceforth it would be a criminal act for serfs to present petitions against their masters. Those who violated this law were to be beaten with the knout and sent to forced labor in Siberia.[18] Serfs could still denounce their owner if they presented evidence that he was treasonous, or plotting an attempt on the life of the tsar, or evading taxes by not having serfs entered on the assessment lists.[19] These exceptions were of small moment. Catherine's decree had stripped the serfs of the only legal weapon they had to protect themselves against the wilfulness of their masters.

Early in the nineteenth century a Frenchman who had lived in Russia for many years, wrote that the serfowner's domination over his peasants was greater than that of any sovereign in the world. He pointed out that the authority of a crowned despot was limited by law, custom, and public opinion, but in Russia

16 Kropotkin, *Memoirs*, pp. 10–11.

17 *Ulozhenie*, Chapter II, sect. 13.

18 *PSZ*, XXVIII, no. 12966, pp. 334–36. Later legislation mildened these penalties.

19 *SZ*, 1857, IX, sect. 1036.

these forces supported and furthered the prerogatives of the seigniors.[20] He was scarcely exaggerating. For, as Empress Catherine II herself explained in a letter to her friend Denis Diderot, Russian serfowners were ''free to do in their estates whatever seemed best to them, except to give the death penalty which is prohibited to them.''[21] She could have added that the death penalty, too, was meted out by serfowners under the guise of ordering a serf to be whipped. If enough blows were given the victim died, but that of course was not the master's fault.

20   Passenans, *La Russie,* I, 86–87.

21   Quoted in Schkaff, *La question,* p. 58.

QUIET VILLAGES
AND
GROWING TOWNS

Even before the onset of industrialism, town life in western Europe was beginning to develop a style and a tenor of its own. But with their poorly developed network of roadways and their uncomfortable vehicles, Europeans still moved inland at a pace no faster than a walking person or a horse-drawn carriage. Communication between one region and another was dreadfully slow, with the result that most towns were obliged to survive on their own resources and those of the surrounding countryside. Nevertheless, commerce and trade were assuming an importance only hinted at in earlier centuries. Above all the towns served as a marketplace. Yet even those outside of the main cities were becoming complex social organisms in their own right. The shopkeepers, tradespeople, and merchants who thrived there were fully conscious of their nonrural way of life. Historians can now describe this gradual growth of civic tradition and identify some of the urban social types who were other than transient or relocated peasants.

John Crofts reminds us of the sheer physical obstacles that had to be surmounted in order to construct a primary system of roadways. Without these arteries of communication it was every horseman for himself. Construction of viable highways capable of supporting heavily loaded wagons was halting and erratic. All-weather streets in the towns were usually so few as to be a curiosity rather than a convenience. Still, the road-map of Europe was being slowly redrawn.

Roger Hart illustrates how imperceptible this change actually was, even in England, to the majority of villagers. Most people preferred to leave the hazards and discomforts of travel to entrepreneurial types whose business it was to move from place to place. Rural-village life, meanwhile, continued in a more accustomed routine of labor and leisure, an existence more often glorified by romantic poets than carefully investigated by social historians. Hart reconstructs the eating and drinking habits of English people in the eighteenth century, an age in which the pub, the pint of gin, and the poorhouse became national institutions.

W. H. Lewis draws some distinctions between England and France and demonstrates that within France (as elsewhere on the Continent) legal and social conditions varied greatly from town to town. Here we encounter the first meaningful use of the term "bourgeois." We are also able to trace the origins of municipal government as it developed under the somewhat reluctant and never financially disinterested aegis of monarchy. Finally, by accompanying Lewis on a walking tour of late seventeenth-century Paris we can gain some sense of the mixture of revulsion and admiration that the large town must have given its citizens and visitors.

It would be overwrought to find in these developments a great social mutation; what we perceive, rather, is an embryonic stage of change. Except in isolated instances, the pace of life by the end of the eighteenth century had not been altered for most Europeans since medieval times. But clearly there was already a movement, a stirring that the dramatic political events after 1789 were to accelerate.

THE ROADS

The Tudor governments had made some effort to deal with the problem of the roads, and the system of repair by statute labor under parish overseers, set up by the acts of 1555 and 1563, worked well enough in remote country places to survive until the nineteenth century. What they had failed and perhaps without the help of Dutch engineers could not have attempted to do, was to establish any standard or prescribe any technique of road-making; and this was a fatal omission.

It is clear from the methods of repair usually adopted that a road was hardly regarded as a structure at all. It was commonly thought of as a strip of land upon which no member of the community had the right to sow his peas, or stack his manure, or dig his marl. It is true that over-thrifty individuals frequently tried to use it in this way; but public opinion was against them for the simple reason that once a highway was blocked the King's lieges had a statutory right to make their way over the land adjoining to their destination.[1] This right was well understood by the public of the seventeenth century, and was exercised so freely as to constitute a serious menace to agriculture. A gentleman like Sergeant Hoskins, contemplating a journey by coach in 1627, would order his servants as a matter of course "to study the coach-way; where to break hedges, and how to avoid deep and dangerous ways";[2] and Justice Ellwood's coachman "seeing a nearer and easier way than the common road through a cornfield, and that it was wide enough to run without damaging the corn," turned into the cornfield without hesitation.[3] In winter especially, when a highway had become in parts impassable the traffic was compelled to use "driftways on trespass through the neighboring enclosures," with the result that the original line of the road was sometimes forgotten and superseded. "Travellers begge passage through another's grounds in winter" says Thomas Adams in a sermon of 1630, "for avoydance of the Miry wayes, and so long use it on sufferance that at last they plead it by Prescription, and hold it by Custome." The problem was particularly grievous in the close-farming districts of the southeast, where the hedges and

From John Crofts, *Packhorse, Waggon and Post: Land Carriage and Communications under the Tudors and Stuarts* (London: Routledge & Kegan Paul Ltd., 1967), pp. 14–17, 19–21, by permission of the publisher.

1   See C. H. Hartman. *The Story of the Roads,* 1927, p. 46.

2   *Memoir of Colonel John Birch* (Camd. Soc.), p. 186.

3   *History of the Life of Thomas Ellwood,* ed. C. Crump, 1900, p. 6.

banks, by confining the traffic to one track, had brought the roads into such an abominable state that they could be used as a potent argument against the enclosure system. Fitzherbert tries to meet the objection by suggesting that fenced-in lanes should be used only where the ground is stony and dry, and that where it is soft "at every hedge that goeth overthwart the highway, there to make a gate. . . . And then hath every man the whole close to ride, carry or go in as they had before."[4] Wherever possible the traffic trampled out a wide verge of land "thrown in, as it were, for an overplus to the highway." In Sussex especially Defoe says he had seen "the road, sixty to a hundred yards broad, lie from side to side all poached with cattle, the land of no manner benefit, and yet no going with a horse but at every step up to the shoulders, full of sloughs and holes and covered with standing water."[5]

In the open-farming districts the traveler was free to pick his way to a much greater extent, but the result often was that the line of the road evaporated in an abstract right of way. This year the approach to the village might be straight forward across the fallow; but next year the fallow (following the usual rotation) might have been ploughed in long strips separated by balks or furrow leys, and the traveler might have to make a wide detour to reach his destination. A witness before the Star Chamber in the reign of James I testified that "sometymes when the common feilds of Ladbrooke (in Warwickshire) lay open, the passengers . . . did in their jornies . . . passe and goe over the said comon feilds now and then upon one furrow ley and sometymes uppon another furrow ley as they would, but they did notwithstanding usually keepe neare one place." He said that "passengers doe the like in other common fields," but nevertheless gave it as his opinion "that there is and may be a high and common way through such places."[6] No doubt he was right, but it was evidently difficult in such districts even for the local farmers to say exactly where the road lay, and for the stranger it must often have been impossible. "Travellers know no highwaies in the common fields" complains an agriculturist of the period, and much land was "spoiled and trampled down in all wide roads where coaches and carts take liberty to choose for their best advantage." The tendency of the traffic to "fan out" wherever possible was particularly noticeable over heaths and commons. Arthur Young, writing in 1760, could remember the time when carriages approaching Norwich from the south "would sometimes be a mile abreast of each other in pursuit of the best track." Carriers crossing Salisbury Plain in 1689 were "about two miles apart" when they were caught in a blizzard. Travelers to Brigg in Lincolnshire were guided by a land lighthouse; and those benighted on their way to Barton on Humber listened for the tolling of a bell.[7]

Evidently then, it was to the interest of the agricultural community that a

4 *Surveyenge,* Ch. XL.
5 Defoe. *Essay on Projects,* 1697.
6 *Star Chamber Proc.:* James I, 68, file 3.
7 Prothero. *The Pioneers and Progress of English Farming,* 1888, pp. 44, 56.

thoroughfare, where it existed, should be kept clear. Nobody expected it to be good going. Indeed it seems to have been generally accepted in some districts that the worst possible way between two given points was along the common road. But as long as it was free from certifiable obstructions, and not demonstrably an impassable slough, it enabled Tom Touchy to take the law of any man who trespassed on the land adjoining. And to many a remote and stagnant and self-supporting village this was its sole value. The inhabitants did not use it themselves. They did not want to go anywhere. They were sometimes quite ignorant even of the name of a parish six miles farther along the road.[8] As far as they were concerned it was simply a strip abandoned to the stranger-public in return for their undisturbed occupation of the fields on either side. . . .

The effect of this growing traffic problem was to maintain and even to intensify the social and intellectual contrast between London and the provinces. The spirit of national unity fostered by Elizabeth's government and the successful contest with Spain had found a focus and a rallying point in the life of the capital. Here the spectacle of English wealth and English power, English law and English genius, might be seen not in dim vision or hopeful outline but as a thing achieved, solid and incontrovertible. Here were the beginnings of a social sense that ignored the old class distinctions, and of an intellectual freemasonry that drew together under the same starry heaven of wit the nobly born exquisite and the bricklayer's son. But this dazzling scene was becoming the more inaccessible the brighter it shone. A widening circle of mud and misery, caused by those very activities that gave the city its wealth and prestige, tended to insulate the capital from the life and thought of the country as a whole. A hundred miles from London they were still living in the fifteenth century; two hundred miles away they were hardly out of the fourteenth. While Ben Jonson was refining upon points of scholarship at the Devil Tavern Sir Thomas Metcalfe of Wensleydale was laying siege to Raydall House with forty armed retainers; blazing away at the windows as though the War of the Roses was still in full swing;[9] and while fashionable congregations listened to the theological subtleties of a Sanderson or a Jeremy Taylor, an old man at Cartmel Fell was assuring his minister that he had indeed "heard of that man you speak of (Jesus Christ) once at a play at Kendall, called Corpus Christi play, where there was a man on a tree, and blood ran down."[10]

To bridge this enormous gulf many things were needed besides better roads—better education, an effective journalism and a more regular system of communications. Meanwhile the carrier did what he could. For more than a century he was the community's sole champion against its inveterate enemies, the wind and the rain. While the citizen took his evening pipe, and the tired farmer dozed by his fire, the carrier's gangs were still splashing thigh-deep through Mimm's Wash, or unpinning the wheels of their wagons to haul them

8   *H. M. Com.* Clements, p. 222; and compare *Diary of Celia Fiennes,* ed. Griffiths, p. 81.

9   *Journal of Nicholas Assheton,* 1617–18 (Chetham Soc.).

10   *Life of John Shaw* (Surtees Soc., 1875), p. 138.

one by one out of Dunchurch Lane; or their clanging pack-trains were vanishing into the wintry heights of the Pennines, there to plod on, hour after hour, along tracks known only to the curlews, until at last their bells would be heard again on Hartside, bringing news from London down the long zigzag path into Melmerby and the Valley of the Lune.

For most country dwellers the carrier was the only regular means of contact with the outside world, and the recurring freshets of news that he brought stirred the sleeping pool of local opinion like the return of the tide, enabling its inhabitants to glow momentarily with a sense of the open sea. He was also, no less, the channel of rumor, and must often have done something to foment that extraordinary propensity to groundless panic which seems to have afflicted most country places in the seventeenth century. "To tell news after the carrier" had become a proverbial way of describing a futile undertaking. The carrier had told all there was, and sometimes a good deal more. "Simondsall news" was what they called it in Gloucestershire.

> The clothiers, horsecarriers and wainmen of this hundred who weekly frequent London, knowinge by ancient custome that the first question, after welcome home from London, is "What newes at London?" doe usually gull us with feigned inventions, devised by them upon those downes; which wee either then suspecting upon the report, or after findinge false, wee cry out "Simondsall newes." A generall speach betweene every cobler's teeth.[11]

But this was peace-time fooling. At moments of crisis when the public was terrified by rumors of a hideous Popish Plot, or of a disbanded Irish army storming across the country and burning folk in their beds, the arrival of the London carrier on his usual day, reporting all quiet on the road, must have had a steadying effect. If the carrier could keep his day, things could not be so bad; and thus his stubborn figure, plodding along the roads which most of them would never travel, and through regions which they hardly knew by name, became the symbol and almost the assurance of an immutable order. . . .

11 J. Smyth. *Lives of the Berkeleys,* III, 30.

—ROGER HART————————————————————————

THE VILLAGE

With few and bad roads, the villages of eighteenth-century England were self-contained and inbred. A village had to be able to clothe and feed itself, provide work for all, and look after its old and sick. Conditions had hardly changed since Shakespeare's day. Village women made the cloth—spinning, weaving and sewing. They also baked the bread from locally grown corn, brewed the beer, salted meat for winter and sometimes helped in the fields. The men made nearly all their own equipment, for example axes, shears, knives, saws, spades, hoes, wagons and carts, hurdles for the sheep-pens, woven baskets. They dug stone and chalk for building cottages and barns. Wages, where paid at all, were very low, perhaps 6s. or 7s. a week; most village workers received payment in kind, shelter, corn, milk, sometimes fish, rarely meat, wool. They were at least more or less immune from the wild fluctuations in the price of bread and other products which hit eighteenth-century townspeople so hard. Every village had one or two craftsmen for special jobs, such as a blacksmith, potter, joiner, weaver, maltster or tanner, depending on local needs and resources. Buying and selling with other villages or towns in the same county was rare. Work was hard—up at dawn and to bed at sundown. Children had to help as soon as they were strong enough to hold a broom or carry timber.

Relaxations and pleasures were few, perhaps fishing, snaring rabbits, a little poaching. A visit to the market or fair in a distant town would be an experience of a lifetime.

Those villagers who farmed three or four acres of their own in the common fields could afford a little more independence of the local squire. Those squires who wanted to make improvements to the property by enclosures often complained about it. One wrote, "If you offer them work, they will tell you that they must go to look up their sheep, cut furzes, get their cow out of the pound or, perhaps, say that they must take their horse to be shod that he may carry them to the horse race or a cricket match." In his book *Horse-Houghing Husbandry* (1731), the great agriculturalist Jethro Tull agreed: "The deflection of [workmen] is such that few gentlemen can keep their lands in their own hands but let them for a little to tenants who can bear to be insulted, assaulted, kicked, cuffed and Bridewelled with more patience than gentlemen are provided with. . . . It were more easy to teach the beasts of the field than to drive the ploughman out of the way.''

Rural housing, if such it can be called, was very primitive. Villagers lived in hovels made of stones piled up and covered with thatch or brushwood, or of cheap local materials, such as ''mud and stud'' in clay districts, or wood on the edge of the great forests such as Wychwood, Wyre, Sherwood, Rockingham, Knaresborough and elsewhere (many of which have since disappeared). The structures were barely weatherproof, and few have survived from Johnson's time into the present century. Brick cottages were unknown until the next century. Cottages were tiny, perhaps one living room and one bedroom for the entire family. Ceilings were low; the windows were small and without glass, the floor beaten earth, perhaps covered with straw.

Yet to many contemporaries, the English village sometimes seemed set in a Garden of Eden. In *The Deserted Village,* Goldsmith wrote:

> How often have I loitered o'er thy green,
> Where humble happiness endeared each scene!
> How often have I paused on every charm,
> The sheltered cot, the cultivated farm,
> The never-failing brook, the busy mill,
> The decent church that topped the neigbr'ng hill,
> The hawthorn bush, with seats beneath the shade,
> For talking age and whispering lovers made.

But this was a particularly rosy view. What does seem clear, however, is that the English village compared extremely well with villages on the Continent in the same period. The young Comte de la Rochefoucauld wrote on his visit to Norfolk in 1784, ''As always, I admired the way in which in all these little villages the houses are clean and have an appearance of cosiness in which ours in France are lacking. There is some indefinable quality about the arrangement of these houses which makes them appear better than they actually are.''

THE FAMILY AT HOME

Breakfast for most people consisted of just tea and rolls, or bread and butter; sometimes toast would be eaten in winter. Foreigners were surprised at this dish. C. P. Moritz wrote in 1782: ''The slices of bread and butter given to you with tea are as thin as poppy leaves, but there is a way of roasting slices of buttered bread before the fire which is incomparable. One slice after another is taken and held to the fire with a fork until the butter is melted, then the following one will be always laid upon it so that the butter soaks through the whole pile of slices. This is called *toast.*''

People did not usually breakfast until the day had already begun; many rose at six but did not breakfast until ten. Fashionable people often took their breakfast so late that they were able to make calls beforehand; and in Bath and other spas and resorts the whole business of bathing and "taking the waters" usually took place before breakfast. In the first part of the century, breakfast parties were popular. We know from the *Gentleman's Magazine* that public breakfast parties were held at such places as Ranelagh, or Ruchholt near Stratford, or Marylebone Gardens, or Cox's at Dulwich. Bubb Dodington (1691–1772), the diarist, recorded a private breakfast party in his *Diary:* "The Princess of Wales and Lady Augusta attended by Lady Middlesex and Mr. Breton did Mrs. Dodington and me the honor of breakfasting with us. After breakfast, we walked all round my gardens: we came in, and they went into all the rooms . . . it was near three o'clock."

Dodington was not the only person to breakfast so late in the day. Fashionable people thought of the morning as lasting until dinner-time, say two or three in the afternoon. C. P. Moritz wrote in 1782 that "it was usual to walk out in a sort of *negligée* or morning dress, your hair not dressed, but merely rolled up in rollers, and in a frock and boots."

Dinner was the chief meal of the day, eaten at two or three o'clock in the afternoon, although the rich often did not sit down until four or five. The Swiss visitor César de Saussure, who was in England between 1725 and 1730, wrote "an Englishman's table is remarkably clean, the linen is very white, the plate shines brightly, and knives and forks are changed surprisingly often, that is to say, every time a plate is removed. When everybody has done eating, the table is cleared, the cloth even being removed, and a bottle of wine with a glass for each guest is placed on the table." At this point, the ladies retired, leaving the men to propose toasts—a long and solemn ceremony—and smoke clay pipes of tobacco.

C. P. Moritz complained bitterly about the poor standard of English dinners: "An English dinner . . . generally consists of a piece of half-boiled or half-roasted meat; and a few cabbage leaves boiled in plain water; on which they pour a sauce made of flour and butter." English coffee, he called "a prodigious quantity of brown water." The wheat bread, the butter, and Cheshire cheese, however earned praise. The middle classes were heavy beef- and mutton-eaters, although some people ate fish; and oysters became a delicacy. Parson Woodforde leaves an account of a dinner which included a leg of mutton with caper sauce, a pig's face, a neck of pork roasted with gooseberries, and plum pudding. Delicacies included "potatoes in shells," cold tongue, partridge, roast swan ("good eating with sweet sauce"), Parmesan cheese, orange and apple puddings, syllabubs and jellies.

Supper was the last meal of the day, and included the same sort of dishes that were eaten at dinner. In 1726, César de Saussure noticed that "supper is not considered a necessary meal," but by the end of the century, this had changed, and people liked "a late and great dinner" (Johnson). Ordinary people had their supper at eight or nine o'clock, at the end of a long day's work, but the rich often ate supper in the small hours, after a dance or party. Horace Walpole commented in 1777, "The present folly is late hours. . . . Lord Derby's cook lately gave him warning: the man owned he liked his place [job] but said he should be killed by dressing suppers at three in the morning."

The diet of the poor was very plain. At the start of the century, coarse rye and barley bread was eaten a good deal, although the purer bread made from wheat became more widely available later on. Former luxuries such as tea and sugar now came within the means of many people, causing Arthur Young to refer disapprovingly to the "growth of luxury among the poor." Young took a note of some average prices of food during his tour of 1771: bread 1¼ d. a pound, butter 6d. a pound, butcher's meat 3d. a pound, cheese 3d. a pound. These items had to be purchased from wages which were probably only 6s. to 8s. a week.

Daily life in the eighteenth century was an almost nonstop round of work, and more work. Ordinary people rose at 5 A.M. or 6 A.M. and usually worked through until 8 P.M. or 9 P.M. Those families who were self-employed, and paid piece-work, naturally tended to work long hours to scrape money together; those who were employed by others had to work these hours, or be sacked for "idleness." There was no escape from this routine for childen. They were set to work by their parents as soon as they could do anything useful. In towns, very young children might be made to run errands, wash floors, help carry and give other domestic help. In the countryside, they scared birds from the crop fields, picked stones from the soil in readiness for tilling, combed wool and collected rushes for dipping in tallow. Daily life was extremely hard, and children had to play as much a part as the old, sick and destitute in the struggle for existence. There was no idea that children occupied any special place in the home or in society; there were no schools for them to go to, no idea of "education." They were regarded more or less as small adults, and everyone hoped they would grow up as quickly as possible to do their share of work, to learn a useful trade, or perhaps go to sea, as many did, at the age of twelve or less.

Many people felt that the treatment of children was a disgrace to society and encouraged them to become lawless or idle. One man who decided something should be done was Jonas Hanway, who with the help of Sir John Fielding, and others, founded the Marine Society, which trained poor boys for the sea. He also spoke out against the cruelties of chimney-sweep boys, before the time of Bennet and Shaftesbury. But his main self-appointed task was to rescue pauper children. Having studied poor-houses and foundling hospitals abroad, he became a Governor of the Foundling Hospital in London, and helped bring about the Acts of 1761 and 1767. The Act of 1761 obliged parishes to keep registers of their infant poor. The 1767 Act ("the Hanway Act") made parishes send their pauper children under the age of six into the country to be looked after, at not less than 2s. 6d. a week. But many parishes had little interest in really helping, and Hanway himself sadly commented, ''the apprenticeship of some parish children is as great a scene of inhumanity as the suffering of others to die in infancy.''

Marriage in those days was a binding contract for life, always performed by a priest, often at the instructions of the parents. Divorce was extremely rare and difficult to obtain, since it required an Act of Parliament in each case. Bigamy, desertion and other marital offenses were probably more common then than now, partly because women had very few rights they could legally enforce against bad husbands, and partly because of the lack of law enforcement. Yet there are more complaints from the husbands than the wives. Johnson thought, ''Our marriage service is too refined. It is calculated only for the best kind of marriages; whereas, we should have a form for matches of convenience, of which there are many.'' He agreed with Boswell, ''that there was no absolute necessity for having the marriage ceremony performed by a regular clergyman, for this was not commanded in scripture.''

Boswell wrote a little ''epigrammatick song'' which Garrick had had set to music, bewailing the fate of husbands:

A MATRIMONIAL THOUGHT

In the blithe days of honeymoon,
  With Kate's allurements smitten,
I lov'd her late, I lov'd her soon,
  And call'd her dearest kitten.

But now my kitten's grown a cat,
  And cross like other wives,
O! by my soul, my honest Mat,
  I fear she has nine lives!

Later, Boswell ''mentioned to him a dispute between a friend of mine and his lady, concerning conjugal infidelity, which my friend had maintained was by no means so bad in the husband as in the wife. Johnson: 'Your friend was in the right, Sir. Between a man and his Maker it is a different question: but between a man and his wife, a husband's infidelity is nothing. They are connected by children, by fortune, by serious considerations of community. Wise married women don't trouble themselves about infidelity in their husbands.' ''

GIN DRINKERS

The first half of the century saw more gin drunk by the people of Britain than at any other time. Gin was not expensive—certainly more within the means of the ordinary person then than now. The order of the day was, ''Drunk for 1*d.,* dead drunk for 2*d.,* straw for nothing''; the amount consumed was enormous. Henry Fielding wrote in 1751 after two years as a London magistrate, ''Gin . . . is the principal sustenance (if it may so be called) of more than a hundred thousand people in this metropolis. Many of these Wretches there are, who swallow Pints of this Poison within the Twenty Four Hours: the Dreadfull Effects of which I have the Misfortune every Day to see, and to smell too,'' he added. The root of the trouble lay in the last part of the seventeenth century; home manufacturers had been encouraged by the Government in making English spirits from corn, to discourage imports. Alehouses had to be licensed by the magistrates, but the sale of gin went unchecked. In London alone there were perhaps eight thousand places where gin was openly sold, apart from alehouses: stalls and barrows, chandlers and tobacconists were some.

Both drinkers and manufacturers opposed reform; in fact, a £20 retail license fixed in 1720, and a 2s. per gallon duty were lifted in 1733, when wheat-growers protested to Parliament that sales had slumped. But three years later, Parliament returned to the attack, fixing a new license fee of £50, and a tax of 20s. per gallon. In those days, it amounted to virtual prohibition; but due to evasion of payments, violence against informers, and difficulties of administration, Parliament in 1743 again reduced all these charges, though from now on the distillers could not sell their own liquor direct to the public, but had to wholesale it to licensed retailers paying a 20s. license. But outside London, the towns were still very anxious about the effects of gin in increasing lawlessness and idleness, and after Bristol, Salisbury, Rochester, Manchester and Norwich petitioned Parliament a new Act was passed (1751) which stopped the worst excesses. After 1751, the situation began to improve although gin still continued to be as popular a drink as tea is today.

DOWN AND OUT

Parishes, of which England had fifteen thousand, were responsible for looking after their own poor (as well as for their sick, aged and orphans). The Government did not concern itself. Most parishes only contained a few hundred people, and so had small resources. Most relied upon the services of an overseer, appointed by the local magistrates. The poor could apply to the parish for "relief," and the overseer then had to decide whether to give them a few pence from the rates and send them on their way; try to find them work; or threaten them with trouble if they didn't find work themselves. Most people of the time agreed with Daniel Defoe, who said that a "pauper given employment was a vagabond given a favor." So it was, that the ratepayers used the parish workhouses as a way of driving idle beggars to find work for themselves.

Under the Poor Law Act of 1722, parishes were allowed to build their own workhouses, and to put their poor to work. Many parishes turned their poor over to a road-builder or other contractor in exchange for a hire fee; a parish would sometimes let a road-builder put a whole workhouse under marching orders. The parish purse would be protected, the contractor would get workmen—and the poor would probably suffer. As the Quaker John Scott wrote in 1773, "By means of this statute, the parochial managers are impowered to establish a set of petty tyrants as their substitutes, who, farming the poor at a certain price, accumulate dishonest wealth, by abridging them of reasonable food, and imposing on them unreasonable [toil]." The workhouse was often feared as a "House of Terror." As well as the workhouse, there was the poor-house, virtually a doss-house. Crabbe paints a pathetic poor-house scene in *The Village* (1783):

> Theirs is yon House that holds the Parish-Poor,
> Whose walls of mud scarce bear the broken door;
> There, where the putrid vap'rs, flagging, play,
> There Children dwell who know no parents' care;
> Parents who know no children's love, dwell there!
> Heart-broken matrons on their joyless bed,
> Forsaken Wives, and Mothers never wed;
> Dejected widows with unheeded tears,
> And crippled age with more than childhood fears;
> The Lame, the Blind, and, far the happiest they—
> The moping Idiot and the Madman gay.

Henry Fielding in 1753, in his report on the Poor Law, said, "they starve and freeze and rot among themselves." But Dr. Johnson's complacent views were more typical of people of the time. Boswell described their talk on the subject: "He [Dr. Johnson] said, 'the poor in England were better provided for, than at any other country of the same extent . . . Where a great proportion of the people,' said he, 'are suffered to languish in helpless misery, that must be ill-policed [governed] . . . a decent provision for the poor is the true test of civilization.'" In 1750, about £700,000 of parish rates went to the relief of the poor. The middle classes who paid it felt it was a heavy and annoying burden.

Fielding wrote three years later, "Every man who hath any property must feel the weight of that tax which is levied for the use of the poor; and every man of any understanding must see how absurdly it is applied. So very useless, indeed, is this heavy tax, and so wretched its disposition, that it is a question whether the poor or the rich are more dissatisfied . . . since the plunder of the one serves so little to the real advantage of the other; for while a million yearly is raised among the former, many of the latter are starved; many more languish in want and misery; of the rest, many are found begging or pilfering in the streets today, and tomorrow are locked up in gaols and bridewells."

A further attempt at reform was made in 1782, with the passing of Gilbert's Act (Thomas Gilbert, M.P., 1720–98). From now on, the workhouse was to be reserved for the helpless, such as the old, the sick, orphans and unmarried mothers; the able-bodied poor were now exposed to the harsh Vagrancy Laws, under which vagabonds, "unlicensed pedlars" and others faced merciless prison sentences. Towards the end of the century, between three thousand and four thousand vagrants a year were sent to houses of correction; but needless to say, as many more were driven to crime. By 1800 there were over four thousand workhouses and poor-houses in the country.

—W. H. LEWIS————————————————————————

THE TOWN

The latent hostility, or at least divergence of interests, between town and country, probably as old as civilization itself, is rooted in the basic fact that the countryman produces while the townsman consumes. No nation has yet evolved a policy that satisfies both classes, and the France of Louis XIV was less fitted to solve the problem than most. For the encumbering vestiges of feudalism which hampered seventeenth-century France at every turn engendered a friction between the country noble and the town *bourgeois,* which appears scarcely to have existed in the contemporary England. To the English squire the neighboring town was the social and commercial headquarters of the countryside, whilst to the French noble, it was a portion of his *seigneurie* which had enfranchised itself from his yoke, obtained many financial privileges, and was growing steadily richer while he grew poorer and more insignificant. He hated and despised a *bourgeois,* whilst the *bourgeois,* increasing in wealth and importance, asked himself why he should put up with the intolerable insolence of the beggarly squireen. A time came quite early on when a noble who attempted to cane a *bourgeois* in the street would find himself rabbled and hooted out of the town; the noble's only possible retort was to wash his hands of the town and seek the company of his own caste in the fields. In inflicting on himself this voluntary banishment from the town and exclusion from municipal office, the noble made a grave strategic error; had he, like his ancestors, solicited election as mayor or alderman, had the noble and the *bourgeois* realized that they had common interests, the centralizing policy of Richelieu and the later Bourbons would have encountered an obstacle which might very possibly have modified the whole course of seventeenth-century history. Here and there a noble may have had a glimmering of such an

From W. H. Lewis, *The Splendid Century* (London: Eyre & Spottiswoode Publishers, Ltd., 1953), pp. 179–82, 183–84, 191–96, by permission of the publisher and William Morrow & Company.

idea, or at least had an instinct which prompted him to keep a finger in the town pie; Maréchal d'Estrades, for instance, was perpetual Mayor of Bordeaux; the Duc de Grammont, hereditary Mayor of Bayonne; and the Duc de Villeroi had a preponderant influence in the affairs of the City of Lyons. But broadly speaking, the nobles withdrew from the towns, creating a vacuum which was promptly filled by the Crown. Henceforward, the towns were the King's proteges, his chief counterpoise against the nobility, and within the towns grew up a municipal aristocracy to replace the self-exiled nobles. And the towns, though they were far from being democracies, and were under the royal protection, tended to become centers of resistance to arbitrary power, and indeed retained a remarkable degree of independence, even under Louis XIV; the town of Provins, for instance, in 1682 rejected an edict of the Council of State on the ground that it was contrary to the liberties of the province: and the edict was withdrawn.

On the whole, we may say that a well-to-do *bourgeois* of one of Louis XIV's *bonnes villes* was the most comfortably situated man of any estate in the realm, but the fact that the constitutions and problems of no two towns are the same makes generalization very difficult. And indeed conditions of life were often different in different quarters of the same town. Surrounding the town was the *banlieue,* often a considerable area of country; if you lived in one of the thirty-five villages of the *banlieue* of Rouen, you enjoyed the privileges of that city. But not one of the villages of the *banlieue* of Bordeaux enjoyed any municipal privileges at all. Inside the towns themselves the *faubourgs* would often pay the *Taille,* whilst the old municipal area in the center of the town would be exempt; sometimes one *faubourg* would pay *Taille* while another would not. But even the least-favored *faubourg* of the most oppressive town offered a better way of life to the ambitious commoner than did the countryside, and the drift to the towns was as serious a problem to Louis XIV's government as it is to many modern ones.

To become a townsman was by no means easy, for not only did the Crown seek to stay this drift to the city, but the cities themselves kept a sharp eye on intruders who seemed likely, in our language, to "come on the bread line"; as early as 1646 the central government had decreed that any peasant settling in a town must pay *Taille* in his last place of residence for the next ten years, while most of the towns demanded a financial guarantee from the intending settler. For instance, the municipality of Rethel in 1682 refused to allow anyone to take up residence in the town who could not pay a five-franc *Taille.* At Boulogne there was a domiciliary fee of twelve francs, and at Gray in 1698 there was a scale of domiciliary fees ranging from eight to seventeen francs according to the trade of the applicant. On the other hand, a man whose services would be valuable to the town was usually given free domiciliary rights, and was sometimes even offered a salary to settle.

The attitude of the *corps de ville* towards the admission of religious orders within the walls was a cautious one, for the establishment of a new religious house raised all sorts of municipal problems. Would the parish priest's income fall off? Would the revenue of the other houses of religious decline? If the order was a mendicant one, what would be the effect on the town charities? Teaching orders were, however, welcome, and so too were the popular Capuchins, for a curious reason. Fire brigades did not exist before 1699, and, somehow or other, the Capuchins had become expert firefighters; in emergencies, in which the modern Londoner dials "fire," the seventeenth-century householder sent for the Capuchins. Finally, all towns fought hard, but generally unsuccessfully, to prevent the Jesuits settling in their midst.

Domiciliary rights, be it noted, did not make the settler a *bourgeois*. For at this time the word *"bourgeois"* did not mean inhabitant of a *bourg*, and still less was it a derogatory adjective applicable to a political theory distasteful to the speaker. Qualifications were required to become a *bourgeois*, and we may perhaps think of him as a man on whom has been conferred the Freedom of the City. The domiciled man had civil rights, the *bourgeois* had both civil and municipal rights; to become a *bourgeois*, a qualifying period of residence was always required, varying from between five and ten years. At Paris, a *bourgeois* forfeited his rank if he failed to spend seven months each year in the city. In nearly all towns an oath of allegiance to the city was demanded from the new *bourgeois*, and everywhere a sharp lookout was kept for the bogus *bourgeois;* it was much easier in old France to become a sham nobleman than a sham *bourgeois*. . . .

The townspeople fell into three broad divisions: an aristocracy consisting of the officers of justice, financiers, holders of Crown offices, and members of the Parlement if there was one: the merchants, with whom this aristocracy was often at loggerheads: and the artisans, who, by and large, sided with the merchants. The two latter classes were subdivided into trade groups, each forming as it were little republics, self-governing within the city state; thus at Paris the merchants formed seven *corps*, drapers, grocers, silk-merchants, furriers, hatmakers, and wine merchants, all under the general control of the provost of the merchants, who was the senior city magistrate.

The artisan class was split into *corporations*, very roughly corresponding to trade unions, and the member, called a *compagnon*, held a recognized legal status. He was forbidden to form any combination outside his *corporation*, though in fact he was often a member of some secret trade guild as well. It should be noted that while the artisan, the member of a *corporation*, was the social inferior of the tradesman, it not infrequently happened that the artisan was the richer man of the two. In addition to the normal advantages of trades guilds, both *corps* and *corporations* had the benefit of a recognized business court, that of the *Juges-Consuls*, elected by themselves, and empowered to judge all trades disputes. The *corporations* were, of course, more numerous than the *corps*, and in Paris, by 1673, there were sixty of the former to seven of the latter. Organization was a mania in Louis XIV's France, and to live in a town made membership of a *corps* or a *corporation* inevitable. One would have thought that at least the unemployed *rentier* would have been exempt; but not a bit of it. If you were in that happy position, you were automatically a member of the *corps of bourgeois* "living nobly," and liable to be elected to office, under the usual penalties in case of noncompliance. Even prison did not enfranchise you from guild membership; at Troyes in 1643 we find the prisoners, with the approval and indeed encouragement of their keepers, forming themselves into a *corporation,* with a formally elected provost, subprovost, and lieutenant to undertake the proper conduct of their affairs. For each *corps* and *corporation* had, of course, its elected officers, as sumptuously robed as its finances would permit, its patron saint, its annual feast, and its communal Mass. Office-bearing in either, and indeed membership, put the individual to considerable expense. But the system was cherished as clothing the common man in a little brief authority and dignity; "you would have enjoyed," writes Racine from Uzès in 1661, "seeing the carpenter, Gaillard, in his red robe." We need hardly add that, this being old France, the various *corps* and *corporations* spent a great deal of their time in quarrelling with each other over matters of precedence, and that some *corps* and *corporations* had been at law with each other for over two hundred years; and naturally, where trades overlapped, as in the case of the bakers and the pastry cooks, there was endless friction and litigation. The aristocracy of the town quarrelled as energetically as did their inferiors, generally in defense of their beloved precedence, and frequently in public. . . .

Municipal government was least successful in that department of its duty whose efficiency we now take for granted, namely, public hygiene and sanitation. And Paris was perhaps the dirtiest city in France. Paris mud left an indelible stain on all it touched, and from whatever direction you approached the capital, Paris mud could be smelt two miles outside the gates. Only those who have traveled on foot through a Chinese town can form any accurate idea of a Paris street, and the resemblance between the two must have been remarkable. In Paris, the stroller would find the same narrow thoroughfare, carpeted in filth, with the central gutter, or rather succession of stagnant pools, choked with dung, entrails, litter of all kinds: the droves of foraging pigs and poultry, the dark open-fronted cavernous shops, each with its trade sign suspended on a gallows and almost touching that of the shop on the other side of the street: the mounds of human excrement and kitchen rubbish outside the doors, awaiting the arrival of the municipal cart to transport it out of the city, where it will be seized upon for manure by the suburban market gardener: the well-to-do in sedan chairs, whose bearers may at any moment deposit the chair in a midden for greater ease whilst expostulating with a clumsy carter. It was not until I first entered a Chinese city that I suddenly understood why Louis XIV's Parisians always wore scented gloves in the streets.

For this state of affairs the municipality was not entirely to blame. Paris contained several large *seigneuries,* each with full seigneurial rights, and within whose bounds the city was powerless to interfere; worse still, the Parisian *seigneurs* were not as a rule individuals, but religious orders, chapters, *commanderies* and the like, and such bodies are notoriously hard to move. Furthermore, all Parisians offered a stubborn passive resistance to all sanitary regulations, and as the middle of the street invariably formed the boundary between competing jurisdictions, any uniform policy of street cleansing was an impossibility, even had the inhabitants desired it, which they didn't. As early as 1644 it had been enacted that all latrines in the city must be emptied by the municipal scavengers before six in summer and before seven in winter, but with the usual result; the edict was reluctantly obeyed for a few days, then tacitly ignored, and as late as 1697 all household filth was still being disposed of by being flung out of the windows. In 1666 a further law was passed making the provision of sanitary accommodation compulsory in every Paris house; but several years later the city was found to have many tenements housing twenty to twenty-five families, with no sanitary arrangements whatever. In fact, generally speaking, no notice was taken of police regulations in Paris, or in any other city in the kingdom. Some little improvement is however noticeable after La Reynie became lieutenant of police in 1667, and especially after he persuaded Louis to clip the wings of the *seigneuries* in 1674. If La Reynie did not succeed in cleansing the street, he at least made them cleanable by paving them, with the result that heavy rain swept away the worst of the dirt instead of turning an evil smelling mud lane into an impassable bog. An attempt too was made to get builders to conform to a municipal specification for new constructions. But right up to the end of the reign and beyond it, complaints from a not oversensitive generation about the filth and stench of Paris are frequent and vigorous.

That such a street loving age could have tolerated this state of affairs speaks volumes for its insensibility; for to see the stir, to reap the harvest of a quiet eye, to stroll and gossip, was the chief amusement of the *canaille* and the lesser bourgeoisie. The true Parisian loved his dirty streets, and was never happier than when showing them off to a stranger. Let us play country cousin to Berthaud, and under his guidance explore this vanished Paris, going with him first to the Pont Neuf, which offers the appearance of a demented fairground, with more than its noise; the bridge is the rendezvous of *charlatans, passe volants,* quack ointment sellers, toothdrawers, street singers, pimps, cutpurses, cloak-snatchers, conjurors, booksellers, and all, with the exception of the pimps, cutpurses, and cloak-snatchers, yelling, "Come, buy, buy, buy," at the full pitch of their lungs. Equally vociferous are the proprietors of the shooting galleries which line the bridge, who offer you three shots a penny, with the certainty of your winning a magnificent prize. The prize is your choice from an old box filled with battered books, dirty rosettes, nutcrackers, tobacco boxes, flutes, broken masks, seedy hats, and a quantity of other miscellaneous rubbish. A very little of the Pont Neuf goes a long way, and we cross the river, which here serves the triple purpose of open sewer, town drinking-water supply, and the washerwomen's place of business; though by the way, the washing of clothes in the Seine at Paris has been strictly prohibited since 1667. But nobody takes any notice of the edict. Here we are at the palace; not the King's palace of the Louvre, for the word "palace" has not yet acquired its modern meaning; the King's residences are *châteaux,* whilst palaces are law courts. The palace is a favorite strolling place, dirty and ill-smelling, even by Parisian standards, but probably no more disgusting than the Louvre, where visitors relieve themselves not only in the courtyards, but on the balconies, and staircases, and behind the doors.

Complaints of its condition were common as late as 1670, and when in the 'eighties the Court moved out to Versailles, one of the things that most surprised visitors about the new residence was that the King there insisted on the same degree of decency and cleanliness which was to be found in a private house. We find the gallery of the law courts full of little shops, and here is the place where the bookbuyer hunts for bargains, undaunted by the fact that the bookseller, like all other tradesmen, sells her wares by personal canvas, and issues a deafening catalogue of the less salable works while we turn over her stock—*Cassandra,* Arnauld's works, Bellerose, Molière, Montaigne, Rabelais, "Come buy, come buy!" Next door to her a girl is shouting her handkerchiefs and lace, pin boxes, and scissors, and from farther down the gallery come lusty praises of the next stall-keeper's Polish knives, English leather jerkins, and felt hats for wet weather, "as worn in Turkey"; while a rival tries to shout him down with his chant of collars and shirts.

Inside the hall of the palace the turmoil is nearly as great; here a lackey is caning a gingerbread seller, there we are shocked to see a man performing an operation which is not usually conducted in such publicity; not that the publicity shocks us, it is the fact that the man is in full view of a statue of the King. The room is full of attorneys of the lowest standing, and their ragtag and bobtail clientele brief them with a noisy repetitiveness and a wealth of gesticulation against which they are apparently hardened by long practice. The combined bar and restaurant of the palace is open to the public, and here we should have enjoyed our pint of wine, had we been able to shake off our hostess, who is infected with the general mania of shouting her wares, and plagues us unceasingly to order various singularly unattractive dishes; so gulping off our drink we emerge into the street to find ourselves in the middle of a fracas. Traffic, foot, horse, and wheeled, has stopped to take sides in the quarrel between that great lady's coachman and a carter, who has locked his wheel in that of the coach. Both drivers have dismounted to do themselves more justice, and the cloak-snatchers are turning the diversion to account, when a squad of archers puts an end to the entanglement with an impartial distribution of *coups de bâton,* during which we take refuge in a shop. We emerge when the storm is over, and a minute later find ourselves passing the police headquarters, the *Châtelet;* here it behooves us to be both swift and unobtrusive, for the place swarms with archers and attorney's clerks, who have a playful habit of identifying the passer-by as some badly wanted criminal and holding him to ransom. We omit the Place de La Grève from our sightseeing trip, for we have unfortunately hit upon a day when there is nothing to be seen there; had it been yesterday or tomorrow, we could have had the pleasure of watching a batch of women being flogged and branded, or a selection of rascals turned off on the gallows—dancing on air as we call it. For this, too, is one of the sights of Paris. Dr. Patin, writing to the father of his pupil, Noel Falconnet, tells him that the boy has been working so well that tomorrow he is taking him as a treat to see a man broken on the wheel. Forcing our way through a mob of itinerant image sellers, picture sellers, piemen, begging friars, led captains, and loafers, we arrive at the Cemetery of the Innocents where the professional letter-writers sit on the flat tombstones awaiting customers. That young footman has been snared by a pretty face at a window, and is commissioning a declaration of love in as high-flown a style as the writer thinks consistent with a fee of ten sous; the cook-maid in earnest colloquy with that other writer wants to *shoe the mule* as it is called, or in other words seeks his assistance in the preparation of a set of fraudulent housekeeping books; while the squint-eyed fellow in the shabby black suit wants help in drawing up a really taking circular advertising his infallible cure for syphilis.

From the cemetery we make our way to the thieves' market, a dirty, neglected street where the cloak-snatchers take their plunder to be dyed, altered, and sold, and where sometimes one can pick up a bargain. Here, as elsewhere, sales are made by patter, but the fences have a technique of their own. Commonly the dealer in stolen clothes poses as a retired soldier who has had some wonderful strokes of luck in looting; finger over lips he takes us in to the darkest recess of the shop and produces a tarnished cloak, which he took off the Grandee of Spain he shot at Rocroi, wishes he had never brought it home, for its extreme richness makes it difficult to dispose of, even at a sacrificial figure. Or, gentlemen, here is something very special; this pistol I had from a man who had it from the lackey who stole it from M. de Turenne; the actual pistol of the immortal Turenne, just think of that! But we don't think of it, and leaving the shop amidst a shower of curses, we set out for the fish market, the *Halles.*

It would be interesting to discover the connection between fish selling and bad language, which is evidently not peculiar to England; for it is clear from contemporary accounts that "the language of the *Halles*" can be best translated by the single word "billingsgate." Berthaud gives us a sample of a quarrel between two rival fishwives, conducted with a creditable pungency on both sides, but with a freedom of personal criticism and simile which unfits it for reproduction, even in a footnote. A formidable body, these ladies of the *Halles,* and, rather surprisingly, much addicted to hero-worship.

When the Duc de Beaufort was thought to have been taken prisoner by the Turks in 1669, they guaranteed a sum for his ransom that worked out at about seven louis d'or per head for the whole of their guild.

Their present favorite is Monseigneur, who sneaks into Paris as often as he thinks it safe to do so, and is in consequence very popular in the city; last time he was ill, a deputation of the corporation of fishwives went out to Versailles in cabs, were admitted to his sickroom, kissed him, promised to have Masses said for him, and after dining at Monseigneur's expense, was sent back to Paris at his charge. A periodical saunter round the *Halles* is essential to the Parisian man about town who wants to keep up-to-date, for in addition to displaying that animation which is so dear to his heart, the *Halles* is the grand manufactory of the type of story which in modern London is supposed to emanate from the Stock Exchange.

We have now exhausted the free entertainment afforded by the capital, unless you are adventurous enough to go home through the Rue de La Huchette, but most prudent visitors decline this item on hearing that its only interest lies in the fact that it is the residential quarter for the cutpurses and cloak-snatchers.

Court, country, town, which of them would we have disliked least? On the whole one is inclined to think the town.

PEOPLE IN PUBLIC
AND
PRIVATE LIFE

Privacy has always been a luxury and thus the possession only of the happy few. Common people were seldom left to their own devices, whether at work, in their domicile, in their religious practice, or at play. Not only was everyday life to an extraordinary degree communal in conception and practice, there simply was no interior space to which to withdraw. It is a mistake to believe that only modern city dwellers have a sense of being crowded. Except for monks and hermits, in fact, the notion of "getting away from it all" seems to have been conspicuously absent during most of European history. The following essays illustrate this point as they examine forms of amusement, sexual practices, and family life in the seventeenth and eighteenth centuries.

Lilly C. Stone shows the importance that organized games and sports held for all strata of society. These were not the great spectacles of antiquity or modernity; rather, they took the form of fairs, festivals, and public contests. As in medieval times, the Church often provided the occasion for a public gathering, even though clergymen were wont to condemn many innocent and some not so innocent pastimes. Not too much had changed in this regard, it seems, since Bodo's time. We may be surprised to learn how many forms of entertainment in which we engage today were commonplace centuries ago. These include both the sports in which common people could participate (archery, bowling, cricket, handball, soccer, fishing) and those reserved mostly for the upper classes (tennis, golf, fencing, cardplaying, horse racing). As a formalized ritual, of course, hunting was also a pleasure strictly for the well-to-do. The one universal sport was gambling; only the amount of the wagers varied.

Edward MacLysaght is aware that the tendentious nature of his sources requires the utmost caution in generalizing about the state of morality. He focuses on manners and morals in Ireland—marriage, divorce, prostitution, premarital sex, drunkenness—and finds a not unfamiliar blend of prudery and promiscuity. Perhaps the key word in his account is "unscreened": however properly or improperly people conducted themselves, usually their behavior was of necessity in public view.

Philippe Ariès traces the evolution of the family. The pattern of home life, he contends, was set by the higher orders of society and eventually imitated by the poor. Before the eighteenth century even the wealthy were accustomed to severe crowding indoors. Only gradually were separate rooms set aside for special purposes. Until then all the normal functions of life were performed in a single space within four walls. It is interesting to note how the precision of our vocabulary has increased as time has proceeded and people have developed the means and taste for privacy. We are reminded that the nuclear family is a relatively modern invention, one that the majority of humankind could not begin to adopt until very recent times.

Modernization is a relative concept for two reasons: first, because social change has been so various in time, place, and class; second, because there is no fixed point toward which society is converging. No sooner do new social patterns appear than they are being altered in ways complex and unanticipated. If a sharper distinction between the private and public sectors of social discourse is a sign of modernity, it is scarcely one that has gone unchallenged. The recurrent complaints about the atomization of modern life, in fact, suggest the contrary. Innovation often seems, on closer examination, to be no more than a reversion to earlier social forms in a different combination. The truism remains true: change is the only constant.

——LILLY C. STONE——————————————————————————

AMUSEMENTS AND SPORTS

Although sports and pastimes in Shakespeare's Age were far less highly organized than they are today, human nature was much the same, and Englishmen enjoyed many of the activities that still have a place in their recreations. To have an understanding of the social life and customs of a nation, a knowledge of its recreations is essential. The way a people spend their moments of leisure provides a clue to their personalities and qualities of character.

During the years when the Tudors and early Stuarts governed England, roads were poor, travel was difficult and sometimes dangerous, and ordinary folk usually did not go far beyond their parish limits for pleasure. Furthermore, life was hard for the ordinary citizen, and few had time for much leisure. Consequently, both time and opportunity were lacking for organized sports that could attract widespread attendance like a modern football match or modern horse racing. To working men and apprentices many sports were forbidden by statute except on such specified holidays as Christmas, but the laws were not always rigidly enforced.

Despite difficulties and handicaps, however, people of all classes enjoyed a variety of simple sports and amusements. If the Elizabethans had to work long hours at hard tasks, they nevertheless found time for play and gaiety. Fairs, festivals, and church wakes provided opportunities to villagers for many amusements. Everyone could look forward to the local fair, at which vendors of a variety of wares spread out their goods for sale. To the fairs came gleemen, jugglers, tumblers, acrobats, and animal trainers with their beasts: a dancing bear, monkeys, an exotic camel, and an "educated" horse. Traveling showmen also brought freaks, as in the "sideshow" at carnivals today, and sleight-of-hand artists were common. After the buying and selling were over, visitors to the fair, adults and children alike, joined in the activities. Women might dance for a prize, and the men engaged in foot races, bowling matches, wrestling, and other similar competitions. One of the most curious events, at which stout young men sought to show their worth and endurance, was the sport of shin kicking. Before this event the participants rubbed both their boots and shins with blue vitriol to harden them. At the close of the day many a young countryman must have been sore and sorry.

From Lilly C. Stone, *English Sports and Recreations* (Charlottesville, Va.: University Press of Virginia, 1971), pp. 429-35, 445-55, by permission of the publisher. Published for the Folger Shakespeare Library.

Festivals celebrated special occasions, such as the end of the harvest, sheep-shearing, and the beginning of spring. Church wakes were held on a saint's day or the day of dedication of the church. A wake began with the vigil at the church and a service; then followed feasting, drinking, and contests of skill and strength like those at fairs. Originally these celebrations were held in the churchyard, but as the activities became more and more secular the churchyard was abandoned or forbidden. Many of the festivals stemmed from pagan rites, and the church thought to remove the taint of heathenism somewhat by acknowledging and modifying them. With the rise of the Puritans, however, objections grew louder, especially to such celebrations as church ales. On these occasions the church-wardens provided a quantity of malt, some from the church stock and the rest from parishioners. The malt was brewed into beer and ale and then sold to raise money for the church. This practice was condemned vociferously by Philip Stubbes, who complained in his *Anatomy of Abuses* (1583) of a situation in which profit to the church increased in proportion to the consumption of beer and the drunkenness that followed.

Pious Philip Stubbes also spoke out against the revelry that took place on May Day. On the eve of this holiday, or in the early morning hours of the day itself, people were accustomed to go into the forests to gather boughs and branches as decorations for their homes. A Maypole would be cut and drawn into the village by oxen. Each ox had flowers tied to its horns and the pole was decorated with herbs, flowers, and ribbons. When the pole was erected, the dancing began. The morris dance was traditional on May Day with a fiddler, Maid Marian, and ten men dressed with horns and bells. Maid Marian was queen of the May and mistress of the archery games. In later years Robin Hood was introduced, probably as king of the May. Upon such levity Stubbes frowned, but he deplored most of the fact that the young men and girls "run gadding over night to the woods, groves, hills, and mountains" and there spend the night "in pleasant pastimes." He declared on "good authority" (one wonders if his own) that of a hundred maids going out scarcely a third returned in the state of virginity.

Archery occupied an important place in the May-Day activities, for it was virtually the national sport. Laws discouraged other physical exercises so that men would not be diverted from the practice of archery. From the time of Edward III when the value of the longbow was effectively demonstrated, it was thought wise to have all the men of England ready as trained archers in case of war. By the beginning of the seventeenth century the usefulness of archery in war was declining. As R. Barret says in *The Theory and Practice of Modern Wars* (1598) "they [archers] may serve to some sorts of service, but to no such effect as any of the fiery weapons," but the victories of the longbow at Crécy, Poitiers, and Agincourt were not quickly forgotten, and every man was expected to own a longbow and to practice regularly. Shooting contests were held to stimulate interest, and even churchwardens' accounts sometimes include expenses for making archery butts. Butts were mounds of earth, banked with turf. Against this mound was placed a white disk for a target. Shooting at these taught accuracy. To learn to "keep a length" the archers practiced "prick" or "clout" shooting, which meant shooting at a target eighteen inches in diameter, stuffed with straw. This mark was placed at a distance of 160 to 240 yards. "Roving" was to shoot in the open, at no mark, and at unknown distances.

Archery was praised as good for all men, great or poor. Gervase Markham in *The Art of Archery* (1634), dedicated to Charles I, calls it an honest and wholesome sport, and much earlier, in *Toxophilus* (1545), Roger Ascham referred to archery as "the most honest pastime of all" and a cure of evil gaming. Ascham, who was at one time tutor to Elizabeth I, felt that a genuine effort should be made to teach archery because, truth to tell, the interest in archery was waning. He felt that many disobeyed the royal laws for lack of knowledge of how to shoot. Christina Hole suggests in *English Sports and Pastimes* that enthusiasm died out because laws commanded the practice of archery instead of leaving it to the pleasure of sportsmen.

An act passed in 1541 in the reign of Henry VIII shows us to what extent the government favored archery. After declaring that all able men under sixty must own a longbow and practice shooting, the act continues with a list of activities which are banned: "That no manner of person or persons . . . shall for his or their gain . . . keep . . . or maintain, any common house, alley, or place of bowling, quoiting, cloish, kayles, half-bowl, tennis, dicing, table, or carding, or any other manner of game prohibited by any statute heretofore made, or any unlawful new game now invented or made, or any other new unlawful game hereafter to be invented, found, had or made. . . ."

In spite of this act gaming houses were kept open, and the various sports flourished. Bowling was probably the most popular. Robert Crowley, printer and Puritan preacher as well as poet, testifies that bowling was not suppressed. In his *One and Thirty Epigrams* (1550), appeared this poem on bowling:

Two sorts of alleys
In London I find;
The one against the law,
And the other against kind.
The first is where bowling
Forbidden, men use,
And wasting their goods,
Do their labor refuse.
But in London (alas!)
Some men are devilishly
Suffered to profess it
As an art to live by. . . .

Two types of bowling were popular then as now. The favorite was played on bowling greens. Bowling in alleys, similar to the modern game, was also common. Bowling greens were often included as part of the gardens in the estates of the gentry, but bowling was not a sport for the rich alone. Besides having alleys in the supposedly illegal gaming houses, men also played at bowls in the open country, according to Gervase Markham's description in *Country Contentments* (1615): "There is another recreation . . . that is, bowling, in which a man shall find great art in choosing out his ground and preventing the winding, hanging, and many turning advantages of the same, whether it be in open wild places or in close alleys; and in this sport the choosing of the bowl is the greatest cunning; your flat bowls being the best for alleys, your round biased bowls for open grounds of advantage, and your round bowls like a ball for greenswards that are plain and level." Charles Cotton, who in the later seventeenth century wrote *The Complete Gamester* (1674), "borrowed" this passage from Markham. Cotton, however, does add a caution against gambling at a bowling match. In his advice on learning the game he states that "practice must be your best tutor . . . ; and that I shall say, have a care you are not in the first place rooked out of your money." Cotton's comments on the weird postures assumed by bowlers as the bowl is rolling down the alley, and the cries to go further or stop shorter, suggest that a bowler of the sixteenth century would not feel out of place in a twentieth-century bowling alley.

Many of the bowling terms, such as "rub," "jack," or "kiss," can be found in Shakespeare, and it appears probable that he was a knowledgeable bowler. A "rub" is anything that diverts the ball from its course (as in Hamlet's soliloquy: "Ay, there's the rub"); a "jack" (also "master" or "mistress") is a small bowl placed as a mark at which to aim; and a "kiss" occurs when one bowl touches another (as in *Cymbeline,* II.i.: "Was there ever man had such luck! When I kissed the jack, upon an up-cast to be hit away!").

Kayles, cloish, and loggats were all closely allied to bowling. In the game of kayles there were six or more pins set up in a straight row. Instead of bowling a ball at the pins, the object was to knock the pins down by throwing a stick at them. Cloish also consisted of setting pins in a row, but a bowl was used to knock them down. In loggats, a game popular with boys and country folk, bones were substituted for the pins, and another bone was thrown at them. Shakespeare has a reference to this sport in the grave-digging scene where Hamlet comments: "Did these bones cost no more the breeding but to play at loggats with 'em?"

Men and boys of the sixteenth century, like their counterparts in other ages, enjoyed various forms of ball games. The variety of games played with balls was great, but often the same game appeared in different sections of the country under different names. As early as 1598 one finds a reference to cricket being played fifty years before. Cricket perhaps was an outgrowth of stoolball and clubball. In playing stoolball, a bowler tried to hit a stool with a ball. One player tried to defend the stool with his hand. In some localities a bat was used. In this game, however, there were no runs. Another game with overtones of cricket was trapball. A ball was placed in a spoon-shaped piece of wood. When the spoon was hit, the ball would rise and was hit into the field. Opponents tried to catch the ball, or to bowl the ball in to hit the trap.

Handball is probably the oldest form of ball game. Many games were derived from it, including fives and a form of tennis. Fives was played against a wall or church tower. This led to complaints from ministers against the delinquent boys who not only did not attend church but disturbed the service by playing ball against the church walls! Rules apparently differed in various geographical areas, as at Eton, where the buttresses from the wall formed two additional sides, and the game called "Eton Fives" developed.

Football was not unknown to the Elizabethan age, but it is hardly recognizable as the game we know today. The main similarity is that a ball, usually a bladder filled with air and encased in leather, was used, and the object was to get the ball across a goal line. What happened in between was nothing short of chaos, or, as Sir Thomas Elyot says in *The Book Named the Governor* (1531), "nothing but beastly fury and extreme violence." There were few if any rules, and each team could have an unlimited number of players. Often there were interparish contests, in which case much of the parish might be commandeered for the playing field, as one set of players tried to kick the ball into the opposing parish. On other occasions an open field or common was used. If the game was a parish affair, it was usually played on a holiday or feast day. At Chester a game was always played at Shrovetide, and legend has it that it commemorated the kicking about of the head of a captured Dane. Often it was a contest between two special groups of people, such as married men and bachelors. At Inverness, Scotland, an annual game was played between the married and the single women—and it is reported that the married women usually won!

Football was another sport prohibited by law to the working man as early as 1349 and as late as Elizabeth's reign. James I in *Basilicon Doron* (1599), a book of instructions for his son, forbids the prince to play football because he thought it "meeter for laming than making able the users thereof." Philip Stubbes gives us a vivid description in his *Anatomy of Abuses* of what happens during a game which he considers a "bloody and murdering practice."

> For doth not everyone lie in wait for his adversary, seeking to overthrow him and to pick him on his nose, though it be upon hard stones, in ditch or dale, in valley or hill . . . he careth not so he have him down . . . so that by this means, sometimes their necks are broken, sometimes their backs . . . legs . . . arms. . . .
>   . . . They have the sleights to meet one betwixt two, to dash him against the heart with their elbows, to hit him under the shortribs with their gripped fists, and with their knees to catch him upon the hip and to pick him on his neck, with a hundred such murdering devices. . . .

Such a commentary suggests that Stubbes himself had been involved at least once in a friendly game of football. . . .

Fishing was as popular with Tudor Englishmen as it is with men of the atomic age. These fishermen of old had just as much trouble catching fish as men of all centuries, although modern editors of Elizabethan fishing treatises contend that fish have grown craftier over the years. Methods and equipment were somewhat different then. Although fishing rods could be bought at the haberdasher's, the various books on the subject describe the rod and line with such care that it is evident that many Elizabethans were given to making their own. Rods were of three types, according to Markham's *Pleasures of Princes* (1614): of two pieces, the lower being nine to ten feet and the upper about a yard long; of one whole piece, which meant a short rod good only for narrow streams; of many pieces, usually made of cane, that fit into one another. The line was made of horsehair with threads of silk intertwined. Some years later Robert Venables in *The Experienced Angler* (1662) preferred a line of either horsehair or silk, but not a mixture.

Until the middle of the seventeenth century fishermen had no reels. Since the line was attached to a loop at the end of the rod, it was not possible to play the trout until it tired. Even when reels did appear, they were used more for salmon than for trout.

Elizabethan fishermen did not favor fishing upstream with a dry fly. Upstream angling was first mentioned by Venables and then with disapproval. He believed that in casting upstream one's line was more likely to hit the water before the fly, or at least the line would be visible, and in either case the fish would be frightened away—all of which argues the inexpertness of Venables as a fly-caster or the poor quality of the equipment then available.

Various baits were used, and Venables suggests that once a week a fisherman, if he had a special fishing spot, should cast in all sort of food, such as corn boiled soft, grain dipped in blood, or worms. Then the fish would be less suspicious of bait. Live baits consisted of such delicacies as red worms, maggots, flies, grasshoppers, hornets, wasps, and snails. Dried wasps, clotted blood of sheep, corn, seed, cheese, berries, cherries, or pastes were used as dead bait. For those who preferred fly-fishing, books told how to make one's own flies. According to Izaak Walton's classic, *The Compleat Angler,* "if he hit to make his fly right, and have the luck to hit, also, where there is store of trouts, a dark day, and a right wind, he will catch such store of them as will encourage him to grow more and more in love with the art of fly-making." This implies a big "if," but all writers on fishing stress the virtues a fisherman must have, the foremost being patience. As Markham writes: "Then he must be exceeding patient and neither vex nor excruciate himself with losses or mischances, as in losing the prey when it is almost in the hand, or by breaking his tools."

One unusual form of fishing was "tickling," in which a fisherman cautiously ran his arm under a bank until he touched a trout and then slowly tickled it until he was in a position to seize it.

Fishing was a sport sufficiently in favor to receive the blessing of university authorities in a day when sports had only a small place in university life. Sir Simonds D'Ewes mentions in a diary kept at Cambridge that angling was one of the pleasures that he enjoyed. D'Ewes also mentions a few other sports which served "as antidotes to disastrous diseases" and of course did not interfere with studies, unlike the experience of Sir Andrew Aguecheek in *Twelfth Night,* who laments: "I would I had bestowed that time in the tongues that I have in fencing, dancing, and bearbaiting."

Sports in which the students participated in their leisure time included tennis, shovegroat (shuffleboard), cards, bowling, jumping, and running. They seem to agree with Robert Crowley's idea of how a scholar should amuse himself.

> To fish, to fowl, to hunt, to hawk,
> Or on an instrument to play;
> And some whiles to commune and talk,
> No man is able to gainsay.
> To shoot, to bowl, or cast the bar,
> To play tennis, or toss the ball
> Or to run base, like men of war,
> Shall hurt thy study nought at all.
> For all these things to recreate,
> The mind, if thou canst hold the mean.

Scottish universities, somewhat more advanced than those below the border, included sports and exercises as a part of the official curriculum. On certain days the students were taken to the fields for organized exercises, and the University of Edinburgh had a tennis court on its grounds. James Melville, whose memoirs dating from the late sixteenth century were published in 1842, states that at school he was taught archery, golf, fencing, running, leaping, and wrestling, and at the University of St. Andrews he played golf and engaged in archery.

Golf was a great recreation in Scotland from early times, though it did not thrive in England until the Stuart kings popularized it there. The treasurer's records in the reign of James IV of Scotland included expenses for golf equipment:

1503, Feb. 3. Item to the King to play at the golf with the Earl of Bothwell	xlii s
1503, Feb. 4. Item to golf clubs and balls to the King	ix s
1503, Feb. 22. Item, xii golf balls to the king	iiii s
1506, Item the 28th day of July for ii golf clubs to the King	ii s

Golf balls at this time were stuffed with feathers and covered with leather.

Tennis was played in both England and Scotland as well as on the continent. In fact, it developed from the French *jeu de paume* or "palm play." In its early stages in the Middle Ages the palm of the hand was used instead of a racket. The hand was gloved, and later strings were stretched between the fingers of the glove. The next step was a crude racket with a handle. For a long time both the hand and the racket were used, but the racket had become sufficiently popular by Chaucer's day to be mentioned in his *Troilus and Criseyde.* The racket was oblong and strung diagonally with only a few strings.

The common people played some form of open-air tennis, but the game was largely the court tennis variety, played in an enclosed court. Because of the expense it was confined for the most part to the gentry and nobility, who could afford to build their own courts. Some public courts, however, were operated by the proprietors of gaming houses. . . .

In a country of inclement weather indoor games were bound to be popular. Furthermore, even the most active could not always be running, leaping, or hitting balls, and there are always those who have no desire to engage in active sports. For moments of less activity there were cards and table games. The origin of card games dates far back in history. Cardplaying had spread over Europe before it crossed the Channel into England. By the fifteenth century card games were common in England, and Edward IV in 1463 forbade the importation of playing cards to protect local cardmakers. By 1496 cardplaying was added to the list of activities forbidden the laboring classes. Henry VII's law read that servants and apprentices could play at cards only during the Christmas holiday, and then only in their master's house. In 1628 a charter was granted the London Company of Makers of Playing Cards.

It is uncertain whether English cards were derived more from French or Spanish cards. They appear to have taken the names of their suits and the symbols from both. The Spanish suits were *espadas* (swords), *copas* (cups), *dineros* (coins), and *bastos* (clubs). In France the suits were *piques* (spears), *coeurs* (hearts), *carreaux* (squares or lozenges), and *trefles* (trefoils). The face cards on French cards were named after various emperors, queens, or famous knights. The knaves appeared in various dress, including armor, depending on the current events of a particular period. Samuel Rowlands in 1612, in his *Knave of Hearts,* indicated that the English jacks were dressed in the costume of Chaucer's time.

We are abused in a great degree;
For, there's no knaves so wronged as are we
By those that chiefly should be our part-takers:
And thus it is my masters, you cardmakers.
All other knaves are at their own free will,
To brave it out, and follow fashion still
In any cut, according to the time:
But we poor knaves (I know not for what crime)
Are kept in piebald suits which we have worn
Hundred of years; this hardly can be borne.
The idle-headed French devised us first,
Who of all fashion-mongers is the worst.

Cardplaying, as well as dicing, was condemned by many. Some claimed it to be an invention of the Devil, and because the cards were named, they described cardplaying as a form of idolatry. John Northbrooke in his *Treatise wherein Dicing, Dancing . . . Are Reproved,* published about 1577, felt that card-playing was not so evil as dicing because there was less trust in chance. But since cardplaying furnished small training for the mind, he saw little good in it. According to him, cheating was prevalent, "either by pricking of a card, or pinching of it, cutting at the nick; either by a bum-card [i.e., a raised or marked card for cheating] finely, under, over, or in the middle, &c. and what not to deceive?" Although moralists condemned cardplaying and rogues cheated, the various games remained extremely popular through the years. Primero was played by Elizabeth I. It was a game at which two or three could play. In this the ace of spades was the best card, as it was always trump in "ombre," which succeeded "primero." Three players could participate in ombre, each receiving nine cards apiece. Trumps were named by the first player. James I liked "maw," which later became known as "five cards." In this game the five of trumps was the best card, the ace of hearts next, then the ace of trumps, and the knave. The ace of diamonds was the worst card unless diamonds were trumps. Two people could play this game—each receiving five cards. "Ruff" and "honor" required four players. Twelve cards apiece were dealt out, leaving four cards in the stack. The top card was turned up and its suit was named as trumps. The player with the ace of trumps could get the stack pile and discard four other cards. As in poker, the player bet on his hand in "post and pair." A poker face and a good bluff often won the game regardless of the cards held.

Dicing was popular and was more condemned even than cardplaying. Thomas Elyot's *Book Named the Governor* has little good to say of this form of play. "And I suppose there is not a more plain figure of idleness than playing at dice. For besides that therein is no manner of exercise of the body or mind, they which do play thereat must seem to have no portion of wit or cunning, if they will be called fair players." John Northbrooke's treatise against dicing objects to it for similar reasons. To him only play which exercises the mind or body is permissible. He cites various laws against dicing but says that royalty sets a bad example, and certainly Henry VIII was an enthusiastic gambler. Nicholas Faret, giving instruction to young gentlemen in *The Honest Man,* indicated that they should know games at hazard, but they should not be gamblers, for as he says, "There are none but great princes (whose condition can never be miserable) which may abandon themselves boldly unto it [gambling]."

The most popular dice game was called hazard. In this game the thrower calls a number between five and nine before throwing. If he throws the number called or a number with a fixed correspondence to it, he "throws a nick" and wins. If he throws two aces or a deuce and ace he "throws out" and loses. If neither, he throws until the first number thrown (the chance) comes up and he wins, or the number first called (the main) comes up, in which case he loses.

Gambling took another form in betting, particularly on horse races. Public races were established by James I, and one of the famous races was the "Bell Course" race which had for a prize a silver bell.

There were other indoor games less harmful to the moral well-being of the participant. Among these was backgammon, called "tables" in Tudor times, probably because the board consisted of two tables hinged together. The ancient game of chess has been a favorite with contemplative men throughout the ages, though James I felt that, far from relaxing a person, chess filled his head with troubles. In England chess assumed its modern shape by Elizabeth's time, a little later than in Europe. Similar to chess was the philosopher's game in which the board was in the form of a parallelogram with squares marked. Instead of chessmen, the counters used had number on them. Each player had twenty-four counters, of which one was a king. The object was to take the opponent's king and make a triumph.

Shovelboard was played on a long table. The flat weights were shoved down the table to reach certain points. This is essentially the same as the shovelboard (or shuffleboard) played on board ship except for the use of the table.

Billiards in its modern form is not too different from the game known to the Elizabethans. The table was covered with a fine green cloth and had six pockets. One difference was that sixteenth-century players used a small ivory arch called a port which stood where the pyramid spot stands now; they also used an ivory peg called a king at the other end of the table. The players had two balls with which they tried to pass the port first and then gently to touch the king.

In the evening, for those men who preferred to pit their skill against the flashing eyes and nimble feet of a pretty girl, the music would sound and the dance would begin—either a "basse" dance in which the dancer's feet did not leave the ground or the "haute" dance which required hops, leaps, kicks, or stamps. A dance could be a dignified movement or a lively form of exercise. The pavan and allemande were stately dances, whereas the galliard and volta or lavolta were more lively. In many of the dances, as in the basse dance and the pavan, the man and woman danced side by side. The courante (sometimes spelled "coranto") presented another form, in which three couples in a straight line faced the onlookers, then each other, and finally turned around again to face the audience.

Dancing, however, was not approved by all. John Northbrooke described dancing as one of the evils of the world. In his diatribe he called this amusement "the vilest vice of all" and then went on to say that "truly it cannot easily be said what mischiefs the sight and hearing do receive hereby . . . ; they dance with disordinant gestures, and with monstrous thumping of the feet, to pleasant sounds, to wanton songs, to dishonest verses."

All sports did not require active participation. One of the favorite pastimes for all was a bearbaiting match or a cockfight. Cockfighting was an old sport. In the early days boys took a cock to their schoolmasters on Shrove Tuesday. Before the masters could claim the cocks, the boys were allowed to fight them in the yard. Or else they engaged in another pastime called cockthrowing, which involved throwing sticks and stones at the cock until it was killed.

The first cockpit was not built until the time of Henry VIII. He liked the sport so much that he added a cockpit to his palace at Whitehall. Drury Lane (or the old Phoenix) Theatre began as a cockpit. Philip Stubbes tells us that houses were erected for the purpose of cockfighting, that flags and pennants would fly on the day of a fight, and that proclamations were sent to announce the coming event.

Bearbaitings were often announced by a parade with the bearward leading the bears through the street, probably accompanied by music and jesters. As early as 1526 Paris Garden in Southwark became a popular resort for bear-baiting and bullbaiting. There the bear or bull was chained to a stake and four or six mastiff dogs were turned loose. As one dog was killed another was set upon the bear. The sight of tearing flesh and spilling blood accompanied by the yelps of the dogs and the growls of the bear evidently gave the crowds great pleasure, for the events were largely attended. Robert Crowley in *One and Thirty Epigrams* gives us a good picture of the event.

> What folly is this, to keep with danger,
> A great mastiff dog and a foul ugly bear?
> And to this only end, to see them two fight,
> With terrible tearing, a full ugly sight.
> And yet me think those men be most fools of all
> Whose store of money is but very small,
> And yet every Sunday they will surely spend
> One penny or two the bearward's living to mend.
> At Paris Garden each Sunday a man shall not fail
> To find two or three hundreds for the bearward's vail.
> One halfpenny a piece they use for to give.
> When some have no more in their purse, I believe.

These brutal sports were favored by royalty, aristocrats, and the lower classes alike. Cockfighting was highly favored by James I, and Elizabeth entertained the French and Danish ambassadors on two different occasions by attending a bearbaiting. The Puritans and the city aldermen objected to this sport, not for humane reasons but because of the disorderliness of the crowds who attended. Bearbaitings were usually held on Sunday, a fact that increased the disfavor of the Puritans. The city aldermen were opposed to any large gathering, for the plague was a bitter enemy and spread easily in crowded areas. It was not until many years later, when the conditions of life improved for many people, that these sports came to be looked upon as brutal. But in the sixteenth and seventeenth centuries, when it was a common experience to see hangings, beheadings, and victims burned at the stake, the sight of dogs and bears tearing at one another must have been only a mild form of amusement.

MARRIAGE AND MORALS

Morals, according to the definition of the Oxford Dictionary, are "habits of life in regard to right and wrong conduct; also *spec.* sexual conduct." In modern parlance the word has come to be used almost exclusively in its restricted sense, but in heading this chapter "Morals" I do not wish to convey that it will deal exclusively with sexual morals, though, writing as I am of the second half of the seventeenth century, it is only to be expected that such evils as perjury, official corruption and even drunkenness will occupy less space than matters coming under the head of the Sixth Commandment.[1]

At that period in the upper classes family alliances were often concluded by the marriage of quite young children. After the ceremony the bride and bridegroom were forthwith taken back to their respective nurseries or schoolrooms to await an age more fitting to matrimony. Marriage in its full sense was common at seventeen and eighteen, and sometimes the parties were brought together at a much earlier age than that. Thus Mr. Berry, in his article on the Jephson family of Mallow, states that the grandmother of William Jephson, who himself was married at twelve years old in 1686, was a bride at twelve and had her first child—his father—at fifteen.[2] This practice was common in England and on the Continent also; it was equally in vogue at the beginning of the century, as is well illustrated by the matrimonial history of the Boyle family,[3] and did not die out till after the time of Queen Anne. In all classes, except the very poor, marriages were usually arranged by the parents.[4] In such a system, where love cannot enter into marriage except occasionally by chance, and where the most which can be hoped for is that common interests and associations may in time engender mutual respect and possibly affection, marital infidelity might well be expected to be very usual, not perhaps among unimaginative rustics of low intelligence, but with a quick-witted and lively people like the Irish. It is well known, of course, that during the eighteenth and nineteenth centuries Ireland was freer of sexual irregularity than any other coun-

From Edward MacLysaght, *Irish Life in the Seventeenth Century: After Cromwell* (New York: Barnes and Noble, 1969), pp. 47-49, 58-63, 66-71, 74-75, by permission of the publisher.

1 The Sixth Commandment in the Catholic Church is the Seventh in the Protestant.

2 *Jnl. of Cork Hist. and Arch. Soc.*, 1906, p. 3, et seq.

3 See Townshend, *Life and Letters of the Great Earl of Cork,* passim.

4 Cf. documents *re* marriage of Charles Carthy and Ellen MacGillycuddy in 1672. MacGillycuddy Papers, folios 75 and 76.

try in the world though not necessarily therefore an island of saints. In the seventeenth century there was unquestionably a greater laxity of morals in this respect, but at no time was the excessive license associated with the Restoration period in England to be found in Ireland. The upper classes who, it must be remembered, were by this time predominately Protestant in religion and more or less English in blood, if they regarded mistresses almost as much as a matter of course as wives, did not indulge in that promiscuity which is the real test of depravity. The ordinary men and women of the country, though they certainly had no very high sense of morality, sexual or otherwise, were on the whole a very decent sort of people, for in weighing evidence on this point, even more than on other subjects, we shall have to take the statements of all our witnesses, except the most reliable, with a good many grains of salt. . . .

The ease with which divorces were obtained was one of the public scandals adversely commented on by writers in the sixteenth, and early seventeenth, century, though stated by Keating in his *Díonbhrollach* to be exaggerated. They were by now altogether less frequent but, if we are to believe the Protestant Archbishops of Armagh and Dublin, were still "decreed by Popish priests resident in Ireland."[5] Dr. Lynch admits the existence of some unnatural vices, the introduction of which into Ireland he attributes to the English soldiery, saying that he himself was ignorant of their very names before he went abroad as a young man.[6] There is no reason to believe that they were at all general in Ireland in his time, any more than the vices retailed for the delectation of readers of the sensational Sunday press are really typical of the countries from which they emanate. Certain laws in force in England against some of these were among the Acts proposed for Ireland in 1611,[7] and in this connection we may note, on the authority of the revised edition of Cowel's Law Dictionary,[8] that a well-known unnatural vice was, with perjury, an offense exempted from the general pardon at the Restoration. Writing in 1698, Henri Mission remarks: "The English say both the word and the thing came to them from Italy and are strangers to England. Indeed they love the fair sex too well to fall into such an abomination. In England as well as almost all other countries, it is a crime punishable with death."[9]

There was, of course, no sensational press, Sunday or periodical, in the seventeenth century, but the State Papers contain quite a number of examples of crimes which would have delighted the editors of the Yellow Press, notably one in which the chief actors finished by unsuccessfully attempting to poison their jailer and eventually paid the penalty, the man being hanged, drawn and

---

5 C. S. P. Ireland, 1663/65, p. 360.

6 See *Cambrensis Eversus*, Chapters IX and XII.

7 *Carew Papers*, Vol. VI, p. 163.

8 Published 1708. This crime was the object of legislation in Ireland in the reign of Charles I. See House of Commons Journal.

9 *Memoirs and Observations* (English edn., London, 1719), p. 20.

quartered and the woman burned presumably alive.[10] Burning alive was a punishment still inflicted, even a hundred years later: thus the notorious Darky Kelly, the proprietor of a Dublin brothel, was tried for murder in 1764 and publicly burnt on Stephen's Green.[11]

Under the Brehon Law incontinency was officially regarded as a misdemeanor. While not actually an offense against the State under English law in Ireland, when free from any element of compulsion, illicit sexual intercourse was subject to penalties which could be imposed by the ecclesiastical authorities, and the courts of the Protestant churches have left many records of sentences involving either excommunications or public humiliation.[12] The latter usually consisted of standing for the greater part of a day in the public place of repentance, in some parishes this ordeal having to be undergone Sunday after Sunday for months, when the guilty person did not show proper signs of contrition.[13]

Prostitutes were to be found in the towns, as probably they have been in all countries and in most ages. Barnaby Rich, writing in 1610 after forty-seven years in Ireland, describing himself as an enemy to Popery but not to Ireland—"let them understand that I love Ireland"—noted that there were in Dublin a number of idle, lazy housewives called tavern keepers, most of them well-known harlots, and remarks that it is rare to find one of the innumerable taverns without a strumpet.[14] In 1644 le Gouz visited Limerick, and remarked: "In this city there are great numbers of profligate women, which I would not have believed on account of the climate." John Stevens, a Catholic like le Gouz, who also saw Ireland more or less under war conditions (1689), is very severe in his comments: "The women were so suitable to the times that they rather enticed men to lewdness than carried the least face of modesty, in so much that in every corner of the town might be said to be a public stew. In fine, Dublin seemed to be a seminary of vice, and an academy of luxury, or rather a sink of corruption and living emblem of Sodom."[15] By way of comment on this we may notice the opinion of Mr. Justice Clodpole in 1668, that Dublin was but the lesser Sodom but pure of Irish (i.e., it was not, in his opinion, an Irish town).[16]

---

10   C. S. P. Ireland, 1666/69, p. 358.

11   Gilbert, *History of Dublin,* Vol. I, p. 94.

12   Dwyer, *History of the Diocese of Killaloe,* pp. 350–66. For survival of public penance well into the eighteenth century, see *Alexander the Coppersmith,* p. 96.

Though not, of course, a member of the Established Church, the famous Quaker, William Edmundson, was excommunicated in 1682 for his persistent refusal to pay tithes. This penalty was accompanied by a sentence of imprisonment. Wight, *Hist. of People Called Quakers in Ireland,* 1653 to 1700. 4th ed., 1811, p. 135. See also Edmundson's *Journal,* Dublin, 1715.

13   See Session Book of Templepatrick Presbyterian Church, Co. Antrim, 1646. Printed Jnl. of R.S.A.I., Vol. LXXXI, pp. 164, 165: also Gilbert, *History of Dublin,* Vol. I, p. 213 and p. 255.

14   *New Description of Ireland,* Introduction, and pp. 70–71.

15   *Journal* (ed. Murray), p. 93.

16   *Carte Papers,* Vol. I, p. 123. Quoted Prendergast, *Cromwellian Settlement,* p. 297.

John Dunton, again, never tires of the subject of sexual looseness in Dublin, but this righteous hypocrite's obvious preference for a pornographic tit-bit to the dull truth detracts greatly from his value as a witness, notwithstanding his undoubtedly keen powers of observation. Nor were the institutions complained of, or enjoyed by our authorities according to their several characters and natures, entirely confined to the largest towns. In Bandon, for instance, one of the presentments of the Grand Jury of the County Cork in 1699 was against "Eliz. Dennis for being a whore and keeping a common bawdy house."[17]

In considering the general question of sexual morality we must keep in mind not only the difference which already existed between rural and urban life, and the difference between class and class, but also the fact that there were two fairly distinct races in Ireland, one constituting a powerful minority upheld by outside power, the other comprising the vast majority, but already descending towards that submergence which was completed a couple of generations later.

The two works known as *The Irish Hudibras* both purport to describe the native Irish in rural surroundings. Both were written by Englishmen, or at least by men of English blood: James Farewell is extremely coarse, but, beyond a reference to venereal disease, he has nothing to say against the morals of the ordinary people. His countrywoman is no doubt a rather revolting figure, but apparently virtuous enough, and it is only the "poor kitchen wench" who is ravished by tories, and unwillingly at that. William Moffet, writing later of the same time, is more explicit. The scurrilous abuse indulged in by his women during their dispute as to which of them belonged to the best family could hardly be equalled in Billingsgate: they accuse each other of indiscriminate relations with grooms and soldiers even after marriage, and one admits premarital indiscretions, but as she married the man afterwards she counts her wanton years no disgrace. "I was," she says, as a *coup-de-grace:*

I was 'tis true for debt in jail
But ne'er got living by my tail.

According to the same author it was their country way to "tumble together without screen from view." The fact that Moffet's book went into several editions is by no means a proof of the truth of the picture he paints, but it does indicate the existence of a market in England, in those days as well as today, for both pornographic literature and anti-Irish propaganda.

There is nothing in the purely native authorities of the time to suggest that the moral standard of the people was particularly low. We have already glanced at the opinions of Keating and Lynch on the Irish people of the previous generation. In common with the clergy, the poets dwell on drink more freely as a theme than sexual looseness. . . .

17 MS. T.C.D. N.3. 20.

Generally speaking, the relations between men and women were very much what they are and always have been. One has only to read the "Love Songs of Connacht," many of which were composed in the seventeenth century, to realize that. They fell in love with all the romance and ardor of their forefathers and of their descendants. Some people were fickle, some constant; there were men without moral principles and women of easy virtue as there are today, and there were just as certainly men and women of high character. The differences lie rather in the circumstances and surroundings than in themselves. We can, in fact, feel reasonably sure that the average man and woman of the time were decent people, the same essentially as the average man and woman of today.

One is struck by the way in which le Gouz in 1644 accepted as a not very startling fact the exaggerated accounts of the massacre of vast numbers of Protestants in Ireland three years before: such an idea horrified men in the seventeenth century little more than the contemplation of statistics of road fatalities does in the twentieth. So, too, the accepted conception of what constituted decency was different at that time from our notions on the subject at the present day, just as the standards in this respect of two highly civilized nations may differ now. In France, for instance, a man may relieve himself or a woman suckle her baby unscreened without comment, whereas in England these things are regarded as outraging the proprieties. In Japan a professional prostitute may marry and become respectable; in fact if we go outside the Christian countries, instances of such discrepancy could be multiplied *ad libitum.*

We know, for example, that in the seventeenth century a certain unpleasant habit was regarded as an unforgivable sin.[18] The commonly accepted word for this is in some dictionaries, but it is stated to be "not in decent use," and there is no convenient polite synonym for it—such as "eructate" for "belch." Both Farewell and Moffet assume the reader's acceptance of this view, and I presume this is what Fynes Moryson had in view when he said: "I would name a great lord among them, who was credibly reported to have put away his wife of a good family and beautiful, only for a fault as light as wind (which the Irish in general abhor), but I dare not name it, lest I offend the perfumed senses of some whose censure I have incurred in that kind."[19]

An English traveler in 1635 was rather shocked when he saw in Waterford "women in a most impudent manner treading clothes with their feet; these were naked to their middle almost, for so high were their clothes tucked about them";[20] and Fynes Moryson described as remarkable a somewhat similar scene

18 Dineley is even more explicit on the subject, he says that it "is so abominated by an Irishman that he either quarrels, or flies from you and crosseth himself"; Page 262 of original MS. (in National Library, Dublin). This passage and others which throw much light on the personal habits of the people, were considered unprintable and omitted from the published edition of his *Observations.*

19 Fynes Moryson, *The Commonwealth of Ireland* (Falkiner), p. 284.

20 Brereton's *Travels,* p. 160.

he witnessed, which from our modern point of view would have seemed considerably more indecorous.[21] Barnaby Rich, too, noted something of the kind, but like John Dunton in Iar Connacht at the end of the century,[22] he was more offended by the proximity of food to the woman's bare thighs than by her nakedness.[23]

To the Irish of the seventeenth century, however, mere nakedness—in its proper place—did not seem any more indecent than the exiguous bathing costumes of today do to us.[24] The habit of sleeping naked dates from early times. It was quite general in Ireland in the seventeenth century; but it was not peculiarly Irish. Wright's *Domestic Manners of the Middle Ages* gives many woodcuts illustrating this custom, several of them belonging to the seventeenth century, from which we may see that ladies of quality in England slept naked,[25] just as the lower orders of society did; and, of course, it is well known that the practice persisted even among quite respectable people well into the nineteenth century.

The sleeping accommodation, where small houses and large families were concerned, has been the subject of frequent comment by travelers and others. "Beds for the most part of the common people," says Dineley, "are of mere straw and that scarce clean, some have ticking stuffed with straw, without sheets, nay they pull off their very shirts so as not to wear them out. These cabins abound with children which, with the man, maid and wife, sometimes a traveling stranger, or pack-carrier, or pedlar or two; aye nine or ten of them together, naked, heads and points."[26] A description of the same custom written in 1841 is so much to the point that I venture to quote it in full: "The floor is thickly strewn with fresh rushes, and stripping themselves entirely naked, the whole family lie down at once together, covering themselves with blankets if they have them, and, if not, with their day clothing; but they lie down decently and in order, the eldest daughter next the wall, furthest from the door, then all the sisters according to their ages. Next the mother, father, and sons in succession, and then the strangers, whether the traveling pedlar, tailor or beggar. Thus, the strangers are kept aloof from the female part of the family; and if there is an apparent community, there is great propriety of conduct. This was the first time my friend had seen the primitive but not promiscuous mode of sleeping (A.D. 1799]. He has, however, often seen it since."[27] Wright states that the taste for

---

21   *Description of Ireland* (Falkiner), p. 226.

22   The incident he describes very closely resembles that mentioned by Moryson.

23   *New Description of Ireland*, p. 40.

24   See *Dublin Scuffle*, p. 401.

25   See woodcut on p. 411, op. cit.

26   *Observations*, p. 21.

27   Rev. Caesar Otway, *Sketches in Erris and Tyrawley*, p. 32. Otway's descriptions of housing and other domestic conditions in 1798, as well as sleeping accommodation—see pp. 28 and 29 of his *Sketches*—are remarkably similar to those of [another observer, John] Dunton exactly 100 years earlier.

domestic privacy grew up in England in the sixteenth century among the upper classes, with a consequent alteration in the accommodation provided in their houses,[28] but such changes occur gradually, and as a rule came to Ireland later than to England.

Referring to the question of nakedness and morals, the remarks of Philip Luckombe, author of a "Tour" in 1779, are of interest. The *Tour* is one of the best of its kind, though not, of course, as important as Arthur Young's or entirely free from the customary condescension of such writers. "From the promiscuous way these people lie together," he writes, "a suspicion naturally arises in a stranger's mind, that incest is unavoidable amongst them. Yet upon the strictest enquiry, I find the fact to be otherwise. They are bred up in such an abhorrence of the turpitude of this crime, that I am inclined to think it is as infrequent here, as among more civilized nations. The better sort of people seem rather surprised that I should entertain such an opinion; which only shews, that what we see practiced in our infancy, though ever so unnatural, makes no impression. A little reflection, however, will remove even the ground of suspicion. Bred up from childhood together, their wonted and innocent familiarity is carried on step by step, without impure emotions being excited. One of these poor souls is no more influenced by the nude bosom of a sister, than in a more affluent state he would be at seeing it covered with gauze. There is no indecency in mere nakedness."[29] This was equally true of an earlier generation. . . .

In 1699 a pamphlet appeared entitled *A Trip to Ireland.*[30] Whether it was printed in Dublin or London is not known, but its authorship is attributed to the celebrated or notorious Tom Brown.[31] For sheer scurrilous abuse this booklet outdoes anything else of the kind I have seen. Dunton could be outrageous enough in his descriptions of the country and its inhabitants, but if his favorable comments were mostly reserved for people whom he regarded at least as his social equals, he does not leave the reader with a perpetual bad taste in the mouth as does the author of *A Trip to Ireland.* This man, who frequently, after the manner of the period, uses without acknowledgment whole passages of the most pornographic parts of Dunton's recently published *Conversation in Ireland,* has nothing good to say of anybody or anything, except the nobility of English origin, for like all his kind he was a toady; he attributes to the Irish "the cruelty of a Spanish inquisitor, the lechery of an Italian, the levity of a Frenchman, the cowardice of a Savoyard, the perfidiousness of a Scotchman, the ignorance of a

28   *Domestic Manners,* p. 442.

29   *A Tour through Ireland, interspersed with Observations on Manners, Customs, etc.,* Dublin, 1780, pp. 164, 165. It would appear that several pages of this book, including the passages here quoted, were taken almost verbatim from Thos. Campbell's *Philosophical Survey of the South of Ireland* (1777, p. 149).

30   Sub-title: "Being a description of the Country, People and Manners, as also some select Observations on Dublin."

31   See Bradshaw Collection, Hib. 4. 699. 2.

Muscovite, and the rebellious temper of a Dutchman.'' Yet surprisingly we find him offering evidence for the defense in the matter of drunkenness. "Drinking,'' he says, "is not so much their vice as some of their neighboring nations, unless their so excessive smoking be reckoned in, to which both the men and women are so generally addicted, yea, the very children, too, that an infant of their breeding shall take more delight in handling a tobacco pipe than a rattle, and will sooner learn to make use of it, than another shall of its sucking bottle.'' A work so contemptible as this is of value to us less for any light it throws on the question of drunkenness than as an example of the semihumorous and wholly obscene sort of scribbling which had a considerable public at the end of the seventeenth century.

—PHILIPPE ARIÈS

FAMILIES AND HOMES

Since everything depended on social relations, one is bound to wonder where people met. They still often met outside, in the street. Not only by chance, because towns were comparatively small, but also because certain streets or squares were promenades where at certain hours one met one's friends, as one does today in Mediterranean towns. The teeming crowds of the Corso or the Piazza Major were to be found in squares which are now deserted or crossed by pedestrians who, even when they loiter, are unknown to one another. The present-day tourist finds it hard to recognize the Place Bellecour at Lyons in this description of it given by an Italian traveler of 1664, the Abbé Locatelli:[1] "Men and women were walking about arm in arm, holding one another as one holds a child. . . . A woman gave her arm to two men, a man his arm to two women. Unaccustomed as we were to these manners [the good priest came from Bologna where people were more reserved than in Lyons], we thought we had entered a brothel . . . I noticed how gay they all were, and at the entrance to the

From Philippe Ariès, *Centuries of Childhood: A Social History of Family Life,* trans. Robert Baldick (New York: Alfred A. Knopf, Inc., 1962), pp. 390–91, 393–95, 398–404, by permission of the publisher and Jonathan Cape Ltd., London.

1   Locatelli, *The Adventures of an Italian priest,* edited by W. Blunt, London, 1956.

promenade, I saw them take each other by the arm, which they held bent like the handle of a basket, and they walked about in this way.'' The surprise felt by this seventeenth-century Bolognese at the sight of this laughing population walking about arm in arm is the same as that which we experience today when we mingle with an Italian crowd.

People met in the street; where did they forgather? In nineteenth-century France, and modern France too, the men often gather together in the café. Contemporary French society remains unintelligible unless one recognizes the importance of the café: it is the only meeting-place which is accessible at any time, as regular as a habit. The English equivalent is the "public house" or pub. The society of the sixteenth and seventeenth centuries was a society without a café or pub: the tavern was a place of ill repute reserved for criminals, prostitutes, soldiers, students on the spree, down-and-outs, and adventurers of every sort—it was not frequented by decent people, whatever their station in life.[2] There were no other public places except private houses, or at least certain private houses: the big houses in either the town or country. . . .

The big house fulfilled a public function. In that society without a café or a "public house," it was the only place where friends, clients, relatives and protégés could meet and talk. To the servants, clerics and clerks who lived there permanently, one must add the constant flow of visitors. The latter apparently gave little thought to the hour and were never shown the door, for the seventeenth-century pedagogues considered that the frequency and the time of these visits made a regular time-table, especially for meals, quite impossible. They regarded this irregularity as sufficiently harmful for children's education to justify sending them to college, in spite of the moral dangers of school life. The constant coming and going of visitors distracted children from their work. In short, visits gave the impression of being a positive occupation, which governed the life of the household and even dictated its mealtimes.

These visits were not simply friendly or social: they were also professional; but little or no distinction was made between these categories. A lawyer's clients were also his friends and both were his debtors. There were no professional premises, either for the judge or the merchant or the banker or the business man. Everything was done in the same rooms where he lived with his family.

Now these rooms were no more equipped for domestic work than they were for professional purposes. They communicated with one another, and the richest houses had galleries on the floor where the family lived. On the other floors the rooms were smaller, but just as dependent on one another. None had a special function, except the kitchen, and even then the cooking was often done in the hearth of the biggest room. Kitchen facilities in the towns did not allow of many refinements, and when there were guests, dishes were bought ready-cooked from

---

2   But Lagniet, in his *Proverbes,* depicts a tavern in which a child does not seem out of place.

the nearest caterer. When Hortensius, Francion's master, wanted to entertain some friends, he told his servant: "Go and ask my neighbor the tavern-keeper to send me some of his best wine together with a roast." Now he said this because as it was already very late, and seeing that the latest to arrive had brought a hurdy-gurdy, he realized that he would have to offer supper to all the people in his room. Francion went out with the servant. At the tavern-keeper's, "we found nothing to suit us and we just bought some wine. We decided to go to the cook-shop on the Petit Pont. The servant bought a capon, and as he also wanted a sirloin of beef, went into all the cook-shops to see if he could find a good one."

People lived in general-purpose rooms. They ate in them, but not at special tables: the "dining table" did not exist, and at mealtimes people set up folding trestle-tables, covering them with a cloth, as can be seen from Abraham Bosse's engravings. In the middle of the fifteenth century the humanist architect Alberti,[3] very much a *laudator temporis acti,* recalled the manners of his childhood: "When we were young . . . the wife would send her husband a little jug of wine and something to eat with his bread; she dined at home and the men in the workshop." He must not be taken literally, for this custom was still common in many artisan and peasants homes at the time he was writing. But he contrasted this simple custom with urban usage at the time: "the table put up twice a day as for a solemn banquet." In other words, it was a collapsible table, like so many pieces of furniture in the early seventeenth century.[4]

In the same rooms where they ate, people slept, danced, worked and received visitors. Engravings show the bed next to a dumb-waiter loaded with silverware, or in the corner of a room in which people are eating. A picture by P. Codde (1636) shows a dance: at the far end of the room in which the mummers are dancing, one can make out a bed with the curtains around it drawn.[5] For a long time the beds too were collapsible. It fell to the apprentices or pages to put them up when company was expected. The author of *Le Chastel de joyeuse destinée* congratulates the youths "dressed in the livery of France" on their agility at setting up beds.[6] As late as the early seventeenth century Héroard wrote in his diary on March 12th, 1606: "Once he [the future Louis XIII] had dressed, he helped to undo his bed." March 14th, 1606: "Taken to the Queen's apartments, he was lodged in the King's bedchamber [the King was away fighting] and helped to take his wooden bed round to the Queen: Mme de Montglat installed her bed there to sleep there." On September 8th, 1608, just before setting out for Saint-Germain, "he amused himself by undoing his bed himself, impatient to leave."[7] Already, however, beds had become less mobile. Alberti, in his

3   P. H. Michel, *La Pensée de L. B. Alberti,* 1930.

4   Père du Colombier, *Style Henri IV et Louis XIII,* 1941, p. 49.

5   P. Codde, reproduced in Berndt, 187.

6   *Jardin de Plaisance,* edited by Droz and Piaget, p. 93.

7   Héroard, op. cit.

regrets for the good old days, wrote: "I remember . . . seeing our most notable citizens, when they went off to the country, taking their beds and their kitchen utensils with them, and bringing them back on their return. Now the furniture of a single room is bigger and more expensive than that of a whole house used to be on a wedding day."[8] This transformation of the collapsible bed into a permanent piece of furniture undoubtedly marks an advance in domesticity. The ornamental bed, surrounded by curtains, was promptly seized upon by artists to illustrate the themes of private life: the room in which husband and wife came together, in which mothers gave birth, in which old men died, and also in which the lonely meditated. But the room containing the bed was not a bedroom because of that. It remained a public place. Consequently the bed had to be fitted with curtains which could be opened or drawn at will, so as to defend its occupants' privacy. For one rarely slept alone, but either with one's husband or wife or else with other people of one's own sex.

Since the bed was independent of the room in which it stood, there could be several in the same room, often one in each corner. Bussy-Rabutin tells how one day, in the course of a campaign, a girl frightened by the troops asked him for protection and hospitality: "I finally told my servants to give her one of the four beds in my room."[9]

It is easy to imagine the promiscuity which reigned in these rooms where nobody could be alone, which one had to cross to reach any of the communicating rooms, where several couples and several groups of boys or girls slept together (not to speak of the servants, of whom at least some must have slept beside their masters, setting up beds which were still collapsible in the room or just outside the door), in which people forgathered to have their meals, to receive their friends or clients, and sometimes to give alms to beggars. One can understand why, whenever a census was taken, the houses of notabilities were always more crowded than the little one-room or two-room apartments of ordinary folk. One has to regard these families, for all that they were giving birth to the modern concept of the family, not as refuges from the invasion of the world but as the centers of a populous society, the focal points of a crowded social life. Around them were established concentric circles of relations, increasingly loose towards the periphery: circles of relatives, friends, clients, protégés, debtors, etc. . . .

The historians taught us long ago that the King was never left alone. But in fact, until the end of the seventeenth century, nobody was ever left alone. The density of social life made isolation virtually impossible, and people who managed to shut themselves up in a room for some time were regarded as exceptional characters: relations between peers, relations between people of the same class but dependent on one another, relations between masters and servants—these

8   P. H. Michel, *L. B. Alberti.*
9   Bussy-Rabutin, *Mémoires,* 3 vols, 1704.

everyday relations never left a man by himself. This sociability had for a long time hindered the formation of the concept of the family, because of the lack of privacy. The development in the sixteenth and seventeenth centuries of a new emotional relationship, or at least a newly conceived relationship, between parents and children, did not destroy the old sociability. The consciousness of childhood and the family postulated zones of physical and moral intimacy which had not existed before. Yet, to begin with, it adapted itself to constant promiscuity. The combination of a traditional sociability and a new awareness of the family was to be found only in certain families, families of country or city notabilities, both nobles and commoners, peasants and artisans. The houses of these notabilities became centers of social life around which there gravitated a whole complex little world. This equilibrium between family and society was not destined to survive the evolution of manners and the new progress of domesticity.

In the eighteenth century, the family began to hold society at a distance, to push it back beyond a steadily extending zone of private life. The organization of the house altered in conformity with this new desire to keep the world at bay. It became the modern type of house, with rooms which were independent because they opened onto a corridor. While they still communicated with each other, people were no longer obliged to go through them all to pass from one to another. It has been said that comfort dates from this period; it was born at the same time as domesticity, privacy and isolation, and it was one of the manifestations of these phenomena. There were no longer beds all over the house. The beds were confined to the bedrooms, which were furnished on either side of the alcove with cupboards and nooks fitted out with a new toilette and hygienic equipment. In France and Italy the word *chambre* began to be used in opposition to the word *salle*—they had hitherto been more or less synonymous; the *chambre* denoted the room in which one slept, the *salle* the room in which one received visitors and ate: the *salon* and the *salle à manger*, the *caméra* and the *sala da pranza*. In England the word "room" was kept for all these functions, but a prefix was added to give precision: the dining-room, the bedroom, etc.

This specialization of the rooms, in the middle class and nobility to begin with, was certainly one of the greatest changes in everyday life. It satisfied a new desire for isolation. In these more private dwellings, the servants no longer left the out-of-the-way quarters which were allotted to them—except in the houses of princes of the blood, where the old manners endured. Sébastien Mercier noted as a recent innovation the habit of ringing for the maidservant. Bells were arranged in such a way that they could summon servants from a distance, whereas they had previously been capable of arousing attention only in the room in which they were rung. Nothing could be more characteristic of the new desire to keep the servants at a distance and also to defend oneself against intruders. It was no longer good form in the late eighteenth century to call on a friend or acquaintance at any time of day and without warning. Either one had days when one was "at home," or else "people send each other cards by their servants." "The post also takes care of visits. . . . The letter-box delivers cards; nothing is easier, nobody is visible, everyone has the decency to close his door."[10]

The use of "cards" and "days" was not an isolated phenomenon. The old code of manners was an art of living in public and together. The new code of manners emphasized the need to respect the privacy of others. The moral stress had been moved. Sébastien Mercier was quick to observe this change: "Present-day custom has cut short all ceremonies and only a provincial stands on ceremony now." Meals were shortened too: "They are much shorter, and it is not at table that people talk freely and tell amusing stories," but in the *salon,* the room to which people withdraw: the "drawing-room." "People are no longer in a hurry to drink, no longer torment their guests in order to prove that they know how to entertain, no longer ask you to sing [the old concerts over dessert of the sixteenth and seventeenth centuries]." "People have abandoned those foolish and ridiculous customs so familiar to our ancestors, unhappy proselytes of an embarrassing and annoying tradition *which they called correct.*" "Not a moment's rest: people tried to outdo each other in politeness before the meal and during the meal with pedantic stubbornness, and the experts on etiquette applauded these puerile combats." "Of all those stupid old customs, that of blessing someone who sneezes is the only one that has lasted down to the present day." "We leave it to the cobbler and the tailor to give each other the sincere or hypocritical accolade which was still usual in polite society forty years ago." "Only the *petit bourgeois* now employs those tiresome manners and futile attentions which he still imagines to be correct and which are intolerably irksome to people who are used to society life."

The rearrangement of the house and the reform of manners left more room for private life; and this was taken up by a family reduced to parents and children, a family from which servants, clients and friends were excluded. General de Martange's letters to his wife between 1760 and 1780 enable us to gauge the progress made by a concept of the family which had become identical with that of the nineteenth and early twentieth centuries. The family had invaded people's correspondence and doubtless their conversations and preoccupations too.[11]

The old forms of address such as "Madame" had disappeared. Martange addressed his wife as "dear *maman*" or "my dear love," "my dear child," "my dear little one." The husband called his wife by the same name that his children gave her: *maman.* His correspondence with his wife was full of details about the

---

10   Sébastien Mercier, *Les Tableaux de Paris,* edited by Desnoitères, p. 194.

11   *Correspondance inédite du général de Martange,* 1756–1782, edited by Bréard, 1898.

children, their health and their behavior. They were referred to by nickname: Minette and Coco. This increasingly widespread use of nicknames corresponded to a greater familiarity and also to a desire to address one another differently from strangers, and thus to emphasize by a sort of hermetic language the solidarity of parents and children and the distance separating them from other people.

When the father was away, he kept himself informed of all the little details of everyday life, which he took very seriously. He waited impatiently for letters: "I beg you, my dear little one, to write just a few words." "Scold Mlle Minette for me for so far neglecting to write to me." He spoke of the joy of seeing his family again very soon: "I look forward to being with you once more in our poor little home, and I should like no responsibility better than that of arranging your room and making our stay pleasant and comfortable." Here we already have the modern taste for domesticity, contrasting the house, the object of enthusiastic pottering, with the outside world.

In this correspondence, questions of health and hygiene occupied an important place. Hitherto people had worried about serious illnesses, but they had not shown this constant solicitude, they had not bothered about a cold, a minor ailment: physical life had not been regarded as so important. "I should be so unhappy if I had no news about your health and that of my little girls." "Although what you tell me about the poor health which you and my poor little girls are enjoying is not as comforting as a father's heart might wish. . . ." "I am not very happy about what you tell me about our little boy's pains and loss of appetite. I cannot recommend you too earnestly, dear child, to procure some Narbonne honey for both him and Xavière, and to rub their gums with it when they are in pain." This was the anxiety of parents over their children's teething troubles: it could have interested a few old women in Mme de Sévigné's time, but it had not hitherto been given the honors of a place in a staff officer's correspondence. "My daughters' colds worry me. . . . But it seems to me that the weather finally took a turn for the better this morning." Vaccination against smallpox was discussed then as inoculation against poliomyelitis is today. "I leave it to you to see to Xavière's vaccination, and the sooner the better, because everybody is satisfied with the vaccination." He advised his wife to drink "Sedlitz water," "the salts of the same name," and lemonade, and also to mix vinegar or brandy with her water, to guard against infection.

One of the girls had got married in Germany. In a letter to her "dear sweet *maman*" of January 14th, 1781, she explained her long silence: "First of all the two youngest had whooping-cough for two months, so badly that every time they coughed they went purple in the face and the blood came bubbling out of their nostrils. After that illness, my little girl and Xavier caught the worst brain fever you could imagine." The doctors had given up hope of saving Xavier: "The poor child suffered all it is possible to suffer." However, in the end he was saved: "Thanks to the Supreme Being, all three have been returned to me." Nobody would now dare to seek consolation for losing a child in the hope of having another, as parents could have admitted doing only a century before. The child was irreplaceable, his death irreparable. And the mother found happiness in the midst of her children, who no longer belonged to an intermediary region between existence, and nonexistence: "The company of my little ones is my sole delight." Here we see the connection between the progress of the concept of childhood and the progress of hygiene, between concern for the child and concern for his health, another form of the link between attitudes to life and attitudes to death. . . .

Between the end of the Middle Ages and the seventeenth century, the child had won a place beside his parents to which he could not lay claim at a time when it was customary to entrust him to strangers. This return of the children to the home was a great event: it gave the seventeenth-century family its principal characteristic, which distinguished it from the medieval family. The child became an indispensable element of everyday life, and his parents worried about his education, his career, his future. He was not yet the pivot of the whole system, but he had become a much more important character. Yet this seventeenth-century family was not the modern family: it was distinguished from the latter by the enormous mass of sociability which it retained. Where the family existed, that is to say in the big houses, it was a center of social relations, the capital of a little complex and graduated society under the command of the paterfamilias.

The modern family, on the contrary, cuts itself off from the world and opposes to society the isolated group of parents and children. All the energy of the group is expended on helping the children to rise in the world, individually and without any collective ambition: the children rather than the family.

This evolution from the medieval family to the seventeenth-century family and then to the modern family was limited for a long time to the nobles, the middle class, the richer artisans and the richer laborers. In the early nineteenth century, a large part of the population, the biggest and poorest section, was still living like the medieval families, with the children separated from their parents. The idea of the house or the home did not exist for them. The concept of the home is another aspect of the concept of the family. Between the eighteenth century and the present day, the concept of the family changed hardly at all. It remained as we saw it in the town and country middle classes of the eighteenth century. On the other hand, it extended more and more to other social strata. In England in the late eighteenth century, agricultural laborers tended to set up house on their own, instead of lodging with their employers, and the decline of apprenticeship in industry made possible earlier marriages and larger families.[12]

12 J. Ashton, *La Révolution industrielle,* p. 173.

Late marriage, the precariousness of work, the difficulty of finding lodgings, the mobility of journeyman labor and the continuation of the traditions of apprenticeship, were so many obstacles to the ideal way of middle-class family life, so many obstacles which the evolution of manners would gradually remove. Family life finally embraced nearly the whole of society, to such an extent that people have forgotten its aristocratic and middle-class origins.[13]

13 H. Bergues, P. Ariès, E. Hélin, L. Henry, M. Riquet, A. Sauvy, J. Sutter, *La Prévention des naissances dans la famille, ses origines dans les temps modernes.* Institut National d'Études Démographiques, Cahier no. 35, 1960. Cf. also R. Prigent, *Le Renouveau des idées sur la famille.* Institut National d'Études Démographiques, no. 18, 1954.

SUGGESTED READINGS

Ancient

BALSDON, J. P. V. D., *Life and Leisure in Ancient Rome* (New York: McGraw-Hill, 1969)

——, *The Romans* (New York: Basic Books, 1965)

BOWRA, C. M., *The Greek Experience* (London: New English Library, 1957)

CARCOPINO, JEROME, *Daily Life in Ancient Rome*, trans. E. O. Lorimer (New Haven: Yale University Press, 1940)

CROWELL, FRANK, *Everyday Life in Ancient Rome* (London: B. T. Batsford, 1961)

EHRENBERG, VICTOR, *Society and Civilization in Greece and Rome,* Martin Classical Lectures, Vol. 18 (Cambridge, Mass.: Harvard University Press, 1964)

FROST, FRANK T., *Greek Society* (Lexington, Mass.: Heath, 1971)

JONES, A. H. M., *The Greek City from Alexander to Justinian* (Oxford: Clarendon Press, 1966)

LEVI, MARIO A., *Political Power in the Ancient World,* trans. Jane Costello (New York: NAL, 1965)

LOT, FERDINAND, *The End of the Ancient World and the Beginnings of the Middle Ages* (New York: Barnes & Noble, 1953)

MATTINGLY, HAROLD, *The Man in the Roman Street* (New York: Norton, 1966)

PAOLI, U. E., *Rome: Its People, Life and Customs,* trans. R. D. MacNaghten (New York: McKay, 1963)

ROBINSON, C. E., *Everyday Life in Ancient Greece* (Oxford: Clarendon Press, 1933)

ROSTOVTZEFF, M. I., *The Social and Economic History of the Hellenistic World,* 3 vols. (Oxford: Clarendon Press, 1941)

——, *The Social and Economic History of the Roman Empire,* 2nd ed., rev. P. M. Fraser, 2 vols. (Oxford: Clarendon Press, 1957)

TREBLE, HENRY A., & K. M. KING, *Everyday Life in Rome in the Time of Caesar and Cicero* (Oxford: Clarendon Press, 1930)

WALCOT, P., *Greek Peasants, Ancient and Modern: A Comparison of Social and Moral Values* (New York: Barnes & Noble, 1970)

Medieval and Renaissance

ADAMS, JEREMY DUQUESNAY, *Patterns of Medieval Society* (Englewood Cliffs, N.J.: Prentice-Hall, 1969)

BENNETT, H. S., *Life in the English Manor* (Cambridge: Cambridge University Press, 1956)

BLOCH, MARC, *Feudal Society,* tr. by L. A. Manyon (Chicago: University of Chicago Press, 1961)

BOISSONADE, PROSPER, *Life and Work in Medieval Europe,* tr. by Eileen Power (New York: Harper & Row, 1964)

BROOKE, CHRISTOPHER, *The Structure of Medieval Society* (New York: McGraw-Hill, 1971)

BURKE, PETER, *Tradition and Innovation in Renaissance Italy: A Sociological Approach* (London: B. T. Batsford, 1972)

BURKHARDT, JACOB, *The Civilization of the Renaissance in Italy* (New York: Modern Library, 1954)

CHEYETTE, FREDRIC L., ed., *Hardship and Community in Medieval Europe* (New York: Holt, Rinehart and Winston, 1968)

D'HAUCOURT, GENEVIEVE, *Life in the Middle Ages,* tr. Veronica Hall (New York: Walker, 1963)

DUCKETT, ELEANOR S., *Death and Life in the Tenth Century* (Ann Arbor: University of Michigan Press, 1967)

DULY, GEORGES, *Medieval Marriage: Two Models from Twelfth-Century France* (Baltimore and London: Johns Hopkins, 1978)

FERGUSON, WALLACE K., *Europe in Transition 1300–1520* (Boston: Houghton Mifflin, 1962)

GIES, FRANCES, and GIES, JOSEPH, *Life in a Medieval City* (New York: Thomas Y. Crowell, 1969)

HASTINGS, MARGARET, *Medieval European Society 1000–1450* (New York: Random House, 1971)

HAY, DENYS, *The Medieval Centuries* (London: Methuen, 1964)

HUIZINGA, J., *The Waning of the Middle Ages* (New York: Doubleday, 1949)

LOPEZ, ROBERT S., *The Birth of Europe* (London: Phoenix House, 1967)

MOREWIDGE, ROSMARIE THEE, ed., *The Role of Women in the Middle Ages* (Albany: State University of New York Press, 1975)

PIRENNE, HENRI, *Economic and Social History of Medieval Europe,* tr. I. E. Clegg (New York: Harcourt Brace, 1937)

POSTON, M. M., *The Medieval Economy and Society* (London: Weidenfeld and Nicholson, 1972)

SOUTHERN, R. W., *The Making of the Middle Ages* (New Haven: Yale University Press, 1953)

THRUPP, SYLVIA L., ed., *Early Medieval Society* (New York: Appleton-Century-Crofts, 1967)

Early Modern

ASHLEY, MAURICE, *The Golden Century: Europe 1598–1715* (London: Weidenfeld and Nicolson, 1969)

ASTON, TREVOR, ed., *Crisis in Europe 1560–1660* (New York: Doubleday, Anchor, 1967)

ERLANGER, PHILIPPE, *The Age of Courts and Kings: Manners and Morals 1558–1715* New York: Harper & Row, 1967)

GREGG, PAULINE, *Black Death and Industrial Revolution* (London: George G. Harrap, 1976)

HOLDERNESS, B. A., *Pre-Industrial England: Economy and Society 1500–1750* (London: J. M. Dent, 1976)

HOSKINS, W. G., *The Age of Plunder: The England of Henry VIII, 1500–1547* (London and New York: Longman, 1976)

KAMEN, HENRY A. F., *The Iron Century: Social Change in Europe, 1550–1660* (London: Weidenfeld and Nicolson, 1971)

LADURIE, EMMANUEL LeROY, *The Peasants of Languedoc,* trans. John Davy (Urbana: University of Illinois Press, 1974)

MARSHALL, DOROTHY, *The English People in the Eighteenth Century* (London: Longmans, Green, 1956)

MOUSNIER, ROLAND, *Peasant Uprisings in Seventeenth Century France, Russia and China* (New York: Harper & Row, 1970)

PINCHBECK, IVY, and MARGARET HEWITT, *Children in English Society,* Vol. 1, *From Tudor Times to the Eighteenth Century* (London: Routledge, 1969)

ROWSE, A. L., *The Elizabethan Renaissance: The Life of the Society* (New York: Scribner's, 1971)

SEAVER, PAUL, ed. *Society in an Age of Revolution* (New York: Franklin Watts, 1976)